Forensic Issues in Adolescents with Developmental Disabilities

Forensic Focus

This series, edited by Gwen Adshead, takes the field of Forensic Psychotherapy as its focal point, offering a forum for the presentation of theoretical and clinical issues. It embraces such influential neighbouring disciplines as language, law, literature, criminology, ethics and philosophy, as well as psychiatry and psychology, its established progenitors. Gwen Adshead is Consultant Forensic Psychotherapist and Lecturer in Forensic Psychotherapy at Broadmoor Hospital.

in the same series

Autism Spectrum Disorders through the Lifespan
Digby Tantam
ISBN 978 1 84310 993 8

The Complete Guide to Asperger's Syndrome
Tony Attwood
ISBN 978 1 84310 669 2

Sexual Offending and Mental Health
Multidisciplinary Management in the Community
Edited by Julia Houston and Sarah Galloway
ISBN 978 1 84310 550 3

Therapeutic Relationships with Offenders
An Introduction to the Psychodynamics of Forensic Mental Health Nursing
Edited by Anne Aiyegbusi and Jenifer Clarke-Moore
ISBN 978 1 84310 949 5

Personality Disorder
The Definitive Reader
Edited by Gwen Adshead and Caroline Jacob
ISBN 978 1 84310 640 1

Psychiatry in Prisons
A Comprehensive Handbook
Edited by Simon Wilson and Ian Cumming
ISBN 978 1 84310 223 6

FORENSIC FOCUS 32

Forensic Issues in Adolescents with Developmental Disabilities

Edited by Ernest Gralton

Jessica Kingsley *Publishers*
London and Philadelphia

Material in Chapter 11 from Gralton *et al.* 2008 is reproduced by
permission of the British Journal of Forensic Practice.
Material in Chapter 17 from Gralton, Udu and Ranasinghe 2006 is reproduced
by permission of the British Journal of Forensic Practice.

First published in 2011
by Jessica Kingsley Publishers
116 Pentonville Road
London N1 9JB, UK
and
400 Market Street, Suite 400
Philadelphia, PA 19106, USA

www.jkp.com

Library of Congress Cataloging in Publication Data
Forensic issues in adolescents with developmental disabilities / edited by Ernest Gralton.
     p. cm.
 Includes bibliographical references and index.
 ISBN 978-1-84905-144-6 (alk. paper)
 1. Teenagers with disabilities. 2. Forensic psychology. 3. Teenagers
with disabilities--Services for. I. Gralton, Ernest.
 HV1569.3.Y68F67 2011
 614'.15--dc22

                                    2011005787

British Library Cataloguing in Publication Data
A CIP catalogue record for this book is available from the British Library

ISBN 978 1 84905 144 6

Printed and bound in Great Britain

To my wife Eira, for her patience.

Royalties from the sale of the book will go to
Kids Company – www.kidsco.org.uk

CONTENTS

Chapter 1

COMPLEX CO-MORBIDITIES IN ADOLESCENTS WITH DEVELOPMENTAL DISABILITIES AND FORENSIC NEEDS

Ernest Gralton

INTRODUCTION

Adolescents with developmental disabilities who have forensic needs are a complex population presenting unique challenges to those who care for them. Those who are referred to secure psychiatric services often have a variety of co-morbid disorders, some unrecognised for long periods due to difficulties in carrying out comprehensive assessments (Barlow and Turk 2001) or due to the phenomenon of 'diagnostic overshadowing' where abnormal behaviours that are the result of developmental disability are attributed to the presence of intellectual disability alone (Mason and Scior 2004).

Psychiatric disorders are up to four times more prevalent in adolescents with intellectual impairment than adolescents without impairment (Emerson and Hatton 2007); however, only a limited proportion of young people receive any form of specialist service (Dykens 2000; Emerson 2003a; Tonge and Einfeld 2001; Wright, Williams and Richardson 2008). Diagnoses amongst this population often include developmental problems like autism and attention deficit hyperactivity disorder (ADHD), developmental dyspraxia/developmental coordination disorder, Tourette's and tic disorders. In addition to this, a number of environmental insults, notably developmental trauma (including neglect and physical and sexual abuse), head injury and substance misuse, are common. Some have also gone on to develop a variety of formal mental illnesses including atypical affective disorders, anxiety disorders (including complex post-traumatic stress disorder (PTSD) and developmental trauma disorder) and a range of psychoses, although these are not always easy to recognise.

RESEARCH EVIDENCE

The prevalence of most of these aforementioned disorders is increased in delinquent adolescents (Kazadin 2000). Diagnosis can be more difficult and response to psychiatric treatment can be idiosyncratic because of communication impairments and the presence of multiple disorders (Berney and Allington-Smith 2010; Kutscher 2005). Some authors have used aspects of Chaos Theory and metaphors like 'interweave' to try to explain the complex interactions of co-morbid disorders in this population and the individuality of each case (Blakemore-Brown 2002). There is a general recognition that more complex models of understanding these young people are now required (Emerson 2003b).

Developmentally disabled adolescents are a particularly difficult group to research as there are complex ethical issues and problems with parental consent, difficulties with control groups and a lack of appropriate specific tools and outcome measures. The research basis on which to develop treatments for adolescents with developmental disorders with forensic needs is therefore still very limited (Hall 2000) and much evidence for interventions is therefore extrapolated from mainstream adolescent or adult developmentally disabled populations.

These young people often find themselves as the ultimate excluded patient population, both from research and from services, on the basis of cognitive impairment, age, instability in terms of accommodation and consistent care. They often find themselves in care at an early age as their complex developmental problems overwhelm the parenting capacity of families, particularly those who are already compromised by parental absence or familial mental disorder. Exclusion from school is three times more common in UK prisoners with developmental disabilities than those without (Talbot 2008). They have significantly more placements outside the family home than their non-disabled peers (Hall 2000).

Developmentally disabled adolescents are significantly overrepresented in populations of adolescent offenders (Hall 2000) but they are often not identified (Ford *et al.* 2008). Around one in five young offenders probably has an IQ less than 70 (Chitsabesan *et al.* 2006) but individuals with significant developmental disability are routinely unrecognised even when in custodial settings (Brier 1994; Talbot 2008). They are more problematic to manage in prison settings than their more intellectually able peers (Smith *et al.* 1990) and the range of available prison-based programmes are not generally adapted to meet their needs. Overall the criminal justice system in the UK comprehensively and routinely fails offenders (including adolescents) with a developmental disability (Talbot 2008).

Mental disorders and their manifestations

The interaction of several developmental and acquired mental disorders produces presentations that are difficult to assess in a single cross-sectional interview as an outpatient (Hall 2000). Key developmental history is often missing in the case of young people who are no longer living with biological parents, particularly those who have had multiple foster and residential placements.

The relationship between ADHD and a higher risk of delinquent behaviour is now well recognised. Adolescents with ADHD are up to five times more likely to be arrested than peers without ADHD (Satterfield *et al.* 1994). It is likely that the symptoms of impulsivity and hyperactivity (rather than inattention) are linked to antisocial behaviour (Bambinski, Hartsough and Lambert 1999). Although ADHD symptoms tend to improve over time, this is by no means universal or uniform in the population (Marsh and Williams 2004). The majority of individuals with ADHD still have one disabling symptom in early adulthood (Weiss *et al.* 1985) which means they are likely to retain significant symptoms throughout adolescence.

A common example of complex co-morbidity in this population is ADHD and developmental dyspraxia (also known as developmental coordination disorder – DCD); around half the children with ADHD have this particular co-morbidity (Martin, Piek and Hay 2006). This co-morbidity has a worrying outcome in early adulthood in relation to criminal behaviour, alcohol misuse and personality disorder (Rasmussen and Gillberg 2000). However, the co-morbid diagnosis of DCD is frequently unrecognised (Kadesjö and Gillberg 2003).

Children with DCD obtained significantly poorer scores on measures of attention and learning (reading, writing and spelling) than comparison children. They have a relatively high level of social problems and are at risk for problems in attention, learning and psychosocial adjustment (Dewey *et al.* 2002).

Deficits in attention, motor control and perception (DAMP), described by Gillberg (2003), affect about 1.5 per cent of the population of school age children. Children classified as having DAMP invariably fulfil criteria for ADHD and DCD and also commonly have symptoms of autistic spectrum disorders (Clarke *et al.* 1999). Children diagnosed with this disorder unsurprisingly have a higher risk of poor outcomes by early adulthood, including delinquency, and have a higher incidence of intellectual impairment and visual motor perception. Childhood-onset DAMP is associated with an increased incidence of psychiatric disorders and combinations of personality disorder (Hellgren *et al.*1994).

A number of researchers have shown that many of these developmental disorders tend to cluster together. A large number of medical, psychiatric and motor and behavioural decontrol syndromes are associated with autistic spectrum disorders (Gillberg and Billstedt 2001). ADHD and autism are common co-morbidities with Tourette's disorder (Kadesjo and Gillberg 2000). Children with ADHD and motor disorders are more likely to have severe ADHD-combined type and other neurodevelopmental and behavioural problems (Tervo *et al.* 2002).

Other authors have described a very similar group of children with multiple problems with affective and anxiety regulation, poor attention and impulsivity, social impairment, impaired cognitive processing and impaired neuro-maturation that they describe as the 'multiple complex developmental disorder' (Ad-Dab'bagh and Greenfield 2001).

There are a range of difficulties in making multiple co-morbid diagnoses, not least is trying to attribute individual symptom clusters to disorders whose symptoms may overlap.

How these developmental disorders influence developing personality and behaviour is a complex and difficult question. There is no question, however, that they can have a significant and adverse impact. Childhood-onset neuropsychiatric disorders, including learning disability, ADHD, tics and autism spectrum disorders, form complex co-morbid patterns with adult personality disorders including psychopathic traits, mood disorders and substance abuse. The results support the notion that childhood-onset social and behavioural problems form a highly relevant psychiatric symptom cluster in relation to pervasive adult violent behaviour (Soderstrom *et al.* 2004; Vizard *et al.* 2004). It may be that right hemispheric dysfunction and visuospatial difficulties in particular are a marker for persistent conduct problems (Raine *et al.* 2002). A significant proportion of adult patients detained in high secure hospitals have childhood-onset neuropsychiatric disorders (Soderstrom and Nilsson 2003). Many of these factors have been identified as being at high risk for developing severe personality disorder in adulthood, and some researchers have proposed a new developmental disorder to describe some of these young people (Vizard *et al.* 2004).

Alcohol related neurodevelopmental disorders like foetal alcohol syndrome are not uncommon in this group and can affect about one per cent of children in the general population (Sampson *et al.* 1997) and they are probably the leading known cause of developmental disability in the Western world (Mattson and Riley 1998). They are associated with a wide variety of neuro-behavioural problems (Mattson and Riley 1998). Common associations are hyperactivity and deficits in visuospatial functioning, verbal and nonverbal learning and executive function (Riley and McGee 2005), as well as high rates of birth defects including sensori-neural deafness and visual impairment (Elliott *et al.*

2008), deficits in adaptive behaviours and social skills (Crocker *et al.* 2009), and sensory processing abnormalities and problem behaviours (Franklin *et al.* 2008). Interventions should logically target the clinical and neuropsychological deficits seen most commonly in these conditions but there is still only limited evidence to support specific interventions (Peadon *et al.* 2009).

There are some genetic disorders that can have behavioural phenotypes or particular clusters of behavioural symptoms, although they are by no means invariable. Velo-cardio-facial syndrome can present with developmental delay and ADHD symptoms (Shprintzen 2000) and significant coordination difficulties (Swillen *et al.* 1999). Fragile X syndrome can be associated with autistic spectrum disorders (Rogers *et al.* 2001). William's syndrome has been associated with problems with attention and concentration, anxiety and social impairment (Udwin and Yule 1991). Cornelia de Lange syndrome can present with mild and borderline intellectual functioning and is associated with hyperactivity, autistic symptoms, aggression and sleep disturbance (Berney, Ireland and Burn 1999). Although these disorders are relatively uncommon in adolescents with developmental disorders and forensic needs, they are worth recognising when they occur and there can be issues around genetic counselling that can involve the wider family. There is still, however, limited evidence around the response to the treatment of individual phenotypes.

This group of young people can also have a range of other neurological disorders including complex sleep disorders (Wiggs and France 2000) and obsessive compulsive disorder, including conditions of autoimmune origin like Paediatric Autoimmune Neuropsychiatric Disorder Associated with Streptococcus (PANDAS), which can complicate their presentation (Moretti *et al.* 2008). Young people with complex developmental disorders have a higher incidence of epilepsy (Pellock 2004) and can present with a variety of epilepsy-related psychiatric disorders (Blumer, Montouris and Davies 2004). They also have an increased overall incidence of physical health problems that require specific enquiry and investigation (Boyle, Decoufle and Yeargin-Allsopp 1994; Lennox, Rey-Conde and Faint 2008).

Attachment

Ideas from both attachment theory (Bowlby 1988) and schema therapy (Young, Klosko and Weishaar 2003) can be helpful in describing how a variety of adverse experiences in childhood (including neglect and abuse) can profoundly affect brain organisation and future relationships, and lead to the development of core maladaptive schemas (strongly held pervasive emotional and cognitive beliefs). These then further exacerbate the pre-existing developmental impairments in this population. These schemas are likely to be linked to emotional memories within the hippocampal/amygdala midbrain system which can trigger powerful involuntary emotional responses in individuals (LeDoux 1998). A variety of maladaptive schemas can lead to major problems with the control of arousal and anger in young people. They may have a seemingly disproportionate arousal response to a variety of triggers (which can be minor or even unidentified by the individual). This in itself can sometimes make it particularly difficult to use tools like behavioural analysis to implement appropriate behavioural programmes for this group of impaired young people.

Exposing children to violence (including sexual abuse) has been shown to significantly impair their emotional, behavioural and cognitive development and is associated with anxiety, fear, aggressive and antisocial behaviour, sexual aggression, substance misuse and a failure to acquire social competence (Itzin 2006; Skuse *et al.* 1998). There are also significant alterations in threat perception demonstrated by studies that show that physically abused children are more sensitised to facial displays of anger (Pollak and Sinha 2002). A history of childhood maltreatment is significantly and consistently associated with violence in delinquent adolescents in recent studies (Lansford *et al.* 2007; Mersky and Reynolds 2007).

The likely biological mechanisms for the disruption of the process of brain development involve the elevated levels of stress neurohormones (De Bellis *et al.* 1999b). Catecholaminergic and steroid hormones are known to modulate the overall process of neuronal migration, differentiation and synaptic proliferation. Chronically elevated glucocorticoids cause disruption to dentritic growth and neuronal connections in animal models (Sapolski 2003). Children with histories of abuse continue to excrete significantly higher amounts of catecholamine and cortisol than controls (De Bellis 1999a), indicating chronic dysregulation of the body's stress and arousal control systems. Maltreated children have smaller intracranial and cerebral volumes, smaller midsaggital areas of the corpus callosum and larger lateral ventricles than controls (De Bellis 1999a).

Case description

The example of Robert demonstrates the range of problems and the potential co-morbidities of young people with developmental disabilities who offend. His story, although fictional, is by no means unusual.

Robert is a 15-year-old boy who was detained in a secure training centre (STC) in the UK, a secure establishment for younger adolescents up to the age of 17 who offend established by the Youth Justice Board as an alternative to prison or secure social service homes. STCs are described as constructive and education focused.

Robert has been convicted of a number of violent offences in the community and for setting fire to a building site. In the STC he is isolated from his peers as he is engaging in persistent deliberate self-harm by cutting himself or tying ligatures around his neck. He also assaulted his peers, and staff who attempted to prevent him from self-harming. The visiting psychiatrist prescribed the antidepressant fluoxetine, which he took only intermittently, but the staff describe his behaviour as deteriorating rather than improving. Since his arrest his mother has also refused to have any contact with him.

Robert is the second youngest of six children. He has three older half brothers; one has a learning disability, the second recently joined the army and the third, the eldest, died of binge alcohol abuse at the age of 19. His mother has a history of mild learning disability, alcohol misuse and depression and has had several admissions to psychiatric hospital including after the birth of Robert. His father has been imprisoned for violent offences, his whereabouts are unknown and he has had no contact with Robert for at least three years. His older sister, aged 21, is developmentally normal and is a single mother with two small children. Robert's younger brother is in primary school and has a Statement of Special Educational Need, requiring extra academic assistance. The family had been known to social services for some years prior to Robert's birth due to concerns about neglect and exposure to domestic violence.

Robert's mother's pregnancy was unremarkable except that she complained that he was very active and 'kicked me hard when he was in there'. There was also some concern that his mother may have consumed a significant amount of alcohol during the pregnancy although she denies this. The delivery was difficult with meconium-stained liquor and evidence on fetal heart monitoring of distress. In addition he needed resuscitation with oxygen post delivery and was nursed in a special care baby unit for 24 hours. He returned home with his mother after five days; all his siblings had been bottle fed and there was no attempt to breast feed. Concern was soon raised by the health visitor about his mother's care of Robert. He was often left for long periods in unchanged nappies and he was failing to thrive. There was also concern about the state of the house and his mother was often found sitting in the lounge smoking and apparently uninterested in Robert.

At six weeks Robert's mother was admitted to the local psychiatric hospital and treated with fluoxetine for postnatal depression. Robert was initially cared for by his maternal grandmother and then returned to his mother's care a few days before her discharge from the mother and baby unit in hospital. Robert was monitored at home by the health visitor. His sleep was reported as very erratic, he was an irritable infant, his motor control was poor and speech development was noted to be slow. He was walking at 15 months, and his activity levels were significantly higher than his siblings. He was constantly climbing on furniture, pulling things off tables, biting his siblings and was prone to prolonged tantrums. His dietary intake was restricted and he would often eat only crisps and 'jelly snakes', refusing to eat any fruit or vegetables. His toilet training was delayed – he was still in nappies at night until the age of five years due to faecal soiling. He was intermittently enuretic until the age of 14 years. He would refuse to use utensils and would feed himself exclusively with his fingers. He was unable to tie his shoelaces on entry to secondary school and was not able to learn to ride a push bike. He was excessively sensitive to some noises; on one occasion he nearly ran into a bonfire as he was so distressed by the noise of exploding fireworks. He would also scream loudly if the vacuum cleaner was turned on.

On several occasions from the age of four years he was found by neighbours outside the house having 'escaped', dressed in minimal clothing. His mother was noted on some visits to smell of alcohol. There were reports from neighbours of frequent shouting and screaming and the sound of breaking objects at the home address. There were reports of significant damage to the fabric of the house, including holes, kicked-in doors, broken windows and fragments of electrical appliances. Robert attended hospital on a number of occasions with bruising to his head. His mother said he had climbed up on a curtain rail and fallen off, or had fallen when he tried to escape out a window. On one occasion he was hit by a car when he ran out onto the road, and was taken to hospital by ambulance with concussion and kept overnight for observation. Robert was spending time being looked after by his maternal grandmother and various family friends. The exact duration of these periods was unknown but thought to be weeks at a time.

When Robert was six his father was arrested and sentenced to prison for eight years following a violent attack with a weapon on a neighbour.

Robert briefly attended nursery school, but was excluded after a couple of weeks for persistent aggression, including hitting and biting the other children. He went on to primary school. Again there were major problems with his interactions with his peers, with frequent aggressive responses. He was unable to attend or concentrate in school and he had to be separated from his peers at the back of the classroom. He was excluded in the second year after he tried to strangle a female peer with a skipping rope. He remained at home for a few months, then he moved to another primary school where he was assessed and given a Statement of Special Educational Need on the basis of cognitive impairment. He was given some additional help by a classroom assistant for ten hours per week. He had major problems holding a pen and forming letters. He needed additional help with recognising his letters and learning to read.

Each time his classroom assistant left and was replaced he was initially angry and aggressive toward the new one. However, with the help of a sympathetic head teacher he was sustained with some difficulty in primary school until the age of ten years. There was a record of a single visit at school from a community psychiatric nurse from his local child and adolescent mental health services when he was around seven years old. His family were subsequently offered family therapy but did not attend any appointments and his case was closed.

At the age of 11 he made the transition to a large local comprehensive secondary school which had a total intake of 1500 pupils. Almost immediately Robert had major difficulties. He was subject to bullying by older pupils due to his poor personal hygiene. He was in constant trouble for fighting with his peers. He was often found wandering about the school unaware of which lesson he was supposed to be attending. When he did manage to find the right lesson he was rude and disruptive to the teachers and was frequently sent out to see the head teacher. He did not attend his detentions. He was aggressive toward his learning support assistant who refused to work with him. He refused to take part in any physical education or sporting activity. He started refusing to attend school or absconded from the premises and spent the day in a nearby wood. He had a number of temporary exclusions lasting a week at a time until, at the end of the first year, he climbed onto the roof of the school and threatened to jump off. This episode required a response by the police and fire service. He was then permanently excluded.

Robert then remained at home for eight months with no educational input. His mother had little control over him and had his younger brother to look after at home. Robert spent long periods roaming the streets or spending time in a rough shelter he had built himself in the wood. He befriended some homeless men and it is believed that he drank alcohol and smoked cannabis with them. It is believed that one of them probably raped him on several occasions although Robert only made partial disclosures about this.

Robert was then placed in a specialist school for children with emotional and behavioural disturbance, travelling 15 miles by taxi each day. He was often late for the taxi or his behaviour was so disruptive while in the taxi that the firm refused to continue to take him.

At this time, when he was 12, his mother confessed to social services that she could no longer cope with him. Robert was taken into temporary foster care. He had three placements, none lasting longer than two weeks as the foster carers were unable to cope with his aggression and he placed their other children at risk. In the last home he was thought to have suffocated the pet cat.

He was then placed at a residential boarding school 100 miles from home. He appeared more subdued and staff felt initially that he was settling in well. Then Robert started to abscond. On one occasion he closed a major motorway by threatening to jump from a bridge. On another occasion he nearly caused a major accident by collecting up traffic cones he found on the road. After just three months he was permanently excluded. As no other placement was available he was transferred as an emergency to the local council's residential children's home where he refused to go to bed at the allotted time, threatened staff with aggression and regularly absconded. He then moved 200 miles away to an independent organisation specialising in residential care for troubled adolescents. He had three separate placements within this service, was arrested on several occasions for stealing alcohol from local shops and was reported approaching female members of the public demanding money and sex. In residential settings female staff would report that he would inappropriately touch them. Staff reported that no sanction was effective in controlling this behaviour and Robert thought that their concern was amusing, laughing about it. In one setting he threatened staff with knives and held them hostage in the kitchen, requiring police intervention. Just before his arrest he set fire to a nearby partially completed building causing £500,000 damage.

PRACTICE ISSUES

What is increasingly clear is that there is a group of children with learning disabilities and complex developmental problems who are particularly difficult to assist in community settings and are more likely to go on to develop significant problems with offending behaviour.

Children with a range of developmental disabilities and behavioural problems are much more difficult to parent. Studies show they significantly increase the stress of caregivers (Baker *et al.* 2003) and have a serious negative psychological, social and economic impact on the family (Emerson 2003b). This makes them more likely to overwhelm the available parenting resources and make them subject to punitive responses by caregivers. Punitive responses have been found to increase child aggression (Stormshak *et al.* 2000) and can result in a negative feedback loop leading to early entry into care and multiple placements.

In these young people with multiple problems the individual co-morbidities may in themselves not necessarily be severe. However, when a number are present together in one individual they 'interweave' to produce a unique and more serious disability than might otherwise be expected (Blakemore-Brown 2002). Aggression is more common in individuals with autistic spectrum disorders (Berney 2004); this may be due to a number of interacting factors including social naivety, impaired understanding of body language and facial expression, increased baseline arousal, cognitive rigidity and a variety of sensory abnormalities. DCD is a major handicap for a young person in terms of interacting appropriately in his or her environment and performing a range of day-to-day skills (Cermak and Larkin 2002). The same young person with co-morbid ADHD and DCD will find that the dyspraxia will significantly worsen his or her social impairment due to difficulties managing a variety of social tasks that involve coordinated motor function. Impulsiveness and inattention associated with ADHD will additionally impact on a similar variety of motor and other social tasks as well as impair executive function abilities like problem solving and understanding the consequences of actions. Specific sensory problems (often associated even with mild autistic disorders) can further complicate the picture. Hypersensitivity to particular sounds, inability to tolerate some types of clothing or refusal to eat particular foods can puzzle parents and carers who may feel the young person is being 'oppositional' for no particular reason and thus may inappropriately respond. Simple tasks that most people take for granted, like eating a meal in a socially appropriate way or negotiating physical space so as not to trip over or bump into others, can be a major challenge for these young people. It also impairs their ability to engage in a range of sporting activities (Gillberg 2003) that are important in social development, self-esteem building and social cohesion. It is not difficult to see how these difficulties can lead to marginalised young people with poor self-esteem who elicit punitive responses from adults (including parents and other authority figures). They are then at high risk to engage in aggression and other risk behaviour alone or with peers, finding themselves in frequent conflict with the wider community.

Physiological arousal

The biological systems for maintaining appropriate levels of arousal are cumulatively compromised by both developmental disorders like ADHD and autism and acquired problems like head injury and chronic PTSD/developmental trauma. These young people are therefore very prone to suddenly 'flip' into very high states of arousal where there is increased risk of self-harm and aggression. These states of high arousal can be prolonged and sustained, particularly in the case of young people with significant abuse and neglect histories. Attempts to keep them safe, particularly with physical restraint, can exacerbate their arousal and dissociation, especially if they were held down as part of a previous physical or sexual trauma. A vicious cycle can then ensue where more restraint leads to higher and more prolonged arousal requiring yet more restraint. This is extremely worrying because there is the potential for serious adverse consequences for young people including physical injury and death (Mohr, Petti and Mohr 2003).

High arousal levels lead to the shutdown of areas of the brain involving language and communication as part of the flight/fight response (Le Doux 1998). Helping young people to control their arousal and keeping it at an appropriate level is one of the key challenges to managing this complex population. Young people are often unable to engage in a whole variety of psychosocial treatments unless this issue can be successfully addressed. Alternative methods of maintaining safety, including the use of safe low stimulus environments and adjunctive pharmacological treatment, may be necessary.

The criminal justice system

The trajectory into the criminal justice system for these adolescents is likely to be complex, haphazard and dependent on a range of environmental and legal variables (Hall 2000). In the UK early diversion from the criminal justice system, particularly for mentally disordered people, was encouraged by the Butler Committee from the mid-1970s (Laing 1999) and subsequently by the Reed Report (Maguire *et al.* 1997). Specific services were subsequently established to achieve diversion (Riordan *et al.* 2000). For developmentally disabled adolescents, however, there were often no appropriate local services to divert to. This has led to delays in treatment and continued risk behaviour in community settings. Paradoxically processing through the criminal justice system with pressure from the court is sometimes the only way for an adolescent with developmental disabilities and forensic needs to access appropriate secure care. Local child and adolescent mental health services may be able to address one aspect of a young person's needs (e.g. ADHD) but are often unable to deal with complex co-morbid problems requiring individualised solutions including complex risk management and skill building across a wide range of domains.

Obtaining information

The information available about the individual can vary from the sparse to the overwhelming. There are a number of potential sources of information including records from child health, general practice, social services, education (including educational psychology), child and adolescent mental health, pre-sentence reports, professional reports for court, criminal records, prison medical records and a variety of 'incident' and other reports from a range of services and settings. In some cases the history is chaotic and it can be difficult to establish who was caring for the young person at any point when he or she has had multiple short placements or periods where he or she may have been outside any parental control. Often important information can emerge many months after an initial assessment.

Instruments

As the initial engagement with developmentally disabled adolescents with forensic problems is often difficult we are often dependent on data collected from informants such as parents, carers, prison officers, and so on. Instruments that structure this informant data may be helpful in relation to screening for complex disorders in a young person with developmental disabilities and forensic needs on initial assessment. Unfortunately there are very few instruments that are specifically designed for this population. In addition these young people can spend so little time in each placement that it can be difficult to obtain an informant who has known them for a long enough period to rate them reliably. None are diagnostic instruments but they can give valuable information that might support a particular or range of diagnostic co-morbidities.

Developmental Behaviour Checklist

The Developmental Behaviour Checklist (DBC) (Einfeld and Tonge 1995) is a 96-item questionnaire which is completed by parents or other primary carers or teachers, reporting problems over a six-month period. The DBC shares the structure of the Child Behaviour Checklist (Achenbach and Edelbrock 1984). The items are completely independently derived from a study of the medical files of 7000 intellectually handicapped children and adolescents seen in a developmental assessment clinic.

The DBC has five subscales: disruptive/antisocial, self-absorbed, communication disturbance, anxiety and social relating as well as a total behaviour problem (TBP) score. It was revised in 2002 to take account of three levels of developmental disability: mild, moderate and severe.

The DBC is sensitive in measuring changes in behaviour in relation to the TPB. It is particularly sensitive in recognising a number of autistic features in young people with significant developmental disability. It appears a little less sensitive in capturing a wider range of problems in relation to adolescents who are in the upper end of the mild and in the borderline learning disability range.

Clinical Assessment of Behaviour

The Clinical Assessment of Behaviour (CAB) (Bracken and Keith 2004) has three versions: two 70 item parent and teacher versions and a longer 170 item extended parent version. It is a comprehensive assessment tool for the objective evaluation of children and adolescents between the ages of 2 and 18 which provides a measurement of the young person's adjustment, psychosocial strengths and weaknesses. It provides an overall score, or CAB behavioural index (CBI), and a number of other scores looking at specific 'scales and clusters' of strengths and weakness, using T scores to compare the results to a standardised population. It is designed to assist in identifying young people who are in need of behavioural and psychiatric interventions and assists in the differential diagnosis of a number of childhood and adolescent psychiatric disorders. It has specific clinical clusters that assist in the identification of symptoms of anxiety, depression, anger, aggression, bullying, conduct problems, ADHD, autistic spectrum behaviours and the presence of specific and generalised cognitive impairment. There are scores for a variety of adaptive skills including social abilities, and also more recent scales for emotional disturbance and social maladjustment. The CAB can give an indication of the likely presence of a number of disorders including autistic spectrum disorders, ADHD, intellectual impairment and affective illness.

Behaviour Rating Inventory of Executive Function

The Behaviour Rating Inventory of Executive Function (Gioia *et al.* 2000) is an 86 item questionnaire designed for carers and teachers of children aged 5–18 that allows an assessment of executive function. It is designed for a broad range of children including those with learning disabilities, attentional disorders, traumatic brain injury, pervasive developmental disorders and other developmental and neurological conditions. It uses age-corrected T scores on a number of individual clinical scales: shift, emotional control, initiate, working memory, plan/organise, organisation of materials and monitor. There are three composite scores: Behavioural Regulation Index (BRI), Metacognition Index (MI) and Global Executive Composite (GEC), an overall composite score. Executive function impairments are common in the population of developmentally disabled adolescents with forensic needs and relate to a variety of disorders that are likely to be co-morbid including ADHD and autism. This instrument can give an indication of the likely presence and degree of executive function impairment.

Interview

Interviewing and assessing this group of adolescents is an art that is not easy to acquire. Particular skills are required. For example, in interviewing young people an interviewer may have to be far more flexible and initially non-directive in order to establish appropriate rapport (Coupey 1997; Morrison and Anders 2001). Adolescents with a forensic history may rapidly enter into a style of communication that mirrors many of the problematic relationships they have had with adults in the past (particularly with those they perceive to hold positions of authority). These can range from the withdrawn and uncommunicative to the overtly hostile and aggressive. Initial questions following introduction like 'Did you know I was coming to see you today?' may be helpful, as on a surprising number of occasions the young person may have had no idea. Ideas from solution focused brief therapy can be helpful in trying to engage young people in the form of trying to understand any interests or goals for the future they may have (Gralton, Udu and Ranasinghe 2006). 'What is stopping you from doing that?' or 'What will you need to do to be able to do that?' may be a much more indirect and non-threatening way of coaxing information about risk behaviours and other concerning symptoms. It is often helpful to have an adult with whom the young person has a reasonable relationship to be present. It is preferable that the adult remain a passive support in the background rather than active in the interview, unless the young person is completely silent. Occasionally there is a significant risk of aggression during the interview and arrangements should be made to ensure that the interviewer is able to summon assistance if it is required.

Pharmacological treatment of complex co-morbid disorders

It is important to understand the difficulties and limitations of diagnosis in young people with complex co-morbid problems, particularly in relation to pharmacological treatment. There has been criticism of the medical model as a way of trying to understand complex disorders in childhood (Sroufe 1997), particularly in the context of interpreting symptom clusters within a developmental perspective. All systems that try to understand or predict complex human behaviour have limitations. The medical model should not be employed as an exclusive tool within any model of care for these complex young people. They will invariably require a variety of assessments from a range of professional perspectives, particularly with a view to looking at risk and outcome over time. However, most of the evidence for the use of pharmacological agents is based on diagnostic categories and it is not possible to engage in rational prescribing without using this model.

It is often important to decide what are the priority issues in terms of risk behaviour and which condition is likely to be contributing to these risk issues that might take precedence in terms of pharmacological treatment. The side effect profile of medication used to treat a priority diagnosis may need to be taken into account so that it ameliorates rather than exacerbates a co-morbid disorder. Occasionally a particular medication may be indicated as a treatment in more than one co-morbid disorder and rational prescribing would suggest that this agent should be higher up the treatment algorithm than another.

Compliance is always likely to be a major concern once young people move back into the community (Lloyd *et al.* 1998) and a simple pharmacological regime is more likely to be adhered to in the longer term than a complex one. Many of the psychotropic medications that are used with young people are technically 'off licence' which does not mean they cannot be prescribed but does mean that there is less information available about their effect on adolescents. There has been a significant increase in the amount of prescribing for adolescents in both the US and the UK since the early 1990s but there is still limited information about the response to some psychotropic medications, particularly antipsychotics (Doerry and Kent 2003; Johnson and Clarke 2001; Popper 2002).

Pharmacological treatment of young people with complex co-morbidity is difficult and there may be the danger that a clinician will resort to poly-pharmacy to try to address all the co-morbid issues. There is also a risk that as young people change placement and see a variety of clinicians they can acquire a cumulative cocktail of medications where there is no clear rationale or prescribing responsibility. This approach is rarely successful, and has particular risks in relation to an increased likelihood of adverse effects (Woolston 1999) and poorly understood interactions between medications, particularly those with shared receptor profiles. The evidence for efficacy in this population is still limited and the use of atypical antipsychotic medication in particular is controversial (Patel *et al.* 2005), particularly around the risk of dyskinesias (Malone *et al.* 2002) and weight gain (Stigler *et al.* 2004).

There is, however, significant evidence to support the use of low dose risperidone in young people with significant conduct disorder (Findling 2000), ADHD and disruptive behaviour disorders in cognitively impaired children (Aman, Binder and Turgay 2004; Snyder *et al.* 2002; Van Bellinghen and de Troch 2001) and those with serious behavioural problems associated with autism (Findling, Maxwell and Wiznitzer 1997; McCracken *et al.* 2002).

Children with learning disability and ADHD respond to methylphenidate (Handen *et al.* 1990; Payton *et al.* 1989), but may require higher doses (Pearson *et al.* 2003) and their response can be more variable, especially at the lower levels of intellectual ability (Aman, Buican and Arnold 2003).

Methylphenidate and clonidine alone and in combination have been provisionally shown to be effective for children and adolescents with ADHD with conduct disorder and aggression (Connor 2000). However, methylphenidate can exacerbate bipolar disorder (Koehler-Troy, Strober and Malenbaum 1986) and there is some evidence that stimulant treatment may be associated with the development of bipolar disorder independent of ADHD (DelBello *et al.* 2001).

Clinicians should remember that ADHD is a condition that generally improves or at least remains static over time. They should consider the possibility of an atypical bipolar disorder (rapid cycling or mixed affective) in young people who have developmental histories consistent with ADHD that is 'getting worse' even when it is tempting to describe it as conduct disorder or emerging personality disorder.

Agents that block the effects of stress neurohormones may be useful adjuncts to the treatment of young people with neglect and abuse who have demonstrated aggressive and other offending behaviour. Perry (1994) has advocated the use of the alpha adrenergic blocker clonidine for children with histories of trauma and abuse due to its effect on noradrenergic autoreceptors to inhibit the firing of cells in the reticular activating system, thus reducing the release of brain noradrenaline. Clonidine has been used to treat severely and chronically abused and neglected children, reportedly improving disturbed behaviour by reducing aggression, impulsivity, emotional outbursts, and oppositional behaviour (Harmon and Riggs 1996). The lipid soluble beta blocker propranolol has been used for established post-traumatic stress disorder in adults (Taylor and Cahill 2002) and has the best evidence for treatment of aggression post-brain injury both in the short and longer term (Fleminger, Greenwood and Oliver 2003). Propranolol has also been successfully used for aggression in children and adolescents (Kuperman and Stewart 1987; Sims and Galvin 1990). There is some limited evidence for the use of sodium valproate in young people with persistent aggression (Golden, Haut and Moshe 2006) without a definitive diagnosis of bipolar disorder.

CONCLUSIONS

It is important to recognise co-morbid disorders, as psycho-education is always the first and most important part of any plan for intervention (Gillberg 2003). Unless there is an appreciation of the complexity around the interacting disorders, those who are intervening can misattribute symptoms or behaviours, draw inappropriate conclusions and may respond in ways that are at best, unhelpful, and may even exacerbate risk behaviour. Services that care for these young people need to have a sophisticated assessment process that can take account of all these complex phenomena or they risk recreating the responses that have contributed to their problems. They will also need a range of multidisciplinary interventions in order to make a sustained and positive impact on these troubled young people (Gralton et al. 2008). These assessments need to be integrated into an overall formulation of the young person. There needs to be a consistent underlying model or philosophy of care that addresses, as far as possible, all the underlying issues.

REFERENCES

Achenbach, T.M. and Edelbrock, C.S. (1984) 'Psychopathology of childhood.' *Annual Review of Psychology 35*, 227–256.

Ad-Dab'bagh, Y. and Greenfield, B. (2001) 'Multiple complex developmental disorder: The multiple and complex evolution of the childhood borderline syndrome construct.' *Journal of the American Academy of Child and Adolescent Psychiatry 40*, 8, 954–964.

Aman, M.G., Binder, C. and Turgay, A. (2004) 'Risperidone effects in the presence/absence of psychostimulant medicine in children with ADHD, other disruptive behaviour disorders, and subaverage IQ.' *Journal of Child and Adolescent Psychopharmacology 14*, 2, 243–254.

Aman, M.G., Buican, B. and Arnold, L.E. (2003) 'Methylphenidate treatment in children with borderline IQ and mental retardation: Analysis of three aggregated studies.' *Journal of Child and Adolescent Psychopharmacology 13*, 1, 29–40.

Baker, B.L., McIntyre, L.L., Blacher, J., Crnic, K., Edelbrock, C. and Low, C. (2003) 'Pre-school children with and without developmental delay: Behaviour problems and parenting stress over time.' *Journal of Intellectual Disability Research 47*, 4–5, 217–230.

Bambinski, L.M, Hartsough, C.S. and Lambert, N.M. (1999) 'Childhood conduct problems, hyperactivity-impulsivity and inattention as predictors of adult criminal activity.' *Journal of Child Psychology and Psychiatry 40*, 3, 347–355.

Barlow, F. and Turk, J. (2001) 'Adolescents with learning disability and psychiatric illness: Two case reports.' *Clinical Child Psychology and Psychiatry 6*, 1, 125–135.

Berney, T. (2004) 'Asperger syndrome from childhood into adulthood.' *Advances in Psychiatric Treatment 10*, 341–351.

Berney, T. and Allington-Smith, P. (2010) *CR 163: Psychiatric Services for Children and Adolescents with Learning Disabilities.* London: Royal College of Psychiatrists.

Berney, T.P., Ireland, M. and Burn, J. (1999) 'Behavioural phenotype of Cornelia de Lange syndrome.' *Archives of Disease in Childhood 81*, 333–336.

Blakemore-Brown, L. (2002) *Reweaving the Autistic Tapestry.* London: Jessica Kingsley Publishers.

Blumer, D., Montouris, G. and Davies, K. (2004) 'The interictal dysphoric disorder: Recognition, pathogenesis, and treatment of the major psychiatric disorder of epilepsy.' *Epilepsy and Behaviour 5*, 6, 826–840.

Bowlby, J. (1988) *A Secure Base: Clinical Applications of Attachment Theory.* Hove: Brunner-Routledge.

Boyle, C.A., Decoufle, P. and Yeargin-Allsopp, M. (1994) 'Prevalence and health impact of developmental disabilities in US children.' *Pediatrics 93*, 3, 399–403.

Bracken, B.A. and Keith, L.K. (2004) *Clinical Assessment of Behavior Professional Manual.* Lutz, FL: Psychological Assessment Resources.

Brier, N. (1994) 'Targeted treatment for adjudicated youth with learning disabilities: Effects on recidivism.' *Journal of Learning Disabilities 27*, 4, 215–222.

Cermak, S. and Larkin, D. (2002) *Developmental Coordination Disorder.* Boston, MA: Cengage Learning.

Chitsabesan, P., Kroll, L., Bailey, S., Kenning, C. *et al.* (2006) 'Mental health needs of young offenders in custody and in the community.' *British Journal of Psychiatry 188*, 534–540.

Clark, T., Feehan, C., Tinline, C. and Vostanis, P. (1999) 'Autistic symptoms in children with attention deficit hyperactivity disorder.' *European Child and Adolescent Psychiatry 8*, 1, 50–55.

Connor, D.F. (2000) 'A pilot study of methylphenidate clonidine or the combination in ADHD comorbid with aggressive oppositional defiant or conduct disorder.' *Clinical Pediatrics 39*, 1, 15–25.

Coupey, S.M. (1997) 'Interviewing adolescents.' *Pediatric Clinics of North America 44*, 6, 1349–1364.

Crocker, N., Vaurio, L., Riley, E.P. and Mattson, S.N. (2009) 'Comparison of adaptive behavior in children with heavy prenatal alcohol exposure or attention-deficit hyperactivity disorder.' *Alcoholism Clinical and Experimental Research 33*, 11, 2015–2023.

De Bellis, M.D., Baum, A.S., Birmaher, B., Keshavan, M.S. *et al.* (1999a) 'Developmental traumatology, part I: Biological stress systems.' *Biological Psychiatry 45*, 1259–1270.

De Bellis, M.D., Keshavan, M.S., Clark, D.B., Casey, B.J. *et al.* (1999b) 'Developmental traumatology, part II: Brain development.' *Biological Psychiatry 45*, 1271–1284.

DelBello, M.P., Soutullo, C.A., Hendricks, W., Niemeier, R.T., McElroy, S.L. and Strakowski, S.M. (2001) 'Prior stimulant treatment in adolescents with bipolar disorder: Association with age at onset.' *Bipolar Disorder 3*, 2, 53–57.

Dewey, D., Kaplan, B.J., Crawford, S.G., Wilson, B.N. (2002) 'Developmental coordination disorder: Associated problems in attention, learning, and psychosocial adjustment.' *Human Movement Science 21*, 5, 905–918.

Doerry, U.A. and Kent, L. (2003) 'Prescribing practices of community child and adolescent psychiatrists.' *Psychiatric Bulletin 27*, 407–410.

Dykens, E.M. (2000) 'Psychopathology in children with intellectual disability.' *Journal of Child Psychology and Psychiatry 41*, 407–417.

Einfield, S.L. and Tonge, B.J. (1995) 'The developmental behavior checklist: The development and validation of an instrument to assess behavioral and emotional disturbance in children and adolescents with mental retardation.' *Journal of Autism and Developmental Disorders 25*, 2, 81–104.

Elliott, E.J., Payne, J., Morris, A., Haan, E. and Bower, C. (2008) 'Fetal alcohol syndrome: A prospective national surveillance study.' *Archives of Disease in Childhood 93*, 9, 732–737.

Emerson, E. (2003a) 'Prevalence of psychiatric disorders in children and adolescents with and without intellectual disability.' *Journal of Intellectual Disability Research 47*, 1, 51–58.

Emerson, E. (2003b) 'Mothers of children and adolescents with intellectual disability: Social and economic situation, mental health status, and the self-assessed social and psychological impact of the child's difficulties.' *Journal of Intellectual Disability Research 47*, 4–5, 385–399.

Emerson, E. and Hatton, C. (2007) 'Mental health of children and adolescents with intellectual disabilities in Britain.' *The British Journal of Psychiatry 191*, 6, 493–499.

Findling, R.L. (2000) 'A double-blind pilot study of risperidone in the treatment of conduct disorder.' *Journal of the American Academy of Child and Adolescent Psychiatry 39*, 4, 509–516.

Findling, R.L., Maxwell, K. and Wiznitzer, M. (1997) 'An open clinical trial of risperidone monotherapy in young children with autistic disorder.' *Psychopharmacology Bulletin 33*, 155–159.

Fleminger, S., Greenwood, R.J. and Oliver, D.L. (2003) 'Pharmacological management for agitation and aggression in people with acquired brain injury.' *Cochrane Database of Systematic Reviews 1*, Art. No.: CD003299.

Ford, G., Andrews, R., Booth, A., Dibdin, J., Hardingham, S. and Kelly, T.P. (2008) 'Screening for learning disability in an adolescent forensic population.' *Journal of Forensic Psychiatry and Psychology 19*, 3, 371–381.

Franklin, L., Deitz, J., Jirikowic, T. and Astley, S. (2008) 'Children with fetal alcohol spectrum disorders: Problem behaviors and sensory processing.' *American Journal of Occupational Therapy 62*, 3, 265–273.

Gillberg, C. (2003) 'Deficits in attention, motor control, and perception: A brief review.' *Archives of Disease in Childhood 88*, 904–910.

Gillberg, C. and Billstedt, E. (2001) 'Autism and Asperger syndrome: Coexistence with other clinical disorders.' *Acta Psychiatrica Scandinavica 102*, 5, 321–330.

Gioia, G.A., Isquith, P.K., Guy, S.C. and Kenworthy, L. (2000) *Behaviour Rating Inventory of Executive Function Professional Manual.* Lutz, FL: Psychological Assessment Resources Inc.

Golden, A.S., Haut, S.R. and Moshe, S.L. (2006) 'Nonepileptic uses of antiepileptic drugs in children and adolescents.' *Pediatric Neurology 34*, 6, 421–432.

Gralton, E., Muchatuta, A., Morey-Canellas, J. and Drew-Lopez, C. (2008) 'Developmental traumatology: Its relevance to forensic adolescent settings.' *British Journal of Forensic Practice 10*, 2, 33–39.

Gralton, E., Udu, V. and Ranasinghe, S. (2006) 'A solution-focused model and inpatient secure settings.' *British Journal of Forensic Practice 8*, 1, 24–30.

Hall, I. (2000) 'Young offenders with a learning disability.' *Advances in Psychiatric Treatment 6*, 278–285.

Handen, B., Breaux, A.M., Gosling, A., Ploof, D.L. and Feldman, H. (1990) 'Efficacy of methylphenidate among mentally retarded children with attention deficit hyperactivity disorder.' *Pediatrics 86*, 6, 923–929.

Harmon, R.J. and Riggs, P. (1996) 'Clonidine for posttraumatic stress disorder in preschool children.' *Journal of the American Academy of Child and Adolescent Psychiatry 35*, 1247–1249.

Hellgren, L., Gillberg, C., Bagenholm, A. and Gillberg, C. (1994) 'Children with deficits in attention, motor control and perception (DAMP) almost grown up: Psychiatric and personality disorders at age 16 years.' *Journal of Child Psychology and Psychiatry 35*, 7, 1255–1271.

Itzin, C. (2006) *Tackling the Health and Mental Health Effects of Domestic and Sexual Violence and Abuse.* London: Home Office and Department of Health.

Johnson, J. and Clark, A.F. (2001) 'Prescribing of unlicensed medicines or licensed medicines for unlicensed applications in child and adolescent psychiatry.' *Psychiatric Bulletin 25*, 465–466.

Kadesjö, B. and Gillberg, C. (2000) 'Tourette's disorder: Epidemiology and comorbidity in primary school children.' *Journal of the American Academy of Child and Adolescent Psychiatry 39*, 5, 548–555.

Kadesjö, B. and Gillberg, C. (2003) 'The comorbidity of ADHD in the general population of Swedish school age children.' *The Journal of Child Psychology and Psychiatry 42*, 4, 487–492.

Kazadin, A.E. (2000) 'Adolescent Development, Mental Disorders, and Decision Making in Delinquent Youths.' In T. Grisso and R.G. Schwartz (eds) *Youth on Trial: A Developmental Perspective on Juvenile Justice.* Chicago, IL: University of Chicago Press.

Koehler-Troy, C., Strober, M. and Malenbaum, R. (1986) 'Methylphenidate induced mania in a prepubertal child.' *Journal of Clinical Psychiatry 47*, 11, 566–567.

Kuperman, S. and Stewart, M.A. (1987) 'Use of propranolol to decrease aggressive outbursts in younger patients.' *Psychosomatics 28*, 315–319.

Kutscher, M.L. (2005) *Kids in the Syndrome Mix of ADHD, LD, Asperger's, Tourette's, Bipolar and More!* London: Jessica Kingsley Publishers.

Laing, J.M. (1999) *Care or Custody? Mentally Disordered Offenders in the Criminal Justice System.* Oxford: Oxford University Press.

Lansford, J.E., Miller-Johnson, S., Berlin, L.J., Dodge, K.A., Bates, J.E. and Pettit, G.S. (2007) 'Early physical abuse and later violent delinquency: A prospective longitudinal study.' *Child Maltreatment 12*, 3, 233–345.

Le Doux, J. (1998) *The Emotional Brain.* London: Wiedenfield and Nicolson.

Lennox, N.G., Rey-Conde, T. and Faint, S.L. (2008) 'A pilot of interventions to improve health care in adolescents with intellectual disability.' *Journal of Applied Research in Intellectual Disabilities 21*, 484–489.

Lloyd, A., Horan, W., Borgaro, S.R., Stokes, J.M., Pogge, D.L. and Harvey, P.D. (1998) 'Predictors of medication compliance after hospital discharge in adolescent psychiatric patients.' *Journal of Child and Adolescent Psychopharmacology 8*, 2, 133–141.

Maguire, M., Morgan, R. and Reiner, R. (1997) *The Oxford Handbook of Criminology.* Oxford: Oxford University Press.

Malone, R.P., Maislin, G., Choudhury, M.S., Gifford, C. and Delaney, M.A. (2002) 'Risperidone treatment in children and adolescents with autism: Short- and long-term safety and effectiveness.' *Journal of the American Academy of Child and Adolescent Psychiatry 41*, 2, 140–147.

Marsh, P.J. and Williams, L.M. (2004) 'An investigation of the individual typologies of attention deficit hyperactivity disorder using cluster analysis of DSM-IV criteria.' *Personality and Individual Differences 36*, 1187–1195.

Martin, N.C., Piek, J.P. and Hay, D. (2006) 'DCD and ADHD: A genetic study of their shared aetiology.' *Human Movement Science 25*, 1, 110–124.

Mason, J. and Scior, K. (2004) '"Diagnostic overshadowing" amongst clinicians working with people with intellectual disabilities in the UK.' *Journal of Applied Research in Intellectual Disabilities 17*, 2, 85–90.

Mattson, S.N. and Riley, E.P. (1998) 'A review of the neurobehavioral deficits in children with fetal alcohol syndrome or prenatal exposure to alcohol.' *Alcoholism: Clinical and Experimental Research 22*, 2, 279–294.

McCracken, J.T., McGough, J., Shah, B., Cronin, P., Hong, D., Aman, M.G., Arnold, L.E., Lindsay, R., Nash, P., Hollway, J., McDougle, C.J., Posey, D., Swiezy, N., Kohn, A., Scahill, L., Martin, A., Koenig, K., Volkmar, F., Carroll, D., Lancor, A., Tierney, E., Ghuman, J., Gonzalez, N.M., Grados, M., Vitiello, B., Ritz, L., Davies, M., Robinson, J. and McMahon, D. (2002) 'Risperidone in children with autism and serious behavioral problems.' *New England Journal of Medicine 347*, 5, 314–321.

Mersky, J.P. and Reynolds, A.J. (2007) 'Child maltreatment and violent delinquency: Disentangling main effects and subgroup effects.' *Child Maltreatment 12*, 3, 246–258.

Mohr, W.K., Petti, T.A. and Mohr, B.D. (2003) *Canadian Journal of Psychiatry 48*, 5, 330–337.

Moretti, G., Pasquini, M., Mandarelli, G., Tarsitani, L. and Biondi, M. (2008) 'What every psychiatrist should know about PANDAS: A review.' *Clinical Practice and Epidemiology in Mental Health 4*, 13. Available at http://archive.biomedcentral.com/content/pdf/1745-0179-4-13.pdf, accessed on 25 December 2010.

Morrison, T.F. and Anders, J. (2001) *Interviewing Children and Adolescents: Skills and Strategies for Effective DSM-IV Diagnosis.* New York: Guilford Press.

Patel, N.C., Crismon, M.L., Hoagwood, K. and Jensen, P.S. (2005) 'Unanswered questions regarding atypical antipsychotic use in aggressive children and adolescents.' *Journal of Child and Adolescent Psychopharmacology 15*, 2, 270–284.

Payton, J.B., Burkhart, J.E., Hersen, M. and Helsel, W.J. (1989) 'Treatment of ADDH in mentally retarded children: A preliminary study.' *Journal of the American Academy of Child and Adolescent Psychiatry 28*, 5, 761–767.

Peadon, E., Rhys-Jones, B., Bower, C. and Elliott, E.J. (2009) 'Systematic review of interventions for children with fetal alcohol spectrum disorders.' *BMC Pediatrics 9*, 35.

Pearson, D.A., Santos, C.W., Roache, J.D., Casat, C.D., Loveland, K.A., Lachar, D., Lane, D.M., Faria, L.P. and Cleveland, L.A. (2003) 'Treatment effects of methylphenidate on behavioural adjustment in children with mental retardation and ADHD.' *Journal of the American Academy of Child and Adolescent Psychiatry 42*, 2, 209–216.

Pellock, J.M. (2004) 'Understanding co-morbidities affecting children with epilepsy.' *Neurology 62*, 5 Suppl 2, 17–23.

Perry, B. (1994) 'Neurobiological Sequelae of Childhood Trauma: PTSD in Children.' In M. Murburg (ed.) *Catecholamine Function in Post-traumatic Stress Disorder: Emerging Concepts.* Arlington, VA: American Psychiatric Press.

Pollak, S.D. and Sinha, P. (2002) 'Effects of early experience on children's recognition of facial displays of emotion.' *Developmental Psychology 38*, 5, 784–91.

Popper, C.W. (2002) 'Child and Adolescent Psychopharmacology at the Turn of the Millennium.' In S. Kutcher (ed.) *Practical Child and Adolescent Psychopatharmacology.* Cambridge: Cambridge University Press.

Raine, A., Yaralian, P.S., Reynolds, C., Venables, P.H. and Mednick, S.A. (2002) 'Spatial but not verbal cognitive deficits at age 3 years in persistent antisocial individuals.' *Development and Psychopathology 14*, 25–44.

Rasmussen, P. and Gillberg, C. (2000) 'Natural outcome of ADHD with developmental coordination disorder at age 22 years: A controlled, longitudinal, community-based study.' *Journal of the American Academy of Child and Adolescent Psychiatry 39*, 11, 1424–1431.

Riley, E.P. and McGee, C.L. (2005) 'Fetal alcohol spectrum disorders: An overview with emphasis on changes in brain and behavior.' *Experimental Biology and Medicine 230*, 6, 357–365.

Riordan, S., Wix, S., Kenney-Herbert, J. and Humphreys, M. (2000) 'Diversion at the point of arrest: Mentally disordered people and contact with the police.' *Journal of Forensic Psychiatry 11*, 3, 683–690.

Rogers, S.J., Wehner, E.A. and Hagerman, R. (2001) 'The behavioral phenotype in fragile X: Symptoms of autism in very young children with fragile X syndrome, idiopathic autism, and other developmental disorders.' *Journal of Developmental and Behavioral Pediatrics 22*, 6, 409–417.

Sampson, P.D., Streissguth, A.P., Bookstein, F.L., Little, R.E., Clarren, S.K., Dehaene, P., Hanson, J.W. and Graham, J.M. Jr. (1997) 'Incidence of fetal alcohol syndrome and prevalence of alcohol related neurodevelopmental disorder.' *Teratology 56*, 317–326.

Sapolski, R.M. (2003) 'Stress and plasticity in the limbic system.' *Neurochemical Research 28*, 1753–1742.

Satterfield, T., Swanson, J., Schell, A. and Lee, F. (1994) 'Prediction of antisocial behaviour in attention deficit hyperactivity disorder boys from aggression/defiance scores.' *Journal of the American Academy of Child and Adolescent Psychiatry 33*, 185–190.

Shprintzen, R.J. (2000) 'Velo-cardio-facial syndrome: A distinctive behavioral phenotype.' *Mental Retardation and Developmental Disabilities Research Reviews 6*, 2, 142–147.

Sims, J. and Galvin, M.R. (1990) 'Pediatric psychopharmacologic uses of propranolol: Review and case illustrations.' *Journal of Child and Adolescent Psychiatric Nursing 3*, 1, 18–24.

Skuse, D., Bentovim, A., Hodges, J., Stevenson, J., Andreou, C., Lanyado, M., New, M., Williams, B. and McMillan, D. (1998) 'Risk factors for the development of sexually abusive behaviour in sexually victimised adolescent boys: Cross sectional study.' *British Medical Journal 317*, 175–179.

Smith, C., Algozzine, B., Schmid, R. and Hennly, T. (1990) 'Prison adjustment of youthful inmates with mental retardation.' *Mental Retardation 28*, 177–181.

Snyder, R., Turgay, A., Aman, M., Binder, C., Fisman, S. and Carroll, A. (2002) 'Effects of risperidone on conduct and disruptive behavior disorders in children with subaverage IQs.' *Journal of the American Academy of Child and Adolescent Psychiatry 41*, 9, 1026–1036.

Soderstrom, H. and Nilsson, A. (2003) 'Childhood onset neuropsychiatric disorders among adult patients in a Swedish special hospital.' *International Journal of Law and Psychiatry 26*, 333–338.

Soderstrom, H., Sjodin, A.K., Carlstedt, A. and Forsman, A. (2004) 'Adult psychopathic personality with childhood-onset hyperactivity and conduct disorder: A central problem constellation in forensic psychiatry.' *Psychiatry Research 121*, 3, 271–280.

Sroufe, L.A. (1997) 'Psychopathology as an outcome of development.' *Development and Psychopathology 9*, 251–268.

Stigler, K.A., Potenza, M.N., Posey, D.J. and McDougle, C.J. (2004) 'Weight gain associated with atypical antipsychotic use in children and adolescents: Prevalence, clinical relevance, and management.' *Pediatric Drugs 6*, 1, 33–44.

Stormshak, E.A., Bierman, K.L., McMahon, R.J. and Lengua, L.J. (2000) 'Parenting practices and child disruptive behavior problems in early elementary school.' *Journal of Clinical Child Psychology 29*, 1, 17–29.

Swillen, A., Devriendt, K., Legius, E., Prinzie, P., Vogels, A., Ghesquiere, P. and Fryns, J.P. (1999) 'The behavioural phenotype in velo-cardio-facial syndrome (VCFS): From infancy to adolescence.' *Genetic Counseling 10*, 1, 79–88.

Talbot, J. (2008) *Prisoners' Voices: Experiences of the Criminal Justice System by Prisoners with Learning Disabilities and Difficulties*. London: Prison Reform Trust.

Taylor, F. and Cahill, L. (2002) 'Propranolol for re-emergent posttraumatic stress disorder following an event of retraumatization: A case study.' *Journal of Traumatic Stress 15*, 5, 433–437.

Tervo, R.C., Azuma, S., Fogas, B. and Fiechtner, H. (2002) 'Children with ADHD and motor dysfunction compared with children with ADHD only.' *Developmental Medicine and Child Neurology 44*, 383–390.

Tonge, B. and Einfeld, S. (2001) 'The trajectory of psychiatric disorders in young people with intellectual disabilities.' *Australia and New Zealand Journal of Psychiatry 34*, 1, 80–84.

Udwin, O. and Yule, W. (1991) 'A cognitive and behavioural phenotype in Williams syndrome.' *Journal of Clinical and Experimental Neuropsychology 13*, 2, 232–244.

Van Bellinghen, M. and de Troch, C. (2001) 'Risperidone in the treatment of behavioral disturbances in children and adolescents with borderline intellectual functioning: A double-blind, placebo-controlled pilot trial.' *Journal of Child and Adolescent Psychopharmacology 11*, 1, 5–13.

Vizard, E., French, L., Hickey, N. and Bladon, E. (2004) 'Severe personality disorder emerging in childhood: A proposal for a new developmental disorder.' *Criminal Behaviour and Mental Health 14*, 17–28.

Weiss, G., Hechtman, L., Milroy, T. and Perlman, T. (1985) 'Psychiatric status of hyperactives as adults: A controlled prospective 15-year follow-up of 63 children.' *Journal of the American Academy of Child and Adolescent Psychiatry 24*, 211–220.

Wiggs, L. and France, K. (2000) 'Behavioural treatments for sleep problems in children and adolescents with physical illness, psychological problems or intellectual disabilities.' *Sleep Medicine Reviews 4*, 3, 299–314.

Woolston, J.L. (1999) 'Combined pharmacotherapy: Pitfalls of treatment.' *Journal of the American Academy of Child and Adolescent Psychiatry 30*, 1455–1457.

Wright, B., Williams, C. and Richardson, G. (2008) 'Services for children with learning disabilities.' *The Psychiatrist 32*, 3, 81–84.

Young, E., Klosko, J. and Weishaar, M.E. (2003) *Schema Therapy: A Practitioners' Guide*. New York, NY: The Guilford Press.

Chapter 2

COMMUNICATION
Obstacles and Opportunities

Carol Reffin

INTRODUCTION

Adolescence is a time of challenges, choices and change. It has been described as a stage in human development which stands out as a period of preparation rather than fulfilment (Modell and Goodman 1990).

Transition from adolescence into adulthood is a significant stage in a young person's life. Young people with developmental disabilities and forensic needs will face great challenges as they enter this stage. Adolescents occupy a variety of cultural niches (Sprinthall and Collins 1994): the economic conditions that they live in, societal values and expectations, community standards and family expectations and relationships. These expectations, opportunities, demands and obstacles that young people encounter exert a powerful influence over their lives and consequent development. Thus it is not surprising that young people with developmental disability, including communication impairment, will inevitably face even greater trials and tribulations.

It is therefore timely and highly relevant to discuss and examine service delivery to this unique population of adolescents. This chapter will provide an overview of speech, language and communication needs of young people with developmental disabilities and forensic needs and how they may present. This population is unique and requires a highly specialised package of care. Communication is crucial to this process, both from the young person's perspective and communication within the team of professionals involved in their care. Communication is something we take for granted. It is a fundamental prerequisite for growth and learning; the ability to communicate is an essential life skill for all children and young people and it underpins a child's social, emotional and educational development (Bercow 2008).

This chapter will cover the role of speech and language therapy with this unique client group, outlining the assessments, intervention and role of the therapist working with them. Language development through the life span and the unique stage of adolescence is also briefly explored as well as a discussion of multi-disciplinary working and its impact on the young person's journey.

RESEARCH EVIDENCE

For many years the primary focus in the field of research around language and communication has been on 'early years', with less attention focused on adolescence. However, it has been pleasing to note that in recent years there has been a change in focus, with studies looking at language and communication needs of adolescents, such as the Bercow report (2008) and studies by Conti-Ramsden and Durkin (2008) and Bryan and Mackenzie (2008) amongst others. Currently there are a limited number of studies and research projects looking directly at speech, language and communication needs of adolescents with developmental disabilities and forensic needs. However, a number of studies, particularly over the last 20 years, have identified links between speech, language and communication impairment and emotional and behavioural difficulties as well as emerging problems of mental health.

The link between language and behaviour is complex and symbiotic. It is widely recognised that adolescents with impaired or impoverished language skills are particularly vulnerable to behavioural, emotional and social difficulties, school exclusion, mental health difficulties and criminal offending behaviours (Clegg et al. 2009; Hartshorne 2006). Research by Prizant et al. (1990) in the field of speech/language therapy and child and adolescent psychiatry has also identified links between communication disorders and an increased risk of developing emotional and behavioural difficulties. The findings of a study by Davis, Sanger and Morris-Friche (1991) suggested that there are often incarcerated youths who have not been identified as having language and learning problems, and that they are a population that would benefit from early assessment. Snowling et al. (2000) felt that young offenders should be viewed as a group to have general verbal deficits.

It is recognised that as many as one-third of children referred for psychiatric intervention will have unsuspected speech and language disorders and one-third of children with communication problems will go on to develop mental illness, if untreated (Clegg, Hollis and Rutter 1999; Cohen 1996). Baker and Cantwell (1987) found that 50–60 per cent of children with speech, language and communication difficulties will fulfil criteria for a mental health difficulty, such as ADHD, psychosis and eating disorders.

Bryan and Mackenzie (2008) have found that a significant percentage of young people in contact with youth justice services have speech, language and communication difficulties, with associated speaking and listening difficulties. There is evidence that shows a relationship between poor literacy skills and juvenile offending (Snowling *et al.* 2000). Oral language competence is known to be linked to literacy skills (Catts *et al.* 2003).

A number of risk factors have also been identified. Recent findings in a study in Australia have highlighted delayed language development as an important risk factor for the development of violent antisocial behaviour in adolescence (Smart *et al.* 2002). A study by Beitchman *et al.* (2001) directly links developmental language disorders and risk for substance abuse and affective disorders in early adulthood, although this study was carried out in young people with a diagnosis of specific language impairment.

Cohen (1996) found that children with unsuspected language impairments showed significantly higher levels of aggression and oppositional behaviour than those whose language impairment had been detected. *Every Child Matters* (ECM) (DfES 2003) identified social isolation as a risk factor for offending and re-offending. Low education and speech and literacy difficulties are risk factors for offending (Tomblin *et al.* 2000). The Bercow review of services (2008) has acknowledged links between language impairment and future risk of offending, noting that if a child does not benefit from early intervention there are multiple risks of lower educational attainment, behavioural problems, emotional and psychological difficulties, poorer employment prospects, challenges to mental health and in some cases a descent into criminality.

The literature search clearly points to the benefits of early intervention and there is now a body of literature and evidence that clearly identifies an increased level of speech, language and communication difficulties with young people in the criminal justice system.

PRACTICE ISSUES

A number of key themes will be explored here, including: how a young person with such complex needs may present; an adolescent's perspective; the experience and impact of multi-disciplinary working; and the role of speech/language therapy and therapeutic intervention.

How a young person presents

Many young people with learning disabilities have already undergone many years of academic and social exclusion, may have poor or distorted feelings of self-worth and often have very little or impaired social success. Kershner (1990) reported that adolescents with learning disabilities have lower levels of academic success and social competence. The young people entering the criminal justice system, namely a medium secure setting, with developmental disabilities are more likely to present in this way.

Communication disability is a feature central to and common across most areas of disability. Competence in oral language and resulting transition to literacy is seen to be crucial as a protective factor in ensuring later academic success, positive self-esteem and improved life chances (Snow and Powell 2002).

These young people with developmental disabilities and forensic needs present with poor conversational skills, limited nonverbal skills and poorly developed social understanding. Hence they are more likely to find peer interaction and forming real friendships very difficult. Language is a central aspect of communication and social interaction and any impairment in communication will have a detrimental effect on their ability to make friends and achieve academic and social competence.

Many young people entering the medium secure setting have a complex background of developmental disabilities, limited social and educational opportunities and a history of social and academic failure, with associated mental health needs. Their speech, language and communication skills are inevitably impaired. As a population they are in danger of being socially excluded and may indeed become permanently marginalised as they grow up without any real hope for the future (Coles 1997).

The young people present with a variety of co-morbid presentations, including attention deficit hyperactivity disorder (ADHD), autistic spectrum disorders (ASD), learning disabilities, developmental dyspraxia, Tourette's, and other mental health illnesses, including schizophrenia, post-traumatic stress disorder, anxiety, psychoses and obsessive compulsive disorder. Typical speech, language and communication difficulties seen may include limited and/or inappropriate social interaction skills, both verbal and nonverbal, pragmatic difficulties, limited or disordered expressive language, poor narrative and discourse skills, memory deficits, disordered or delayed speech, difficulties with abstract language as well as deficits of theory of mind. It is known that deficits related to mental illness, specifically schizophrenia, include reduction in utterances and complexity (De Lisi 2001) as well as disordered structure of language (Covington *et al.* 2005).

An adolescent's perspective

Language development is known to develop well into adulthood so it is essential that there is continued input during the adolescent years. It was once widely believed that language development was complete by late childhood; however, research conducted over the last 30 years has revealed that substantial growth occurs throughout adolescence and well into adulthood (Nippold 2000).

Crucial features of language development, including skills in turn-taking, conversational repair, use of irony and metaphor and the ability to adapt communicative style according to the demands of different contexts, take place in adolescence (Owens 1996). There is also continued development in the areas of syntax, semantics and pragmatics.

Young people's thinking and reasoning skills change in adolescence, including how they think about their social world (social cognition). Peers are viewed as companions who can provide advice, support and feedback. However, the presence of speech and language difficulties will affect the young person's social cognition. Young people with a history of failure both academically and socially will have poor self-concepts by the time they reach adolescence. The measure of our self-esteem is directly related to our communicative competence, so language disordered young people will have difficulties. This lack of self-confidence and self-esteem is present in many of the young people being looked after in medium secure settings.

Social acceptance during adolescence is very important. Young people of today live in a society where everyone is expected to have acquired knowledge and skills in use of the internet and mobile phones. To be socially accepted young people need to be able to understand and interpret others' social messages; many adolescents with speech and language impairments experience significant difficulty in processing information from the social environment (Minskoff 1980). Parker and Asher's study (1987) showed that being disliked by peers and having few friends in childhood is associated with high rates of mental health and behaviour problems in adolescence and adulthood. This is typically seen with the population of young people in the medium secure setting. As Wojnilower and Gross (1988, p.109) stated: 'social competence is now generally acknowledged to be as necessary as academic achievement for children to be prepared to deal with life's challenges'.

If a young person's social network breaks down, this can lead to impairment in his or her mental health, social behaviour and academic performance (Bronfenbremer 1989). It is recognised that language development is instrumental in maintaining interpersonal and social relationships (Paul 1995). Therefore young people with reduced speaking and listening skills in a medium secure setting will be unable to make social relationships and their communication difficulties will affect their engagement with education and therapy.

Communication is central to any close relationship (Asher, Parker and Walker 1996), Asher *et al.* believe that in order to achieve true reciprocity in a friendship it is essential to communicate. Adolescent friendships draw on skills of initiating interactions, responding to others' perspectives and needs, providing social support to each other and disclosing personal information (Steinberg and Morris 2001) and language is integral to this. If antisocial adolescents do form friendships they tend to be with other antisocial individuals and the relationships tend to be less harmonious and short lived (Dishion, Andrews and Crosby 1995). For those who have difficulty communicating it is recognised that some delinquent behaviour provides an alternative way of obtaining peer acceptance and getting along with others (Mouridsen and Hauschild 2009). Winsor (1995) also found that challenging behaviours can serve as communicative functions in students with language disabilities. This is certainly the case with many young people entering a medium secure setting. It has been suggested that the failure to acquire and use developmentally appropriate language skills may indeed contribute to the emergence of nonverbal aggressive behaviours (Davis *et al.* 1991; Sanger *et al.* 2002).

It is clear that young people with a communication impairment are at a disadvantage in making and sustaining appropriate peer relations. Their interactions are infrequent and they generally have poorer discourse skills. Snow (2000) found that adolescents with language problems had an increased chance of delinquency. These findings suggest that failure to succeed academically and socially at school is linked with mixing with similar low-performing peer groups. Interaction and friendships during adolescence make particularly high demands on social communication skills and consequently young people with language and communication difficulties often experience problems with the social demands during unstructured times. In a medium secure setting, this is evident on the wards when the young people have 'free time' and are not attending therapy or education sessions. The Treatment and Education of Autistic and related Communication-Handicapped Children (TEACCH) (Mesibov, Shea and Schopler 2004) therapeutic approach is employed on a ward where many young people have a diagnosis of autism (although this may not be an approach that is used across all medium secure settings). Each young person has a highly structured day with a visual timetable. This provides a sequence of daily activities that is predictable and comprehensible, including unstructured time at the end of the day, when education and therapy sessions have been completed. The Boardmaker software (Mayer-Johnson 2008) produces a symbol based communication system to provide visual support.

Collaboration – working together

When working with young people, a multi-disciplinary way of working is highly recommended (Bercow 2008; DfES 2003). The Royal College of Speech and Language Therapists' guidance, *Communicating Quality 3* (RCSLT 2006), advises that most speech and language therapy will be carried out as part of a multi-disciplinary team and increasingly those disciplines will be employed by different agencies. This is the case whether the service user is a targeted at-risk group or a referred individual.

Speech and language therapists in a multi-disciplinary team are uniquely placed to understand the nature and overall developmental significance of language acquisition in childhood and adolescence. In order to work in a multi-disciplinary way, each profession must be prepared to share their thoughts and findings with others and must acknowledge their professional strengths and weaknesses in order to work truly collaboratively (McCartney 1999). The importance of team working is highly relevant in a medium secure setting and is of great benefit for planning and delivery of therapy. Liaison with other team members is crucial in the care of these young people, allowing the team to jointly assess their needs, deliver joint therapy and appreciate the value of others' input and expert knowledge.

The young people at Malcolm Arnold House, St Andrew's Healthcare, have access to a wide range of professionals from psychiatry, medical staff, occupational therapy, physiotherapy, education, psychology, nursing, art therapy, social work and speech and language therapy. All these professionals are based in one setting which allows them to access each other easily so they can arrange meetings, share resources, discuss and review progress of the young people, and so on. The aim of team working is to offer therapy that is based on a holistic awareness of the patients' needs and to work collaboratively in planning and implementing person-centred goals and clinical care and to provide information about the nature of the communication difficulty (RCSLT 2006). It is widely recognised that collaborative practice is one of the best ways of meeting the needs of children with communication problems (Kersner 1996). Shared knowledge and understanding is crucial for effective communication (Lindsay and Dockrell 2002). This is achievable within a medium secure setting, if each professional is willing to communicate with other members of the team, including the young person and his or her family or carers.

Therapeutic intervention: the role of speech and language therapy

Bryan and Mackenzie's model of service delivery to meet the needs of vulnerable young people (2008) makes excellent recommendations that are highly relevant to this adolescent population. Speech and language therapists are trained to take a holistic view, centred around the young person and his or her speech, language and communication needs. When young people enter the secure setting a comprehensive assessment of their needs is carried out. The purpose of the initial assessment will be explained to them before the assessment begins, at an appropriate level for their cognitive ability. This assessment usually comprises a number of different tasks designed to give a baseline of level of understanding, expressive language skills, verbal memory, language processing speed and literacy skills. This is administered and then followed by a battery of appropriate formal and informal assessments, looking at the following areas of communication as well as eating and drinking: listening and attention, vocabulary, understanding, verbal reasoning, language processing, expressive language skills, memory and literacy skills. A hearing screen is also carried out as there is known to be an over-representation of hearing impairment in this population (Bryan 2004).

The purpose of initial assessment is to identify and collect a range of relevant information including discussion with the young person and consultation with carers, family and colleagues. The speech and language therapist will have to decide if the young person needs intervention and if so examine the impact of the presenting difficulties, identify general risks, and advise where and when the intervention should take place and what form it should take. This includes an assessment of any eating or drinking difficulties as well (RCSLT 2006). A referral is then made to a dysphagia specialist if needed.

This process enables the speech and language therapist to identify specific communication needs. This information is then shared with the team and communication guidelines are drawn up and added to the young person's care plans. A clinical decision is then reached around intervention. The intervention offered within a medium secure setting is needs-led and is a combination of direct and indirect therapy. Direct therapy may be individual and/or group and includes the following: groups to develop emotional literacy, curriculum vocabulary, narrative group, social communication, and thinking skills. It is known that children and young people with language impairments experience difficulties with narratives (Roth and Spekman 1986).

Achieving the production of narratives draws on a range of cognitive and linguistic skills that many young people with developmental disability do not have. The therapy offered is to address this need and to improve their vocabulary, syntax, semantics, memory and sequencing skills, understanding of time, and improve their knowledge of events, and so on. Stringer (2006) found that young people with language disorder and behaviour difficulties benefited from intensive group therapy focusing on narrative development and social skills.

At Malcolm Arnold House, individual therapy is offered for language, dyspraxia, phonology and speech, oral skills and articulation therapy, narrative therapy, vocabulary, memory, listening, dysfluency and voice and any other relevant input. Indirect intervention may include some or all of the following: advice, support and training to staff, joint consultation with other team members, adaptations to the environment, communication guidelines added to each young person's care plan, report writing and attendance at care programme approach (CPA) meetings, attendance at ward rounds, adaptation and differentiation of resources to make them accessible (e.g. working alongside the physiotherapist regarding education of young people around a healthy lifestyle and tackling obesity, and referral to other relevant agencies). In a medium secure setting, the therapist is responsible for making information accessible to all and enhancing communication systems by differentiation of existing resources, therapy programmes and visual support, and for providing advice regarding creating a supportive communication environment.

Speech and language therapists are the lead experts regarding communication and swallowing disorders, which enables them to lead on the assessment, differential diagnosis, intervention with and management of individuals with communication and swallowing disorders (RCSLT 2006).

Being based in the medium secure unit allows the speech and language therapist to provide continuity of support, as the young people are in residential care. The therapist is able to understand the working day, and can view the young people on a day-to-day basis, enabling him or her to create effective and targeted intervention. Working alongside other professionals involved with the young person occurs on a regular basis. The therapist liaises with education staff regarding curriculum vocabulary strategies to use in classroom settings. There is an opportunity for joint working with the psychologists regarding joint training with ward staff, use of social stories around trauma and sexual offending, and so on. The therapist is able to liaise with social workers, facilitate sessions aimed at explaining patients' rights, and work alongside the advocacy team to ensure that information is accessible to this population. Joint therapy sessions with occupational therapy are offered to make activities of daily living accessible, using pictures to sequence each step needed to carry out everyday activities such as getting up, early morning routine, and self-care routines.

The speech and language therapist needs to provide the young people and staff with appropriate communication tools. Simple but effective changes to the way staff communicate with these young people is provided and this significantly improves the experience for the young person concerned. Often intervention takes place as a direct result of a crisis that has occurred on the unit, when it has been necessary to write a social story or use comic strip cartoons as a therapeutic approach (Gray 1994). The use of Boardmaker pictures (Mayer-Johnson 2008) to help the young person to understand or reflect on what has happened is beneficial. Talking Mats (Murphy 1998) have also been effective in therapeutic intervention, enabling the young people to communicate and express their likes/dislikes and their feelings about their environment, education and therapy sessions and their expressed preferences.

Case study

Jane is a 15-year-old girl, admitted to a medium secure setting under section 3 of the Mental Health Act for treatment. Jane needs to remain on the section for her own health and safety and for the protection of others. She has a diagnosis of possible schizophrenia, mild learning difficulties and ADHD. There is a history of domestic violence witnessed at home and her parents have now separated. She is an only child. She coped relatively well in school until she entered secondary education. She was then assessed by an educational psychologist and it was recommended that she receive specialist support.

Jane resented this and disliked having support in the class. She has been physically aggressive towards staff and peers in school. She has a history of poor peer relationships. There is a history of aggressive behaviour also towards property, including her property and that of others. On admission to the unit a risk assessment has been completed that identified a possible link between extreme emotion, an inability to regulate her emotion and lack of empathy with the level and severity of violence displayed. The impact of a communication difficulty in addition to a learning disability increases the incidence of challenging behaviour and/or mental health issues. Language and communication problems are linked with challenging behaviour (Chamberlain, Chung and Jenner 1993).

Cycle of intervention

Initially Jane's care focused on management of her mental illness and challenging behaviour through assessment and intervention by the multi-disciplinary team. Her continuing care focused on the development of appropriate coping skills, as well as working towards achieving her personal goals. Jane was offered a range of therapeutic interventions as part of her individualised care plan, in response to her complex needs.

More than a conversation

Assessment by the speech and language therapist identified some pragmatic impairment, weak word knowledge, some word-finding difficulties and associated difficulties with ADHD including hyperactivity, impulsiveness, organisational problems, impaired executive functions, i.e. skills needed to make a plan and execute it. Intervention focused on initiating structure and boundaries, giving her clear expectations. All interventions were time limited. She was provided with visual support, and offered narrative therapy, inclusion in a social communication group as well as joint work with the occupational therapists regarding budgeting, making snacks and independent self-care skills. She also completed a course of therapy concentrating on vocabulary building. Snow and Powell (2005) found that male young offenders produce narratives that are significantly poorer than male non-offenders with respect to structural and qualitative adequacy of narratives elicited.

CONCLUSION

It is clear that young people with developmental disabilities and associated forensic needs require support that responds to their individual needs, from staff with understanding and experience in working with them. A growing number of people with learning disabilities appear to be in contact with the criminal justice system. Research by the Prison Reform Trust, *No One Knows* (Talbot 2010), identified that 20–30 per cent of offenders have learning difficulties or learning disabilities that interfere with their ability to cope within the criminal justice system. Some people with mild learning disabilities are not having their needs identified because their learning disability is not visible. It is now recognised that plans should be developed in the context of the evidence and recommendations of the Bercow review of services for children with speech, language and communication needs (Bercow 2008).

Traditionally, the majority of therapy offered to these young people is verbally mediated so speech and language therapists should make treatment programmes accessible. It is crucial that training is offered to staff. If the ability to understand and communicate is affected, the young person is inevitably more vulnerable, more suggestible and easily led. As cited in *Positive Practice, Positive Outcomes* (DOH 2010), young people with developmental disabilities will have a significantly reduced ability to understand complex information, learn new skills and cope independently. They need support in carrying out a range of everyday tasks such as filling in forms, following instructions, concentration, telling the time, remembering information, re-telling and explaining events, managing money, making and keeping appointments, and using the telephone. When young people enter the criminal justice system they often lack the language skills needed to understand what is happening to them or the implications of what is being asked of them (Snow and Powell 2004). Milder learning disabilities are less easy to identify immediately and can be hidden, making the young person much more vulnerable. The likelihood of offending is increased when a young person has a learning disability and a mental illness (Lindsay *et al.* 2006). Young offenders with a learning disability and communication impairment are often misunderstood and it has been recognised that an impairment or inability to communicate may often be misconstrued as non-compliance.

Work with children in secure settings is part of the government's overall strategy for improving outcomes for vulnerable children and families, set out in the *Every Child Matters: Change for Children* programme (DfES 2003). There is a specific duty placed on secure establishments to safeguard and promote the welfare of children in their care, following guidance around the ECM five outcomes. The group of professionals involved in their care need to ensure that the young people are healthy, stay safe from harm, achieve their potential, make a positive contribution to the community by engaging in pro-social behaviour and acquire educational skills so they can become more independent. This is an ongoing challenge when working with young people who have such complex needs, but is also a rewarding experience.

REFERENCES

Asher, R., Parker, J.G. and Walker, D.L. (1996) 'Distinguishing friendship from acceptance: Implications for intervention and assessment.' In W.M. Bukowski, A.F. Newcomb and W.W. Hartup (eds) *The Company They Keep*. New York, NY: Cambridge University Press.

Baker, L. and Cantwell, D.P. (1987) 'Factors associated with the development of psychiatric illness in children with early speech/language problems.' *Journal of Autism and Developmental Disorders 17*, 4, 499–510.

Beitchman, J.H., Wilson, B., Johnson, C.J., Atkinson, L. *et al.* (2001) 'Fourteen-year follow-up of speech/language-impaired and control children: Psychiatric outcome.' *Journal of the American Academy of Child and Adolescent Psychiatry 40*, 1, 75–82.

Bercow, J. (ed.) (2008) *The Bercow Report*. Nottingham: DCSF Publications.

Bronfenbremer, U. (1989) 'Ecological systems theories.' *Annals of Child Development 6*, 187–249.

Bryan, K. (2004) 'Prevalence of speech and language difficulties in young offenders.' *International Journal of Language and Communication Disorders 39*, 391–400.

Bryan, K. and Mackenzie, J. (2008) *Meeting the Speech, Language and Communication Needs of Vulnerable Young People*. London: Royal College of Speech and Language Therapists.

Catts, H., Fey, M., Tomblin, M., Bruce, J. and Zhang, X. (2003) 'A longitudinal investigation of reading outcomes in children with language impairments.' *Journal of Speech, Language, and Hearing Research 45*, 60, 1142–1157.

Chamberlain, L., Chung, M.C. and Jenner, L. (1993) 'Preliminary findings on communication and challenging behaviour in learning.' *British Journal of Developmental Disabilities 39*, 118–125.

Clegg, J., Hollis, C. and Rutter, M. (1999) 'Life sentence: What happens to children with developmental language disorders in later life?' *Bulletin of the Royal College of Speech and Language Therapists 571*, 16–18.

Clegg, J., Stackhouse, J., Finch, K., Murphy, C. and Nicholls, S. (2009) 'Language abilities of secondary age pupils at risk of school exclusion: A preliminary report.' *Child Language Teaching and Therapy 25*, 1, 123–139.

Cohen, N.J. (1996) 'Unsuspected language impairments in psychiatrically disturbed children: Developmental issues and associated conditions.' In J.H. Beitchman, N.J. Cohen, M.M. Konstanareas and R. Tannock (eds) *Language, Learning, and Behavior Disorders: Developmental Biological and Clinical Perspectives*. New York, NY: Cambridge University Press.

Coles, M. (1997) *Strategies for Studying*. Carlisle: Cavel.

Conti-Ramsden, G. and Durkin, K. (2008) 'Language and independence in adolescents with and without a history of specific language impairment (SLI).' *Journal of Speech, Language, and Hearing Research 51*, 1, 70–83.

Covington, M.A., Congzhou, H., Brown, C., Naci, L. *et al.* (2005) 'Schizophrenia and the structure of language: The linguist's view.' *Schizophrenia Research 77*, 85–98.

Davis, A.D., Sanger, D.D. and Morris-Friche, M. (1991) 'Language skills of delinquent and nondelinquent adolescent males.' *Journal of Communication Disorders 24*, 4, 251–266.

De Lisi, L.E. (2001) 'Speech disorder in schizophrenia: Review of the literature and exploration of its relation to the uniquely human capacity for language.' *Schizophrenia Bulletin 27*, 481–496.

Department for Education and Skills (DfES) (2003) *Every Child Matters: Change for Children*. Nottingham: Department for Education and Skills (DfES) Publications.

Department of Health (2010) *Positive Practice, Positive Outcomes: A Handbook for Professionals in the Criminal Justice System Working with Offenders with Learning Disabilities*. Learning Disability Specialist Collection. London: Care Services Improvement Partnership.

Dishion, T.J., Andrews, D.W. and Crosby, L. (1995) 'Antisocial boys and their friends in early adolescence: Relationship characteristics, quality, and interactional process.' *Child Development 66*, 1, 139–151.

Gray, C. (ed.) (1994) *Comic Strip Conversations*. Arlington, TX: Future Horizons.

Hartshorne, M. (2006) *The Cost to the Nation of Children's Poor Communication*. 'I Can Talk' Series 2. London: I CAN.

Kershner, J.R. (1990) 'Self-concept and IQ as predictors of remedial success in children with learning disabilities.' *Journal of Learning Disabilities 23*, 6, 368–374.

Kersner, M. (1996) 'Working together for children with severe learning disabilities.' *Child Language Teaching and Therapy 12*, 17–28.

Lindsay, G. and Dockrell, J. (2002) 'Meeting the needs of children with speech, language and communication needs: A critical perspective on inclusion and collaboration.' *Child Language Teaching and Therapy 18*, 8, 91–101.

Lindsay, W.R., Steele, L., Smith, A.H.W., Quinn, K. and Allan, R. (2006) 'A community forensic intellectual disability service: Twelve-year follow-up of referrals, analysis of referral patterns and assessment of harm reduction.' *Legal Criminal Psychology 11*, 113–130.

Mayer-Johnson (2008) *Boardmaker Studio*. Available at http://store.mayer-johnson.com/uk/boardmaker-studio-with-2000-2008-pcs-addenda.html, accessed on 25 December 2010.

McCartney, E. (1999) 'Barriers to collaboration: An analysis of systemic barriers to collaboration between teachers and speech and language therapists.' *International Journal of Language and Communication Disorders 34*, 4, 431–440.

Mesibov, G.B., Shea, V. and Schopler, E. (eds) (2004) *The TEACCH Approach to Autism Spectrum Disorders.* New York, NY: Plenum Publishing.

Minskoff, E.H. (1980) 'Teaching approach for developing nonverbal communication skills in students with social perception deficits. Part I. The basic approach and body language clues.' *Journal of Learning Disabilities 13*, 3, 118–124.

Modell, J. and Goodman, M. (1990) 'Historical perspectives.' In S.S. Feldman and G.R. Elliott (eds) *At the Threshold: The Developing Adolescent.* Cambridge, MA: Harvard University Press.

Mouridsen, S. and Hauschild, K. (2009) 'A long term study of offending in individuals diagnosed with a developmental language disorder as children.' *International Journal of Speech and Language Pathology 11*, 3, 171–179.

Murphy, J. (1998) 'Talking mats: Speech and language research in practice.' *Speech and Language Therapy in Practice*, Autumn, 11–14.

Nippold, M. (2000) 'Language development during the adolescent years: Aspects of pragmatics, syntax, and semantics.' *Topics in Language Disorders 20*, 2, 15–28.

Owens, R.E. (1996) *Language Development: An Introduction.* Fourth edition. Boston, MA: Allyn and Bacon.

Parker, J.G. and Asher, S.R. (1987) 'Peer relations and later personal adjustment: Are low-accepted children at risk?' *Psychological Bulletin 102*, 3, 357–389.

Paul, R. (ed.) (1995) *Language Disorders From Infancy Through Adolescence: Assessment and Intervention.* St Louis, MI: Mosby.

Prizant, B.M., Audet, L.R., Burke, G.M., Hummel, L.J., Maher, S.R. and Theadore, G. (1990) 'Communication disorders and emotional/behavioral disorders in children and adolescents.' *Journal of Speech and Hearing Disorders 55*, 2, 179–192.

Roth, F.P. and Spekman, N.J. (1986) 'Narrative discourse: Spontaneously generated stories of learning disabled and normally achieving students.' *Journal of Speech and Hearing Disorders 51*, 8–23.

Royal College of Speech and Language Therapists (RCSLT) (ed.) (2006) *Communicating Quality 3.* London: RCSLT.

Sanger, D., Moore-Brown, B.J., Montgomery, J.K. and Larson, V.L. (2002) 'Service delivery framework for adolescents with communication problems who are involved in violence.' *Journal of Communication Disorders 3*, 5/3, 293–303.

Smart, D., Vassallo, S., Sanson, N., Dussuyer, I. *et al.* (2002) *Patterns and Precursors of Adolescent Antisocial Behaviour.* Melbourne: Australian Institute of Family Studies.

Snow, P. (2000) 'Language disabilities, co-morbid developmental disorders and risk for drug abuse in adolescence.' *Brain Impairment 1*, 2, 165–176.

Snow, P. and Powell, M. (2002) *The Language Processing and Production Skills in Young Offenders: Implications for Enhancing Prevention and Intervention Strategies.* Canberra: Criminology Research Council.

Snow, P. and Powell, M. (2004) 'Interviewing juvenile offenders: The importance of oral language competence.' *Current Issues in Criminal Justice 16*, 2, 220–225.

Snow, P. and Powell, M. (2005) 'What's the story? An exploration of narrative language abilities in male juvenile offenders.' *Psychology Crime and Law 11*, 239–253.

Snowling, M.J., Adams, J., Bower-Crane, M. and Tobin, V. (2000) 'Levels of literacy among juvenile offenders: The incidence of specific reading disabilities.' *Criminal Behaviour and Mental Health 10*, 4, 229–241.

Sprinthall, N.A. and Collins, W.A. (eds) (1994) *Adolescent Psychology*. Columbus, OH: McGraw-Hill.

Steinberg, L. and Morris, A.S. (2001) 'Adolescent development.' *Annual Review of Psychology 52*, 83–110.

Stringer, H. (2006) 'Facilitating Narrative and Social Skills in Secondary School Students with Language and Behaviour Difficulties.' In J. Clegg and J. Ginsborg (eds) *Language and Social Disadvantage Theory into Practice*. Bognor Regis: Wiley.

Talbot, J. (ed.) (2010) *No One Knows: Prisoners With Learning Difficulties and Learning Disabilities, England and Wales*. London: Prison Reform Trust.

Tomblin, J.B., Zhang, X., Buckwalter, P. and Catts, H. (2000) 'The association of reading disability, behavioral disorders, and language impairment among second-grade children.' *Journal of Child Psychology and Psychiatry 41*, 4, 473–482.

Winsor, J. (1995) 'Language Impairment and Social Competence.' In J. Winsor and Warren S.F. (eds) *Language Intervention: Preschool Through the Elementary Years*. Baltimore, MD: Paul H Brookes.

Wojnilower, D.A. and Gross, A.M. (1988) 'Knowledge, perception, and performance of assertive behavior in children with learning disabilities.' *Journal of Learning Disabilities 21*, 2, 109–117.

Chapter 3

THE APPLICATION OF SENSORY INTEGRATION WITHIN AN ADOLESCENT FORENSIC LEARNING DISABILITY SERVICE

Claire Underwood and Jackie O'Connell

INTRODUCTION

Sensory integration (SI) has been historically considered an intervention for younger children with particular diagnoses. However, it has recently been recognised that following SI principles can help a wide range of people from children through the life stages of adolescence, adulthood and old age (Bundy and Murray 2002). Often young people find it difficult to recognise why they feel a particular way; they just know that they don't feel 'right'. For most people their sensory system develops through exposure to normal childhood experiences, such as playing, going out, using equipment and modelling from the well adjusted adults around them. A high proportion of our young people have not had these experiences thus their sensory systems haven't developed in the same way. Therefore it can be difficult to identify, for example, that they dislike background noise, or find it difficult to tune out. Everyone has a tolerance threshold for a particular sensory input. Unfortunately, for some of our young people, by the time they reach this threshold, they have lost their ability to remain safe and may exhibit challenging behaviours.

Sensory processing is the ability to take in, sort out and make use of information from the world around us. It allows us to make an appropriate adaptive response to meet the demands of the environment. Information is gathered from tactile (touch), vestibular (movement and gravity), proprioceptive (body position), visual, auditory, olfactory (smell) and gustatory (taste) senses. It is a neurological process of receiving, organising and interpreting sensory information resulting in an adaptive and automatic plan of action that can be carried out in response (Ayres

1979). This processing of sensory information is called sensory integration or SI. 'The brain locates, stores, and orders sensations – somewhat as a traffic policeman directs moving cars... When the flow of sensations is disorganised, life can be like a rush-hour traffic jam' (Ayres 1979, p.5).

Following the growing evidence base and interest in the use of SI within mental health settings (Brown *et al.* 2006; Champagne and Stromberg 2004), the application of SI on adolescents with high arousal levels, attachment, trauma and forensic histories plus a developmental disability was explored (particularly in considering whether this would be useful as an alternative technique for de-escalation and containment of aggressive and violent behaviour). This has led to SI theory and practice evolving as an integral part of the therapeutic programme and becoming embedded into the fabric of each unit. This chapter will describe how this approach has been implemented and integrated into the therapeutic programme, including risk, environmental and ethical issues which have arisen as a result of working within a forensic medium secure unit.

RESEARCH EVIDENCE

Within occupational therapy (OT) practice, current theorists rely upon the core writings of Dr A. Jean Ayres (1979, 2005). Dr Ayres brought together her knowledge of neuroscience and OT to pioneer and create the theory, assessments and treatment principles. Over the last 30 years, the concept of SI has continued to be informed, refined and developed by the clinical practice of OTs using a sensory integrative frame of reference. Developments in neuroscience have continued to evolve and shape our understanding and application of the concepts of sensory modulation adding further evidence to the theory of SI. Recent research on the plasticity of the brain past childhood (Bundy and Murray 2002) gives weight to Jean Ayres' theory that SI can influence new neural pathways.

In more recent years the growing scientific evidence base of SI has expanded to a variety of clinical populations including mental health (Brown *et al.* 2006; Champagne 2006; Champagne and Stromberg 2004). Literature also supports SI as an intervention for those with sensory defensiveness and to reduce self-injurious behaviour (Brown, Shanker and Smith 2009; Moore and Henry 2002; Pfeiffer and Kinnealey 2003), which is often a part of the young person's clinical profile. Teaching people to understand and interpret their sensory needs will enable them to change situations and hence the way they are feeling before the need to resort to challenging behaviour (Brown *et al.* 2006; Champagne and Stromberg 2004; Kwok, To and Sung 2003). Currently in America sensory approaches are cited as one of the key strategies to reduce seclusion and restraint as part of a national initiative (Champagne and Stromberg 2004).

SI treatment is often prioritised following a young person's admission as it allows OTs 'to address the underlying issues affecting occupational performance' (Shaaf and Nightlinger 2007, p.245). Helping patients to self-modulate more effectively will increase their ability to engage in more cognitive therapies, improve ability to communicate with others, and improve social skills and general independent functioning (Bar-Shalita, Vatine and Parush 2008; Brown *et al.* 2006). When young people are in a heightened state of arousal or shutdown they can only process information essential for survival; their ability to self-reflect and analyse, their executive functioning, is diminished. Therefore SI facilitates a young person to be calm and alert thus reducing self-injury and enabling them to meaningfully engage in functional activities preparing them for other therapies (Brown *et al.* 2006).

PRACTICE ISSUES

Co-morbidity

Due to the multiple diagnosis and complex nature of the client group it is important to look at the relationship between diagnosis, arousal, attachment and sensory processing disorder.

Of particular relevance and concern is that SI also plays an important role in arousal or 'alertness'. Assessments often indicate that young people have difficulty with sensory modulation which appears linked with their fluctuating arousal levels. Sensory modulation difficulties cause an individual to respond inappropriately and inconsistently with the demands of the situation, thus undermining socially and developmentally appropriate behaviour. Kimball (1999, cited in Bundy and Murray 2002) pointed out that moderate arousal produced an ideal adaptive environmental interaction, but over-arousal led to behavioural disorganisation, anxiety and potentially negative responses. 'Modulation is the process of increasing or reducing neural activity to keep that activity in harmony with all the other functions of the nervous system' (Ayres 1979, p.70). Ayres defined modulation as the 'brain's regulation of its own activity' (1979, p.182). It involves facilitating some neural messages to produce an enhanced response and inhibiting other messages to reduce activity.

Alongside, there's a strong relationship between arousal states and anxiety, and anxiety and sensory defensiveness (Kinnealey and Fuiek 1999; Pfeiffer *et al.* 2005). Symptoms of complex post-traumatic stress disorder (PTSD) and anxiety often present similarly to those associated with sensory defensiveness and share 'a number of behavioural and psychological traits. Hypervigilance and increased levels of arousal, including increased sympathetic nervous activity...' (Kinnealey and Fuiek 1999, p.198). As high anxiety levels in complex PTSD can generate a heightened flight, fight, fright response this equally can be generated from a diagnosis of being sensory defensive. The literature points to the conclusion that 'stress can amplify tactile or sensory defensiveness' (Lane 2002, p.115).

Indeed, clinical experience and assessments have highlighted that sensory defensiveness is a common feature within the clinical profile of this client group. Behaviours often appear to be an avoidance of sensory stimuli and/or a means of self-regulation. These behaviours correlate with a phenomenological study of sensory defensiveness in adults whereby avoidance and engaging in alternative activities (frequently proprioceptive) were used to counteract the effects of distressing input (Kinnealey, Oliver and Wilbarger 1995). The term sensory defensiveness was introduced to describe 'the imbalance between inhibition and excitation within the CNS. The imbalance led to too little inhibition and a consequent flood of input reaching the CNS structures' (Knickerbocker 1980, cited in Lane 2002, p.107). Thus young people will often over-attend to stimuli that others may ignore or adapt to, such as noise on the unit and unexpected touch, typically responding with emotional and behavioural responses including withdrawal (flight), aggression (fight) or fright (irritability/mood swings), at times going into shutdown.

Furthermore, attachment research shows 'the powerful effect interpersonal relationships can have on the development and on-going functioning of self-regulation' (Siegel 1999, p.285). Siegel states 'within the context of an attachment relationship the child's developing mind and the structure of the brain will be shaped' (1999, p.285). Therefore the principles of attachment theory and the interpersonal relationship are crucial in helping a child learn how to self-soothe and nurture oneself. Equally, early attachment can be compromised by severe over- or under-reactions of a child to sensory stimuli. Siegal (1999, p.285) proposes that 'interpersonal relationships can provide attachment experiences that can allow similar neurophysiological changes to occur throughout life'. Therefore the reaction of staff to the young people's presenting behaviours will greatly influence the young person's internal capacity to regulate sensation. Hence training and education of all the multidisciplinary team (MDT) in order to understand how behaviour and emotional difficulties are sensory-based is essential to 'know how to appropriately relate to the child and avoid escalating an already tense and possibly threatening situation' (Bhreathnach 2008, p.5).

We know that sensory processing disorders co-exist with other diagnoses; research has indicated that autism is 'a disorder of the senses where each sense operates in isolation and the brain is unable to organise the stimuli in any meaningful way' (Bogdashina 2003, p.25). Many people with autistic spectrum disorders may be unable to recognise their own sensory needs. Most people can cut out background stimuli and attend to the situation; for some this is not possible, resulting in a multitude of different sensory inputs, perhaps leading to sensory overload. Imagine how difficult it must be to be unable to ignore the noises in the background, sensation of your clothes on your skin and smells within the air. Focusing your attention would then be next to impossible, yet this is often something we expect our young people to do. These findings are congruent with Tomchek and Dunn's (2007, p.198) study detailing the differences in sensory processing of children with and without autism where they concluded that children with autism 'were reported to be inattentive, underresponsive, and sensitive to tactile input. They also were reported to seek sensory input and have difficulty filtering auditory input'.

Similarly, sensory processing disorders have been linked with learning disability, with this population finding it difficult to organise, interpret and respond to sensory input. This can result in people avoiding activities they find difficult to process, or seeking out particular activities in an attempt to activate their higher than normal neurological threshold (Urwin and Ballinger 2005). Often the tactile system is affected, resulting in difficulties maintaining concentration, emotional and behavioural issues and difficulties modulating arousal levels (Urwin and Ballinger 2005).

Several researchers have found links between attention deficit hyperactivity disorder (ADHD) and sensory processing disorders (Adamson, O'Hare and Graham 2006; Chu and Reynolds 2007a). These have been linked on a neurological level, illustrating that poor sensory modulation can influence the behavioural patterns observed in young people with ADHD. Further research supports SI techniques as part of a multimodal treatment programme (Chu and Reynolds 2007a, 2007b).

Assessments

A comprehensive OT assessment affords the ability to offer specific sensory approaches appropriate to each individual's needs, treatment goals and interests. Assessment is important to determine personal preferences, as well as their effectiveness in recognising that a sensory activity that helps one young person unwind may not work for another. Following this, the co-creation and prioritisation of therapeutic treatment goals are determined and options for intervention are explored. The treatment goals are created jointly by the therapist and the service user, where possible. Through a comprehensive assessment of clinical observation, sensory history and standardised tests, the therapist is able to determine how the adolescents' brain is processing the input.

Assessments used include:

- Adult/Adolescent Sensory Profile (Brown and Dunn 2002) – a standardised self-report instrument requiring the service user to have a good understanding of questions asked. Can help to determine whether aspects of sensory processing might be contributing to the occupational performance challenges that young people experience in daily life, such as impaired social function, difficulty in group situations, aversive responses to noise and high stimulus environments.

- Sensory Profile (Dunn 1999) – this includes a carer's questionnaire that is useful when a young person cannot self-report. However, this is not standardised for adolescents.

- Sensory Choices Checklist (Williams and Shellenberger 1996) – helps indicate young persons' sensory preferences/dislikes by asking them to indicate activities that calm or alert them. Choices are used to help establish a sensory diet.

- Sensory Integration Inventory – revised for individuals with learning disabilities (Reisman and Hanschu 1992), an observational tool to screen for clients who might benefit from an SI treatment approach. Needs to be completed by a therapist with a background and sound knowledge of SI theory and practice for accurate interpretation.

- OTA Watertown Developmental/Sensory History for Adults and Adolescents (2nd ed.) (Koomar et al. 1996). The assessment provides a detailed insight into a young person's medical, birth and childhood history, current and past sensory history, general state of arousal, sleep and functional performance with activities of daily living. The difficulty with this assessment has been that therapists do not always have access to this information due to the young person's disruptive childhood and possible absence of attachment figures.

- The Developmental Test of Visual Perception for Adolescents (DTVP-A) (Reynolds, Pearson and Voress 2002) – a visual perceptual screening tool used by OTs. Consisting of a battery of six subtests measuring the interrelated visual-perceptual and visual-motor abilities of the individual. The DTVP-A provides standard scores for each of six subtests, constituting a composite, which is then converted into the following indexes: general visual-perception, motor-reduced visual perception, and visual-motor integration.

From clinical observations of the young people, data gathering and the findings from sensory assessments the information is collated and used to formulate a young person's sensory processing difficulties using the new proposed nosology (Miller *et al.* 2007). This classifies the different sensory processing disorders under one umbrella with differentiated diagnostic sub-types.

Interventions
Individual Occupational Therapy SI (OT-SI)

OT-SI sessions are delivered by OTs who have completed the SI training to ensure they have the relevant skills, knowledge and experience. Following assessment, typical treatment stages considered are based on the protocol used by Pfeiffer and Kinnealey (2003) and recommended by Kinnealey *et al.* (1995): providing insight, administering OT-SI and making recommendations for a sensory diet (Wilbarger 1984).

First, the focus is on psycho-educational intervention, explaining to the young person and care team the findings from the assessments, explanation of SI as a theory and intervention and explanation of arousal levels related to occupational performance.

Second, intervention involves administering individual client centred and client directed OT-SI intervention. Typically these are held weekly for 45 minutes and initially run for 12 weeks before being revised. Typical activities may include:

- resistance work through weight bearing through extended arms and active muscle resistance work (proprioceptive input)

- tactile exploratory play (sand; playdough; shaving foam; rice/beans)

- visual perceptual and ocular motor activities and games

- hand-eye coordination work (organisation of sensory systems to produce a motor response)

- vestibular work (through use of a Swiss ball, balance cushion and hammock swing).

Third, recommendations are made on activities for a sensory diet that can be incorporated into the young person's daily programme and as part of his or her de-escalation care plan. These may include rebound therapy, yoga, multi-gym, swimming plus use of sensory tool kits and sensory rooms.

Sensory diet

The concept of sensory diets was developed by Wilbarger (1984) and has been used within mental health as recommended by Champagne and Stromberg (2004) for individuals with trauma histories and mental illness who may be unaware of the sensory needs and responses. By providing sensory experiences individuals are encouraged to feel grounded and calm/alert.

A sensory diet may include:

- coping and reorientation strategies

- personalised sensory kit – a box individualised with equipment that has been identified and assessed as useful for the young person to help regulate, ground and calm him or her, both for prevention as well as crisis intervention. This may include: relaxation CD, fidget, massage tool, picture/photos of grounding images

- regular daily input, as specified in the individualised care plan which details type and amount of support necessary and how to utilise sensory strategies safely, which is especially important in a forensic setting

- regular involvement in physical activities like yoga, multi-gym and swimming, health walks, etc.

- incorporating sensory strategies into groups such as sensory art and baking

- using sensory strategies as part of the prevention and management of aggression and violence care plan, e.g. massage, vibrating cushion and weighted blanket when arousal levels are high or if there is a trigger.

Sensory rooms

Sensory rooms offer a nurturing, person-centred sensory supportive environment and treatment space. They are effective in offering patients some time out and the opportunity to learn about their own sensory needs. These rooms can be adapted to be either calming or alerting, through the use of different equipment, tailored to individual patient needs (Kwok *et al.* 2003). During the initial assessment sessions patients will have the opportunity to explore lots of different sensory experiences, such as light, touch and sound, while utilising various pieces of equipment (Champagne and Stromberg 2004). Thus relevant equipment can be identified which will calm/relax or heighten arousal levels of individual patients, which can then be incorporated into their daily programmes. Often young people find it difficult to occupy themselves effectively. Due to their individual difficulties, including impairments in social and interaction skills, they find themselves being drawn into altercations which can rapidly escalate. The sensory rooms are especially used in the evenings, when the majority of incidents occur, to engage patients in a relaxing and therapeutic activity. This provides a safe and familiar space for relaxation; with regular use this may reduce the amount of challenging behaviours observed on the ward (Champagne and Sayer 2003).

Sensory stories

Sensory stories incorporate ways of using different sensory strategies to help people with sensory modulation difficulties, particularly those with over-responsive sensory modulation difficulties (Therapro Inc. undated). These stories use any ordinary event or daily activity that a person may engage in, and give the person different sensory strategies that he or she can use to cope with these situations. The techniques use primarily deep pressure touch, active resistance to movement and slow linear activities to provide the calming sensory stimulus that the person needs. These stories can be written for any situation which the young person finds difficult such as going out, brushing teeth, showering, and so on. The stories are laid out with a pictorial sequence and have relevant words. They are designed to be read with the young person about three times per week for regular tasks, and two to three times a day in the week before infrequent tasks, such as going to the dentist. Although research has shown that these can be effective with younger children (Therapro Inc. undated), due to the flexible nature in which these can be designed and utilised it is felt that they could adapted for anyone. The advantages are multifold as the young person can take responsibility and control in regulating his or her arousal levels, applying the appropriate magnitude of input. The strategies are designed to be normalised activities which can be used whilst out in the general community (i.e. these are strategies which may not be noticed by others).

Sensory care plans/de-escalation plans

Using the care programme approach SI techniques have been incorporated into the risk de-escalation care plan to provide strategies and techniques for crisis prevention and reduce seclusion and restraint. These are individualised for each young person based on the person's profile of need. More in-depth sensory care plans are cross-referenced to use within these to instruct the MDT how to implement sensory strategies with the young person. These may include using the sensory room and/or a young person's sensory tool kit as detailed above. The use of the sensory room would be an early stage intervention, utilising the tools relevant for the young person to help him or her to calm and lower arousal levels, thus avoiding the situation escalating further. This method has been seen to be effective in previous studies (Champagne and Sayer 2003).

Sensory considerations within the environment

Our young people have a decreased capacity to tolerate sensory stimuli. They can easily become overwhelmed or irritated by the environment resulting in becoming highly aroused. Therefore within the planning of a Child and Adolescent Mental Health Service (CAMHS) tier 4 adolescent service particular attention and focus is needed on creating therapeutic spaces in order to meet the sensory needs of the young people ensuring the environment is not overstimulating or unpredictable. Staff needs to be aware of environmental stressors/triggers that can ultimately lead to violent behaviour and the need for use of seclusion and restraint. Nurture space is needed through the provision of quiet rooms, chill out, sensory rooms, and so on. Active spaces such as access to courtyards, multi-gym and sports hall facilities for obstacle courses, gross motor activities, and so on, are needed as well. A combination of spaces provides the balance of nurture and challenge, positive risk taking and safety within the context of consistency, boundaries and predictability. Due to restrictions placed on the young people, including home office sections and risk levels, sensory spaces must be available within the secure perimeter of the building. Access to different spaces can help diffuse the highly expressed emotion within the main living area by providing the young person 'time away'. Young people must be offered choices of therapeutic spaces to utilise different sensory spaces according to their needs at the time and depending on their own sensory preferences. Using gym equipment to provide heavy resistance muscle work when feeling aggressive and utilising the sensory room when anxious are some examples.

Other environmental considerations include colour, lighting, noise, distractions, size of the rooms and seating options (Champagne 2006). For example, within a classroom or group setting staff need to consider the amount of visual or auditory distractions in the space and how this might affect the young people's occupational performance. In large, open spaces with poor acoustics and echoing sounds the space may need to be adapted in order to prevent the young people becoming overwhelmed. This is particularly an issue for young people on the autistic spectrum, and those who are sensitive to sound. Sufficient space needs to be provided in order to accommodate basic equipment, such as bean bags and floor mats.

Other sensory-based interventions
Sensory approaches have been incorporated into much of the existing programme at St Andrew's Healthcare to provide a sensory curriculum that runs alongside the therapy and educational programme. These interventions are delivered under the supervision and/or consultation of an OT with SI training. These interventions include:

- Sensory circuits – a 30-minute group at the beginning of the day to help establish a morning routine and facilitate service-users in modulating arousal levels. The group consists of alerting, organising and finally, a calming exercise. Regularly completing these activities will also enhance their understanding of the effects of different sensory stimuli with the eventual goal that they will be able to take a more active role in regulating their arousal levels in the future (Harwood 2009).

- Alert programme – adapted to help the young people 'learn to monitor, maintain, and change their level of alertness so that it is appropriate to a situation or task' (Williams and Shellenberger 1996, p.1–1).

- Groups such as 'chill out group', 'nurture me', 'creative relaxation' or Tai Chi which incorporate sensory approaches to help the young people learn techniques to self-soothe, calm and regulate arousal levels.

- Sensory-based gardening, animal assisted therapy, art, craft and baking sessions to provide a multi-sensory approach.

- Self-care, facilitated jointly by OT and beauty therapy that use activities including massage in recognition of the importance of touch as a therapeutic medium in self-regulation.

- Rebound therapy groups, facilitated by physiotherapy and OT to improve balance, coordination, body and spatial awareness, muscle strength, aerobic fitness, flexibility and exercise tolerance, used to help regulate arousal levels when identified as part of a sensory diet.

- Theraplay®-based interventions incorporating sensory approaches within the activities used under the four dimensions of Theraplay® – structure, nurture, engagement and challenge – in order to help regulate arousal levels and teach service-users to self-soothe (Jernberg and Booth 2001).

Equipment
Within SI theory and practice, the emphasis is on the integration of vestibular, proprioceptive and tactile sensations. Therefore activities and equipment are utilised in OT-SI that focus on these three senses. Proprioceptive input

can have calming, organising and modulating effect, so it can be used when arousal levels are either too high or too low. Unlike other sensory inputs, proprioceptive input is rarely overloading to a nervous system. It is therefore an excellent strategy to use to excite or inhibit arousal levels, for example using proprioceptive input during a group session where everyone seems to be unable to be alert or maintain a level of wakefulness for the session – then using the same strategy for a young person who seems to be becoming more excitable or aroused. The vestibular system also has an important role to play in regulating arousal levels. For example slow rhythmic linear input such as rocking a baby can be the fastest way to calm someone down. Equally, fast arrhythmic, orbital vestibular movement can facilitate heightening arousal levels.

There is a growing body of literature demonstrating the positive impact of healthy physical contact on people of all ages and the importance of touch in healthy child development and in therapy. Touch is an integral part of SI, being the most pervasive of all sensory systems and essential for social, emotional and physiological development, psychological and emotional well-being, regulation of stress and to improve body image (Jernberg and Booth 2001). Krauus (1987), investigating the effects of deep pressure touch on anxiety, stated that researchers' results from animal and human studies 'led them to conclude that pressure is inhibitory not only to the motor system, but to the whole autonomic system' (p.368).

Equipment used at St Andrew's Healthcare:

- tactile trays (rice, lentils, sand)
- trampette
- fidgets
- weighted blankets
- scooter boards
- Swiss balls/logs
- medicine balls and Therabands
- rocker chair
- portable swing
- large spinning disc
- vibrating massage tools/cushion/snake
- messy play (cornflour, shaving foam)
- aroma dough
- ooze tubes, optic fibre lights.

Ethical health and safety considerations

Due to the very nature of working in an adolescent medium secure unit ethical and risk issues have been a constant theme and solutions are needed with guidelines and procedures in place to ensure safe practice.

Due to the fear of allegations and the risk involved for both staff and young people, much concern has been expressed regarding the use of touch in therapy. It is well researched that in healthy child development it is vital that the young person experiences gentle, kind, loving and safe touch. Therefore a clear rationale is in place regarding the therapeutic use of touch with guidelines making it explicit as to how touch can be administered in a safe and therapeutic manner. These have been adapted from the guidelines published in *The Ethical Use of Touch in Psychotherapy* (Hunter and Struve 1998). The aim is for staff to understand how to touch cautiously, to meet the needs of the young person, and to be vigilant as to the effect that touch has on the young person. The guidelines make it explicit when is it appropriate or not advisable to touch, to safeguard when using touch, taking into account sensory sensitivities, preferences and personal history, in order not to re-traumatise the young person. Therapeutic touch is often documented as part of the de-escalation care plan or as part of their sensory diet. Types of touch used include:

- direct – foot/hand/back massage, facial, Indian head massage

- indirect – foot spa, massage tools, brushing, manicure/pedicure, henna art, body painting, hair beading, sand play.

When adhering to the treatment principles of SI, ensuring the environment is safe is paramount at all times and this can never be underestimated within a forensic setting. Due to the high risk behaviours of working with this population suspended equipment including bolster swings and hammocks are not possible. Consequently a portable swing is used but this has restrictions in that it only facilitates gentle linear vestibular movement, and weight restrictions prevent it being used with some young people. Guidelines and staff training are essential for the safe use of sensory rooms, ensuring all equipment is risk assessed and appropriately utilised.

Use of aerosols such as shaving foam and crazy soap used within interventions needs strict supervision due to the potential to set off fire alarms. Stringent infection control policies mean all equipment purchased needs to be washed or sterilised. Brushes are sterilised after each use and weighted and ball blankets (blankets with plastic balls stitched into the cover for an even spread across the blanket) require a washable, fire retardant cover. The challenge has been sourcing equipment that meets these health and safety requirements. Explicit guidelines for use of weighted blankets have been devised, to ensure safe practice. These include assessment by an SI-trained OT and care plans outlining their use in line with the guidance documentation.

Case description

George is 16 years old and was admitted three months ago, under section 37/41, due to increasing levels of physical aggression resulting in a number of serious attacks and a history of self-harm. He has a diagnosis of mood disorder and emerging personality disorder, attachment difficulties, depression, obsessive compulsive disorder and mild learning disability. George was referred for an assessment for SI intervention with OT for two main reasons: first, to assess whether OT-SI could help George regulate arousal levels in order to support him to tolerate his peer group; and second, to look at alternative sensory strategies to help reduce self-harm and aggression leading to a reduction in seclusion and restraint.

Through occupational assessment, interview and observations it appeared that George displays aversive responses in relation to certain sensory stimuli such as unexpected or prolonged noise and withdraws from unanticipated tactile input. Additionally he presents with difficulties in regulating emotions and frequently resorts to antisocial coping strategies in order to manage this dysregulation. Subsequently George was assessed for sensory processing disorder; the Sensory Integration Inventory – revised for individuals with learning disabilities was administered as part of the assessment.

Since admission George has struggled with developing a structure and routine to his day, displaying behaviours including self-harming by cutting and banging his head, which at times appear in response to the ward environment. He spends the majority of his day isolating himself, using the quiet room, sleeping on the sofa and engaging mainly with the nursing staff on an individual basis.

Behaviours observed indicate that when the unit is unsettled, noisy and busy, George will pace the room and engage in self-injurious behaviour including head-banging. On other occasions he spends long periods of time lying on the sofa, or withdraws from his peers sitting by himself listening to his iPod. At the time of the assessment George was refusing to engage in any group but would engage individually with staff. George's fluctuating arousal states appeared to be impacting on all his occupational domains; his under- and over-arousal states appear to impact on his ability to engage fully in daily occupations.

Using the new nosology (Miller *et al.* 2007) the hypothesis is that George appears to have sensory modulation disorder sub-type 1: sensory overresponsivity (SOR) occurring in multiple systems leading to George being sensory defensive to auditory, visual and tactile stimuli. He is sensory over-responsive, meaning he has a low neurological threshold to stimuli, presenting with an averse reaction to stimuli activating the sympathetic nervous system leading to a state of flight, fright or fight. Miller *et al.* (2007, p.137) states 'behaviours in SOR range from active, negative, impulsive, or aggressive to more passive withdrawal or avoidance of a situation'. The hypothesis is that behaviours such as head-banging, pacing and cutting are his attempts to self-regulate his levels of arousal. A diagnosis of sensory defensiveness requires a meaningful cluster of behaviours such as exhibited by George including avoidance of messy play activities, not standing close to people, avoidance of certain textures, adverse reactions to light touch and withdrawal of touch contact. Many of his presenting problems, such as lack of social participation and interaction with his peers and his poor engagement in everyday activities, appear to be due to this.

During twice weekly individual SI sessions deep touch pressure and proprioceptive input were primarily chosen along with linear vestibular input due to the evidence indicating this for sensory defensiveness (Ayres 2005; Fisher and Dunn 1983, cited in Lane 2002; Koomar and Bundy 2002). Within SI intervention activities were chosen that are known to be both calming and organising and feed into the reticular formation within the brainstem. Equipment activities used for proprioceptive and deep touch pressure with George included trampette (mini trampoline), large therapy balls rolled firmly over his back and legs, scooter board, joint compressions, vibrating massage tools, tactile trays, vibrating cushion, hand and back massage providing deep pressure, avoiding light and tickly touch, as 'when addressing sensory modulation dysfunction we use deep touch that is typically calming, and we avoid light or unexpected touch which is often interpreted as noxious or painful' (Koomar and Bundy 2002, p.263). Activities and equipment used were chosen as they required active engagement which gives more enhanced proprioceptive input than passive proprioceptive movement.

Since intervention, George has presented as much calmer, more able to tolerate touch and tactile sensations, for example his hands being dirty, and more able to tolerate his peer group. In order to maintain and improve these functional abilities, ongoing support is given through the use of sensory diet, which includes rebound therapy (trampoline therapy) providing linear vestibular movement, multi-gym and swimming, and sensory approaches being incorporated in the OT groups that he attends such as sensory art and baking. Sensory strategies are now used as part of his prevention and management of aggression and violence care plan, to use when his arousal levels are high or there is a trigger. In addition to this George is offered the opportunity to retreat to a quiet, nurturing space, away from his peers, when he is experiencing sensory overload.

CONCLUSION

A multi-model approach has been found to be the most effective way to implement SI into the service we offer at St Andrew's. This involves a combination of education and training, development of guidelines, procedures and documentation, and establishing and adapting new and existing treatment interventions in order to incorporate sensory approaches as part of the fabric of the service. What has been evident is the motivation of service-users to engage in this type of work, with the service-users clearly voting with their feet.

Our young people's sensory processing difficulties clearly impact on all occupational domains and intervention is multi-dimensional, recognising the relationship SI theory and practice have with attachment, trauma, diagnosis and arousal states. Advanced clinical reasoning skills are required in order to understand and integrate elements of different models and theories in such complex cases, highlighting the need for further research.

REFERENCES

Adamson, A., O'Hare, A. and Graham, C. (2006) 'Impairments in sensory modulation in children with autistic spectrum disorder.' *British Journal of Occupational Therapy 69*, 8, 357–364.

Ayres, A.J. (1979) *Sensory Integration and the Child*. Los Angeles, CA: Western Psychological Services.

Ayres, A.J. (2005) *Sensory Integration and the Child*. Los Angeles, CA: Western Psychological Services.

Bar-Shalita, T., Vatine, J. and Parush, S. (2008) 'Sensory modulation disorder: A risk factor for participation in daily life activities.' *Developmental Medicine and Child Neurology 50*, 932–937.

Bhreathnach, E. (2008) *Sensory Attachment Intervention*. Unpublished handout from Sensory Attachment Intervention Level 1 © training.

Bogdashina, O. (2003) *Sensory Perceptual Issues in Autism and Asperger Syndrome*. London: Jessica Kingsley Publishers.

Brown, C.E. and Dunn, W. (2002) *Adult/ Adolescent Sensory Profile*. San Antonio, TX: The Psychological Corporation.

Brown, S., Shanker, R. and Smith, K. (2009) 'Borderline personality disorder and sensory processing impairment.' *Progress in Neurology and Psychiatry 13*, 4, 10–16.

Brown, S., Shanker, R., Smith, K., Turner, A. and Wyndham-Smith, T. (2006) 'Sensory processing disorder in mental health.' *Occupational Therapy News*, May, 28–29.

Bundy, A.C. and Murray, E.A. (2002) 'Sensory integration: A. Jean Ayres' Theory Revisited.' In A. Bundy, S. Lane and E.A. Murray (eds) *Sensory Integration: Theory and Practice*. Philadelphia, PA: F.A. Davis.

Champagne, T. (2006) *Sensory Modulation and Environment: Essential Elements of Occupation*. Second edition. Southampton, MA: Champagne Conferences and Consultation.

Chamapagne, T. and Sayer, E. (2006) 'Effects of the Use of the Sensory Room in Psychiatry.' In T. Chamapagne (ed.) *Sensory Modulation and Environment: Essential Elements of Occupation.* Second edition. Southampton, MA: Champagne Conferences and Consultation.

Champagne, T. and Stromberg, N. (2004) 'Sensory approaches in inpatient psychiatric settings: Innovative alternatives to seclusion and restraint.' *Journal of Psychological Nursing 42,* 9, 35–44.

Chu, S. and Reynolds, F. (2007a) 'Occupational therapy for children with attention deficit hyperactivity disorder (ADHD), part 1: A delineation model of practice.' *British Journal of Occupational Therapy 70,* 9, 372–383.

Chu, S. and Reynolds, F. (2007b) 'Occupational therapy for children with attention deficit hyperactivity disorder (ADHD), part 2: A multicentre evaluation of an assessment and treatment package.' *British Journal of Occupational Therapy 70,* 10, 439–448.

Dunn, W. (1999) *Sensory Profile User Manual.* San Antonio, TX: The Psychological Corporation.

Harwood, J. (2009) *Sensory Circuits: A Sensory Motor Skills Programme for Children.* New York: DPA.

Hunter, M. and Struve, J. (1998) *The Ethical Use of Touch in Psychotherapy.* Thousand Oaks, CA: Sage Publications.

Jernburg, A. and Booth, P. (2001) *Theraplay®: Helping Parents and Children Build Better Relationships through Attachment-based Play.* San Francisco, CA: Jossey-Bass.

Kimball, J.G. (1999) 'Sensory Integration Frame of Reference: Postulates Regarding Change and Application to Practice. In P. Kramer and J. Hinojosa (eds) *Frames of Reference for Pediatric Occupational Therapy.* Second edition. Baltimore, MD: Lippincott, Williams and Wilkins.

Kinnealey, M. and Fuiek, M. (1999) 'The relationship between sensory defensiveness, anxiety, depression and perception of pain in adults.' *Occupational Therapy International 6,* 3, 195–206.

Kinnealey, M., Oliver, B. and Wilbarger, P. (1995) 'A phenomenological study of sensory defensiveness in adults.' *The American Journal of Occupational Therapy 9,* 5, 444–451.

Koomar, J., Hurwitz, M., Kahler-Reis, R. and Szklut, S. (1996) *Developmental/Sensory History for Adults and Adolescents.* Second edition. Watertown, MA: OTA Watertown.

Koomar, J.A. and Bundy, A.C. (2002) 'Creating direct intervention from theory.' In A.C. Bundy, S.J. Lane and E.A. Murray (eds) *Sensory Integration: Theory and Practice.* Philadephia, PA: F.A. Davis.

Krauus, K. (1987) 'The effects of deep pressure touch on anxiety.' *The American Journal of Occupational Therapy 41,* 6, 366–373.

Kwok, H., To, Y.F. and Sung, H.F. (2003) 'The application of a multisensory Snoezelen room for people with learning disabilities.' *Hong Kong Medical Journal 9,* 2, 122–6.

Lane, S.J. (2002) 'Sensory modulation.' In A.C. Bundy, S.J. Lane and E.A. Murray (eds) *Sensory Integration: Theory and Practice.* Philadephia, PA: F.A. Davis.

Miller, L.J., Anzalone, M.E., Lane, S.J., Cermak, S.A. and Osten, E.T. (2007) 'Concept evolution in sensory integration: A proposed nosology for diagnosis.' *The American Journal of Occupational Therapy 61,* 2, 135–139.

Moore, K.M. and Henry, A.D. (2002) 'Treatment of adult psychiatric patients using the Wilbarger protocol.' *Occupational Therapy in Mental Health 18,* 1, 43–63.

Pfeiffer, B. and Kinnealey, M. (2003) 'Treatment of sensory defensive adults.' *Occupational Therapy International 10,* 3, 175–184.

Pfeiffer, B., Kinnealey, M., Reed, C. and Herzberg, G. (2005) 'Sensory modulation and affective disorders in children and adolescents with Asperger's disorder.' *American Journal of Occupational Therapy 59*, 335–345.

Reisman, J.E. and Hanschu, B. (1992) *Sensory Integration Inventory – Revised for Individuals with Developmental Disabilities*. Hugo, MN: PDP Press.

Reynolds, C.R., Pearson, N.A. and Voress, J.K. (2002) *Developmental Test of Visual Perception, Adolescent and Adult (DTVP-A)*. Austin, TX: Pro-ed.

Shaaf, R.C. and Nightlinger, K.M. (2007) 'Occupational therapy using a sensory integrative approach: A case study of effectiveness.' *American Journal of Occupational Therapy 61*, 239–245.

Siegel, D.J. (1999) *The Developing Mind*. New York, NY: The Guilford Press.

Tomcheck, S.D. and Dunn, W. (2007) 'Sensory processing in children with and without autism: A comparative study using the short sensory profile.' *The American Journal of Occupational Therapy 61*, 190–200.

Therapro Inc. (undated) Sensory Stories. Available at www.sensorystories.com/About.aspx, accessed on 23 June 2011.

Urwin, R. and Ballinger, C. (2005) 'The effectiveness of sensory integration therapy to improve functional behaviour in adults with learning disabilities: Five single-case experimental designs.' *British Journal of Occupational Therapy 68*, 2, 56–66.

Wilbarger, P. (1984) *Planning an Adequate 'Sensory Diet': Application of Sensory Processing Theory During the First Year of Life*. Washington, DC: Zero to Three.

Williams, M.S. and Shellenberger, S. (1996) *How Does Your Engine Run? A Leader's Guide to the Alert Programme for Self-Regulation*. Albuqerque, NM: Therapy-Works.

Chapter 4

MENTAL ILLNESS IN ADOLESCENTS WITH DEVELOPMENTAL DISABILITIES WHO REQUIRE SECURE CARE

Ernest Gralton

INTRODUCTION

Mental illnesses including schizophrenia and bipolar disorder occur in developmentally disabled adolescents. Although there is limited research evidence on the incidence in this population, the rates are likely to be significantly increased in those referred to secure settings. Mental illness can present atypically, not only because there may be issues around the communication of symptoms, but also because there is evidence of significant variance in the clinical manifestations in this population, particularly for bipolar disorder.

RESEARCH EVIDENCE

Mental ill health is over-represented in adults with intellectual disability, particularly those with a pervasive developmental disability (Morgan *et al.* 2008). Conventional diagnostic systems underestimate mental ill health in populations of people with learning disability (Cooper *et al.* 2007). The prevalence is most likely increased by a factor of at least three, and this may still be an underestimate (Smiley 2005). A specific diagnosis becomes progressively more difficult with IQ reduction (Clarke 1999).

Children, including adolescents with developmental disabilities, have a greater risk of experiencing co-morbid psychiatric conditions than their developmentally normal peers (Allington-Smith 2006; Emerson and Hatton 2007; Rutter *et al.* 1976). However, the incidence of psychotic illness (e.g. schizophrenia) does not appear to be significantly higher in children with intellectual disability than their non-disabled peers (Emerson 2003).

The identification of mental illness in adolescents with complex developmental disability is a difficult process. Diagnostic certainty is difficult and diagnoses in adolescents may change with longitudinal follow up, particularly between schizophrenia, schizoaffective and bipolar disorders (Friedlander and Donnelly 2004; Lay, Schmidt and Blanz 1997). Specific instruments such as the Psychiatric Assessment Schedule for Adults with a Developmental Disability (PAS–ADD) have been developed to detect mental illness in adults with learning disability (Moss *et al.* 1993). However, no such instruments exist specifically for developmentally disabled adolescents or children.

Diagnostic overshadowing is a bias amongst clinicians to attribute symptoms of mental health problems to cognitive impairment alone. It has been shown to be an issue in studies involving UK mental health professionals (Mason and Scior 2004) and may lead to a relative underrecognition of mental illness in developmentally disabled young people.

Schizotypal cognitions (including hallucinations and delusions) in adolescents with learning disability should not be accepted as normal and may be a predictor of future psychotic illness (Johnstone *et al.* 2007). Premorbid child social impairment is a known risk factor for developing later schizophrenia (Hollis 2003).

There are some genetic disorders that are associated with learning disability where there is also an increased risk of schizophrenia and bipolar disorder. The two best examples of this are velo-cardio-facial syndrome, which involves a deletion on chromosome 22 (Murphy, Jones and Owen 1999; Papolos *et al.* 1996), and Prader Willi syndrome, which involves a deletion on chromosome 15 (Beardsmore *et al.* 1998; Boer *et al.* 2002).

Epilepsy confers an increased risk of psychiatric disorder; the incidence of epilepsy is increased in people with learning disability. Some types of complex partial epilepsy can produce psychotic symptoms (Sachdev 2007) like paranoia and auditory hallucinations. Complex partial epilepsy needs to be excluded, if at all possible, in those patients presenting with psychotic symptoms or affective illness. Investigations for other organic causes need to include testing for autoimmune conditions like systemic lupus erythematosus and neuroendocrine disorders like hyperthyroidism.

There has been an ongoing debate about the validity of diagnosis of bipolar disorder in adolescents, although a comprehensive recent review of the evidence appears to confirm it does occur in children and adolescents (Youngstrom, Birmaher and Findling 2008). There appears to be a diagnostic difference between the US and the UK, with clinicians in the US more likely to diagnose bipolar disorder in clinical vignettes describing complex cases in children than clinicians in the UK (Dubicka *et al.* 1997). It is accepted that adolescents present with a more complex picture of mixed affective and rapid cycling syndromes (Birmaher *et al.* 2006; Geller *et al.* 2004) and co-morbidity is extremely common (Findling 2008). The existence of bipolar illness in adolescents with developmental disorders has been recognised for many years (McCraken and Diamond 1988). Even international centres of excellence can miss co-morbid mental illness like bipolar disorder in children with developmental disabilities and treatment can lead to substantial improvements in their function and dramatic reductions in the burden of care (Frazier *et al.* 2002).

Mood disorders are more difficult to diagnose; an onset in childhood or adolescence is not uncommon and individuals are much less likely to volunteer symptoms. Diagnosis is more reliant on observation and observer information (Lainhart and Folstein 1994). Rapid cycling bipolar disorder appears to be a more common variant in people with intellectual disability and often has an early, even pre-pubertal, onset (Vanstraelen and Tyrer 1999).

Mood disorders are probably more common in adolescents with autistic spectrum disorders (ASD) and are significantly underdiagnosed (Bradley and Bolton 2006; DeLong and Dwyer 1988). They have been reported with familial types of learning disability and temporal cortical abnormalities (Raghavan, Day and Perry 1995).

Unfortunately patients with intellectual impairment are routinely excluded from studies on adolescent bipolar disorder. A randomised trial for treatment of bipolar disorder in young people with developmental disabilities is very unlikely to become available in the near future; treatment principles need to be derived from related populations (Gutkovich and Carlson 2009). Bipolar disorder is, however, prevalent in children and adolescents with ASD. They have elevated rates of aggression and delinquency, behavioural disorders, depression, obsessive-compulsive disorder and suicidal ideation (Weissman and Bates 2010).

Severe neglect and abuse is increased in those with bipolar disorder and is associated with an early age of onset and more severe disorder (Garno *et al.* 2005), possibly mediated by disturbances in brain growth (Liu 2010). This means that adolescents with histories of attention deficit hyperactivity disorder (ADHD) and developmental trauma (common in our referral population) are probably more likely to go on to develop bipolar disorder and these can present atypically in adolescents with developmental disabilities.

There is concern that antidepressant use can induce sustained bipolar illness in some vulnerable adolescents, possibly those with pre-existing bipolar II disorder (Joseph, Youngstrom and Soares 2009; Pavuluri, Birmaher and Naylor 2005).

The treatment of bipolar disorder that is co-morbid with ADHD is complex and there is no clear research answer to whether methylphenidate or atomoxetine consistently worsen bipolar disorder. Prior stimulant treatment is probably associated with a younger age of onset of bipolar disorder (DelBello *et al.* 2001). Anecdotally, in our disabled adolescent population at Malcolm Arnold House, St Andrew's Healthcare, methylphenidate and atomoxetine can both lead to significant mood instability in patients with bipolar disorder. Caution needs to be applied with co-morbid bipolar illness although there is evidence that ADHD can be treated with stimulants as long as the mood disorder is already stabilised (Findling *et al.* 2007).

Adolescents with bipolar disorder treated with mood stabilisers combined with an atypical antipsychotic appeared to have a greater response than those treated only with mood stabilisers (Azorin and Findling 2007), although evidence for the treatment of adolescents with developmental disabilities is still very limited. There is a significant number of case descriptions in the literature with positive outcomes following treatment with mood stabilisers, but no substantive randomised controlled trial.

In terms of treatment for schizophrenia, risperidone has been shown to be effective in adolescents with schizophrenic illness (Haas *et al.* 2009). However, as with olanzepine, there is concern about adverse effects (particularly weight gain) (Arango *et al.* 2009; Kryzhanovskaya *et al.* 2009) and longer term consequences of elevated prolactin. Quetiapine would be an alternative where there are concerns surrounding prolactin levels (Roke *et al.* 2009).

Case description

Robert, the young person from Chapter 1, was admitted to our inpatient unit under section 3 of the Mental Health Act. Robert initially presented as quiet and withdrawn with minimal interaction with his peers, and for the first 24 hours he appeared relatively safe under one-to-one observation. He slept through his first night. He was not on any psychotropic medication. However, on the evening of the second day Robert was observed to be more irritable and confrontational with staff. He refused staff prompts to stop inciting his peers to become aggressive. He needed restraint and was secluded, where he self-harmed by cutting his arm with a fragment of plastic that he had secreted on his person.

Over the following two weeks staff noted a pattern of significant mood instability, sometimes precipitated by environmental events including prompts from staff. At other times there was no clear precipitant supported by data from the Modified Overt Aggression Scale (Alderman, Knight and Henman 2002). Robert was verbally and physically aggressive to both staff and peers, often without warning. On several occasions Robert was sexually inappropriate, trying to touch the breasts of staff and masturbating in the day area of the ward. On two occasions he was very tearful while in seclusion and tried to place a ligature around his neck. Robert also expressed paranoid ideation about black members of staff trying to harm him.

Robert was placed in our Extra Care facility to segregate him from his peers as there was concern about the risk he presented to other vulnerable young people. A provisional diagnosis of a rapid cycling bipolar disorder was made and he was started initially on risperidone, then sodium valproate was added to his regime. Robert complained of some mild extrapyramidal side effects (tremor) so risperidone was changed to olanzepine.

Robert's mood appeared to stabilise slowly over the next four to five weeks with less irritability, a reduction in aggression and longer periods of mood stability. Robert's appetite increased and a healthy eating plan was added to his care plan. His relationship with his peers improved enough for him to come out of the Extra Care unit and to return to his allocated bedroom. Robert engaged for the first time in remedial education and occupational therapy assessment. Robert still demonstrated significant social impairment and would still engage in some risk behaviour if not carefully monitored by staff. However, his fluctuations in mood are within what would be accepted as normal limits and the members of the multidiscliplinary team agreed there had been a transformation in his overall presentation.

PRACTICE ISSUES

Adolescents with a developmental disability referred to our forensic setting are likely to have a formal mental disorder and a history of neglect and/or abuse. Careful history taking may also reveal one or more relatives with a formal diagnosis or history suggestive of a serious affective disorder.

Complex combination of affective and psychotic symptoms on a background of a developmental disorder (including ASD) with longstanding behavioural problems can produce difficult diagnostic and treatment dilemmas. A common conundrum is the development of severe mood dysregulation in the context of pre-existing ADHD (Carlson 2009). This co-morbidity is not uncommon and has worse outcome than bipolar disorder alone (Ryden *et al.* 2009; Wingo and Ghamei 2007). ADHD is a developmental disorder whose symptoms generally remit over time, so a 'worsening of ADHD symptoms' raises suspicions of the development particularly of a co-morbid mood disorder.

Complex mood disorders are much more common in the population of young people referred to our inpatient secure service than schizophrenic psychoses. Adolescents with developmental disabilities can present with irritability and fluctuating mood over hours rather than distinct periods of elation lasting days or weeks. Paranoid ideation is not uncommon but frank delusions are rare. Physical aggression and self-harm are both associated with significant mood fluctuations. Hypersexuality, including serious sexual offending, is sometimes a consequence of intermittent mood disturbance.

Often assessment in other settings has been cross-sectional with professionals observing adolescents in non-specialist settings including both community and custodial. Rapid cycling or mixed affective disorders are extremely difficult to diagnose in cross-sectional assessments due to the fluidity of symptoms and the tendency for untrained staff to attribute behaviours solely to environmental events. The situation can additionally be complicated by intermittent illicit substance misuse.

There are some dangers with the rigid application of applied behavioural analysis in this complex patient population. Environmental events can clearly de-stabilise mental disorders, including affective disorders. The presence of an environmental event leading to disturbed or agitated behaviour does not rule out the existence of a co-morbid mental disorder, including bipolar affective illness. Good multidisciplinary working and positive interdisciplinary relationships are essential in understanding and devising treatment strategies for this complex population with multiple co-morbidities.

Our patients are always supplemented with omega-3 fatty acids and multivitamins unless there is a specific contraindication, in view of the evidence that they can reduce aggression in adolescents (Gesch *et al.* 2002) and improve mood stability in bipolar disorder (Turnbull, Cullen-Drill and Smaldone 2008).

Risperidone is frequently used in adolescents with developmental disabilities including ASD (Pandina *et al.* 2007) and conduct disorder (Aman *et al.* 2002) so there may be a rationale for it to be the first atypical antipsychotic to be used for bipolar disorder. Olanzepine is also particularly effective and quetiapine is well tolerated.

As has been found by other authors in this area (Gutkovich and Carlson 2009; Kowatch *et al.* 2003) our experience is that combinations of sodium valproate, lithium and carbemazepine are effective in complex rapid cycling and mixed affective bipolar disorder in this population. Sodium valproate is probably the most appropriate for most cases, particularly those with seizure disorder or known organic brain injury. We have so far not had to use combinations of three mood stabilising medications but we have not uncommonly used two mood stabilisers with an atypical antipsychotic before stability is achieved.

Occasionally antidepressants need to be used for persistent depressive symptoms in bipolar disorder in these patients, but the dose needs to be titrated carefully and increased very slowly in combination with a mood stabliser to reduce the risk of precipitating rapid cycling. Often a lower than normal dose is what is required to maintain affective stability.

Weight gain is a particular problem with olanzepine and sodium valproate. Early intervention in diet and exercise is needed to maintain a Body Mass Index (BMI) within reasonable limits before significant weight gain occurs. Blood and ECG monitoring is essential for young people on atypical antipsychotics and mood stabilisers due to adverse cardiac effects including QT prolongation and changes to prolactin, thyroid and lipid profiles.

However, the formal treatment of a mental illness is often only an initial step in a multidisciplinary rehabilitation programme. Typically adolescents who require secure care have multiple deficits and significant treatment needs across a wide range of domains.

CONCLUSIONS

The recognition and appropriate treatment of co-morbid mental illness is very important in the young people with developmental disability referred to secure inpatient services. Co-morbid mental illness, particularly bipolar disorder, can contribute to a variety of serious offending and antisocial behaviours. These adolescents can remain undiagnosed with serious mental illness for months or even years. Appropriate assessment of fluctuating symptoms in community settings can be problematic. It is very difficult to engage a young person in a programme looking at improving a whole range of personal safety and community skills when he or she continues to suffer from significant symptoms of mental illness, particularly rapid mood fluctuation. A trial of pharmacological treatment in an inpatient facility may be appropriate given the increased ability to monitor behavioural and symptomatic change and potential adverse effects.

REFERENCES

Alderman, N., Knight, C. and Henman, C. (2002) 'Aggressive behaviour observed within a neurobehavioural rehabilitation service: Utility of the OAS-MNR in clinical audit and applied research.' *Brain Injury 16*, 6, 469–489.

Allington-Smith, P. (2006) 'Mental health of children with learning disabilities.' *Advances in Psychiatric Treatment 12*, 130–138.

Aman, M.G., De Smedt, G., Derivan, A., Lyons, B. and Findling, R.L. (2002) 'Risperidone disruptive behaviour study group: Double blind placebo controlled study of risperidone for the treatment of disruptive behaviours in children with subaverage intelligence.' *American Journal of Psychiatry 159*, 1337–1346.

Arango, C., Robles, O., Parellada, M., Fraguas, D., Ruiz-Sancho, A., Medina, O., Zabala, A., Bombin, I. and Moreno, D. (2009) 'Olanzapine compared to quetiapine in adolescents with a first psychotic episode.' *European Child and Adolescent Psychiatry 18*, 7, 418–428.

Azorin, J.M. and Findling, R.L. (2007) 'Valproate use in children and adolescents with bipolar disorder.' *CNS Drugs 21*,1019–1033.

Beardsmore, A., Dormant, T., Cooper, S.A. and Webb, T. (1998) 'Affective psychosis and Prader-Willi syndrome.' *Journal of Intellectual Disability Research 42*, 6, 463–471.

Birmaher, B., Axelson, D., Strober, M., Gill, M.K., Valeri, S., Chiappetta, L., Ryan, N., Leonard, H., Hunt, J., Iyengar, S. and Keller, M. (2006) 'Clinical course of children and adolescents with bipolar spectrum disorders.' *Archives of General Psychiatry 63*, 2, 175–183.

Boer, H., Holland, A., Whittington, J., Butler, J., Webb, T. and Clarke, D. (2002) 'Psychotic illness in people with Prader Willi syndrome due to chromosome 15 maternal uniparental disomy.' *Lancet 359*, 135–136.

Bradley, E. and Bolton, P. (2006) 'Episodic psychiatric disorders in teenagers with learning disabilities with and without autism.' *The British Journal of Psychiatry 189*, 361–366.

Carlson, G.A. (2009) 'Treating the childhood bipolar controversy: A tale of two children.' *American Journal of Psychiatry 166*, 18–24.

Clarke, D. (1999) 'Functional Psychoses in People with Mental Retardation.' In N. Bouras (ed.) *Psychiatric and Behavioural Disorders in Developmental Disabilities and Mental Retardation.* Cambridge: Cambridge University Press.

Cooper, S.A., Smiley, E., Morrison, J., Williamson, A. and Allan, L. (2007) 'Mental ill-health in adults with intellectual disabilities: Prevalence and associated factors.' *The British Journal of Psychiatry 190*, 27–35.

DelBello, M.P., Soutullo, C.A., Hendricks, W., Niemeier, R.T., McElroy, S.L. and Strakowski, S.M. (2001) 'Prior stimulant treatment in adolescents with bipolar disorder: Association with age at onset.' *Bipolar Disorders 3*, 2, 53–57.

DeLong, G.R. and Dwyer, J.T. (1988) 'Correlation of family history with specific autistic subgroups: Asperger's syndrome and bipolar affective disease.' *Journal of Autism and Developmental Disorders 18*, 593–600.

Dubicka, B., Carlson, G.A., Vail, A. and Harrington, R. (1997) 'Prepubertal mania: Diagnostic differences between US and UK clinicians.' *European Child and Adolescent Psychiatry 17*, 3, 153–161.

Emerson, E. (2003) 'Prevalence of psychiatric disorders in children and adolescents with and without intellectual disability.' *Journal of Intellectual Disability Research 47*, 1, 51–58.

Emerson, E. and Hatton, C. (2007) 'Mental health of children and adolescents with intellectual disabilities in Britain.' *British Journal of Psychiatry 191*, 6, 493–499.

Findling, R. (ed.) (2008) *Clinical Manual of Child and Adolescent Psychopharmacology*. Washington, DC: American Psychiatric Publishing Inc.

Findling, R., Short, E., McNamara, N., Demeter, C., Stansbrey, R., Gracious, B., Whipkey, R., Manos, M.J. and Calabrese, J.R. (2007) 'Methylphenidate in the treatment of children and adolescents with bipolar disorder and attention-deficit/hyperactivity disorder.' *Journal of the American Academy of Child and Adolescent Psychiatry 46*, 11, 1445–1453.

Frazier, J.A., Doyle, R., Chiu, S. and Coyle, J.T. (2002) 'Treating a child with Asperger's disorder and comorbid bipolar disorder.' *American Journal of Psychiatry 159*, 13–21.

Friedlander, R.I. and Donnelly, T. (2004) 'Early-onset psychosis in youth with intellectual disability.' *Journal of Intellectual Disability Research 48*, 540–547.

Garno, J.L., Goldberg, J.F., Ramirez, P.M. and Ritzler, B.A. (2005) 'Impact of childhood abuse on the clinical course of bipolar disorder.' *British Journal of Psychiatry 186*, 121–125.

Geller, B., Tillman, R., Craney, J.L. and Bolhofner, K. (2004) 'Four year prospective outcome and natural history of mania in children with a prepubertal and early adolescent bipolar disorder phenotype.' *Archives of General Psychiatry 61*, 5, 459–467.

Gesch, C.B., Hammond, S.M., Hampson, S.E., Eves, A. and Crowder, M.J. (2002) 'Influence of supplementary vitamins, minerals and essential fatty acids on the antisocial behaviour of young adult prisoners.' *British Journal of Psychiatry 181*, 22–28.

Gutkovich, Z.A. and Carlson, G.A. (2009) 'Medication Treatment of Bipolar Disorder in Developmentally Disabled Children and Adolescents.' In J.L. Matson, F. Andrasik and M.L. Matson (eds) *Treating Childhood Psychopathology and Developmental Disabilities*. New York, NY: Springer.

Haas, M., Unis, A.S., Armenteros, J., Copenhaver, M.D., Quiroz, J.A. and Kushner, S.F. (2009) 'A 6-week, randomized, double-blind, placebo-controlled study of the efficacy and safety of risperidone in adolescents with schizophrenia.' *Journal of Child and Adolescent Psychopharmacology 19*, 6, 611–621.

Hollis, C. (2003) 'Developmental precursors of child- and adolescent-onset schizophrenia and affective psychoses: Diagnostic specificity and continuity with symptom dimensions.' *British Journal of Psychiatry 182*, 37–44.

Johnstone, E.C., Owens, D.G.C., Hoare, P., Gaur, S., Spencer, M.D., Harris, J., Andre, W., Stanfield, A.W., Moffat, V., Brearley, N., Miller, P., Stephen, M., Lawrie, S.M. and Muir, W.J. (2007) 'Schizotypal cognitions as a predictor of psychopathology in adolescents with mild intellectual impairment.' *British Journal of Psychiatry 191*, 484–492.

Joseph, M.F., Youngstrom, E.A. and Soares, J.S. (2009) 'Antidepressant-coincident mania in children and adolescents treated with selective serotonin reuptake inhibitors.' *Future Neurology 4*, 1, 87–102.

Kowatch, R.A., Sethuraman, G., Hume, J.H., Kromelis, M. and Weinberg, W.A. (2003) 'Combination pharmacotherapy in children and adolescents with bipolar disorder.' *Biological Psychiatry 53*, 11, 978–984.

Kryzhanovskaya, L.A., Robertson-Plouch, C.K., Xu, W., Carlson, J.L., Merida, K.M. and Dittmann, R.W. (2009) 'The safety of olanzapine in adolescents with schizophrenia or bipolar I disorder: A pooled analysis of 4 clinical trials.' *Journal of Clinical Psychiatry 70*, 2, 247–258.

Lainhart, J.E. and Folstein, S.E. (1994) 'Affective disorders in people with autism: A review of published cases.' *Journal of Autism and Developmental Disorders 24*, 587–601.

Lay, B., Schmidt, M.H. and Blanz, B. (1997) 'Course of adolescent psychotic disorder with schizoaffective episodes.' *European Child and Adolescent Psychiatry 6*, 1, 32–41.

Liu, R.T. (2010) 'Early life stressors and genetic influences on the development of bipolar disorder: The roles of childhood abuse and brain-derived neurotrophic factor.' *Child Abuse and Neglect 34*, 7, 516–522.

Mason, J. and Scior, K. (2004) '"Diagnostic overshadowing" amongst clinicians working with people with intellectual disabilities in the UK.' *Journal of Applied Research in Intellectual Disabilities 17*, 2, 85–90.

McCracken, J.T. and Diamond, R.P. (1988) 'Case study: Bipolar disorder in mentally retarded adolescents.' *Journal of the American Academy of Child and Adolescent Psychiatry 27*, 4, 494–499.

Morgan, V.A., Leonard, H., Bourke, J. and Jablensky, A. (2008) 'Intellectual disability co-occurring with schizophrenia and other psychiatric illness: Population-based study.' *British Journal of Psychiatry 193*, 364– 372.

Moss, S., Patel, P., Prosser, H., Goldberg, D. *et al.* (1993) 'Psychiatric morbidity in older people with moderate and severe learning disability. I: Development and reliability of the patient interview (PAS-ADD).' *British Journal of Psychiatry 163*, 471–480.

Murphy, K.C., Jones, L.A., Owen, M.J. (1999) 'High rates of schizophrenia in adults with velo-cardio-facial syndrome.' *Archives of General Psychiatry 56*, 940–945.

Pandina, G.J., Bossie, C.A., Youssef, E., Zhu, Y. and Dunbar, F. (2007) 'Risperidone improves behavioral symptoms in children with autism in a randomized, double-blind, placebo-controlled trial.' *Journal of Autism and Developmental Disorders 37*, 2, 367–373.

Papolos, D.F., Faedda, G.L., Veit, S., Goldberg, R. *et al.* (1996) 'Bipolar spectrum disorders in patients diagnosed with velo-cardio-facial syndrome: Does a hemizygous deletion of chromosome 22q11 result in bipolar affective disorder?' *American Journal of Psychiatry 153*, 1541–1547.

Pavuluri, M.N., Birmaher, B. and Naylor, M.W. (2005) 'Pediatric bipolar disorder: A review of the past 10 years.' *Journal of the American Academy of Child and Adolescent Psychiatry 44*, 9, 846–71.

Raghavan, R., Day, E.K. and Perry, R.H. (1995) 'Rapid cycling bipolar affective disorder and familial learning disability associated with temporal lobe (occipitotemporal gyrus) cortical dysplasia.' *Journal of Intellectual Disability Research 39*, 6, 509–519.

Roke, Y., van Harten, P.N., Boot, A.M. and Buitelaar, J.K. (2009) 'Antipsychotic medication in children and adolescents: A descriptive review of the effects on prolactin level and associated side effects.' *Journal of Child and Adolescent Psychopharmacology 19*, 4, 403–414.

Rutter, M., Tizard, J., Yule, W., Graham, P. and Whitmore, K. (1976) 'Research report: Isle of Wight studies, 1964–1974.' *Psychological Medicine 6*, 313–332.

Ryden, R., Thase, M.E., Straht, A., Aberg-Wistedt, A., Bejerot, S. and Landen, M. (2009) 'A history of childhood attention-deficit hyperactivity disorder (ADHD) impacts clinical outcome in adult bipolar patients regardless of current ADHD.' *Acta Psychiatrica Scandinavica 120*, 3, 239–246.

Sachdev, P.S. (2007) 'Alternating and postictal psychoses: Review and a unifying hypothesis.' *Schizophrenia Bulletin 33*, 4, 1029–1037.

Smiley, E. (2005) 'Epidemiology of mental health problems in adults with learning disability: An update.' *Advances in Psychiatric Treatment 11*, 214–222.

Turnbull, T., Cullen-Drill, M. and Smaldone, A. (2008) 'Efficacy of omega-3 fatty acid supplementation on improvement of bipolar symptoms: A systematic review.' *Archives of Psychiatric Nursing 22*, 5, 305–311.

Vanstraelen, M. and Tyrer, S.P. (1999) 'Rapid cycling bipolar affective disorder in people with intellectual disability: A systematic review.' *Journal of Intellectual Disability Research 43*, 5, 349–359.

Weissman, A.S. and Bates, M.E. (2010) 'Increased clinical and neurocognitive impairment in children with autism spectrum disorders and comorbid bipolar disorder.' *Research in Autism Spectrum Disorders 4*, 4, 670–680.

Wingo, A.P. and Ghamei, S.N. (2007) 'A systematic review of rates and diagnostic validity of comorbid adult attention-deficit/hyperactivity disorder and bipolar disorder.' *Journal of Clinical Psychiatry 68*, 11, 1776–1784.

Youngstrom, E.A., Birmaher, B. and Findling, R.L. (2008) 'Pediatric bipolar disorder: Validity, phenomenology, and recommendations for diagnosis.' *Bipolar Disorders 10*, 1, 194–214.

Chapter 5

WORKING WITH THE FAMILIES OF DEVELOPMENTALLY DISABLED YOUNG PEOPLE DETAINED IN SECURE SETTINGS

Phil Webb and Margaret Mills

INTRODUCTION

At the point of admission to a secure psychiatric unit, a young person's family will usually have had some degree of contact and involvement with the care system over a prolonged period of time. Typically this will have been with his or her local Health and Social Care Service agencies and sometimes with the judicial system, if there has been a forensic history. In some circumstances, the ability to engage with these families will be dependent on how positive or negative these experiences have been.

Many parents or other significant family members of those admitted tend to fit broadly into three categories. The first group is those who feel that the system has let them down in some way and respond with hostility and refusal to co-operate. These families often report that no help was available when it was most needed despite numerous requests, or if it was offered, too little was given and it was usually inappropriate. Many have also had ongoing battles in one form or another with their local authority or health service regarding the care and treatment of their child and usually the relationship with these services has deteriorated significantly. By the time of the young person's admission, and certainly in the initial stage of the assessment period and sometimes throughout the whole of the admission period itself, clinical teams (particularly social workers) may bear the brunt of this animosity. Fuelled by frustration and anger, some families will steadfastly continue to refuse to co-operate with the team or support the treatment process. Generally these families will attempt to undermine any therapeutic intervention that the young person has had. This can have a detrimental effect as these negative attitudes can influence the young people on whether they choose to continue to engage with the clinical team or not. This group is the hardest to work with and are, by default, the most difficult to engage.

The second group tends to be those who have also had good and bad experiences of the system prior to admission but are now relieved that at last their child is now receiving the care and treatment needed – even though in many cases it may have taken a long time and may well have required a significant incident before that help was given. This group generally tends to engage with clinical teams from the outset and our experience is that the outcome for the young person in these cases is often significantly better.

The third group tends to be those who either have had or still have little involvement with their child for a variety of reasons. Typical examples in these cases involve past or current concerns regarding abuse and/or neglect issues and their parenting capacity/ability. This last group tends to be known to local authority Children and Family services. Their children have either been on what was previously called the At Risk or Child Protection Register or, as of 2008, subject to a Child Protection Plan and/or have been subject to care proceedings under section 31 of the Children Act (Children Act 1989) and taken into care. In some cases, the parents themselves have been subject to restrictions regarding contact with their child; in some circumstances this may be because of past offences committed by parents and carers. Some may even have been convicted and placed on the UK Sex Offenders Register.

Clearly these are very broad descriptions, and within all the groups varying degrees of engagement can take place.

RESEARCH

There is little evidence of research into the experiences of support offered to parents and carers of children and adolescents in inpatient psychiatric units. Despite the increase in adolescent inpatient beds due to changes in the Mental Health Act (2007) where a responsibility on local authorities to provide age appropriate psychiatric inpatient care is made, there does not appear to be any guidance on the needs of the parents and carers of these young people. Inpatient psychiatric units themselves may attempt to address the support needs of families and carers by providing questionnaires, which seek to ask their views, but this evidence is sporadic and tends to be used to inform the individual organisations themselves rather than published in peer reviewed journals.

Despite this, a range of family issues are vitally important in relation to the assessment and treatment of young people with developmental disabilities who come into secure settings. A number of studies have suggested that family functioning is likely to be problematic in this population of young people.

Parents of children with disabilities have been found to be more likely to experience stress and depressive symptoms than parents of typically developing children as a result of the increased challenges inherent in their parenting role (Mitchell and Hauser-Cram 2008). Parents of young people with autistic disorders in particular have even higher stress levels, poor quality of life (Mugno et al. 2007) and lower social support (Heiman and Berger 2008) in comparison with parents with children with other types of developmental disabilities. A significant proportion of the elevated risk for psychopathology among children with developmental disability may be due to their increased exposure to psychosocial disadvantage (Emerson and Hatton 2007). Children and young people with learning disabilities are at a disproportionate risk of experiencing mental health problems yet their experience of and access to mental health services can be very uneven (Sin, Francis and Cook 2010). Historically some health services in the UK have not had anyone trained to meet the needs of this complex patient population. Where available, services have often been fragmented and developments haphazard (Wright, Williams and Richardson 2008), with the burden of care of very complex adolescents often shifted to secure social and residential educational providers.

Social alienation is an important factor on the pathway to delinquency (Bailey 1999). The monitoring of young people by parents, their disciplinary styles, the quality of relationships with parents, the psychosocial conditions of parents and cohesion of the family unit have all been correlated with mental health outcomes and behaviour in high risk young people (Ungar 2004). International reviews of the literature have long concluded that children of heavy drinking parents have a variety of adverse long-term consequences including psychoactive substance use, criminality, suicide, depression, personality disorders, as well as psychological and behavioural disturbances (Plant, Orford and Grant 1989). Young offenders have high rates of family breakdown (Chitsabesan et al. 2006) and are more likely to have been exposed to domestic violence (Holt, Buckley and Whelan 2008). Offenders with developmental disabilities who are aggressive are more likely to have been themselves exposed to parental anger and aggression (Novaco and Taylor 2008). Power et al. (2009) evaluated the support of parents of children and young people who deliberately self-harmed and found that effective planned parent support directly correlated with more positive outcomes for their children at least in the short to midterm. An advisory paper by the Child Health Support Group (CHSG) 2005 in Scotland put forward various recommendations for psychiatric inpatient units for children and young people which stated very clearly the need to incorporate and take into account the importance of regular family work when services are planned. Research which has looked at family and carer views within existing inpatient settings has tended to look at children with physical health difficulties focusing on the relationship of the family with the medical profession, that is, treating physicians and nurses. Tarkka, Paavilainen and Lehti (2003) looked at the support offered to families of heart patients with the findings noting that the families were overall dissatisfied with the social support offered by the medical profession. This limited evidence suggests that families should be at the centre of the support set up for the young people and that to exclude them in many cases can be detrimental.

PRACTICE ISSUES

Difficulties in the area of engagement can sometimes be overcome if you are able to engage with the family during the early stages of the admission process. Pre-admission assessment visits are a good starting point. Pre-admission assessments in most cases are conducted at the young person's current location which may be another secure facility, or a residential setting. Depending on the circumstances these can sometimes be carried out in the family home, if this is where the young person still resides. Collecting as much information at this early stage is extremely important and gives a good insight into the family dynamics. Although not always possible, arranging to visit or contact the family as soon as possible prior to admission is very important. It is also useful to link in with any external social worker involved with the family, and obtain access to the local authority files.

The local services have far more information on the family; sometimes a joint visit with them can be a good way to initiate contact and can put the family at ease, particularly if there is somebody they know present during the visit. It is at this point that the clinical team begins to assess the wider needs of the family as well as the needs of the young person. The Common Assessment Framework (CAF) (Department of Health, Department for Education and Employment and Home Office 2000) is widely used in the UK. The CAF assessment process provides a systematic multi-agency approach to analyse and record what is happening to a child within the family and the wider context of the community in which the child lives. The assessment stages involve gathering and analysing information about the three domains of the CAF. The stages are: child's developmental needs, parents' or caregivers' capacity to respond appropriately, and impact of the wider family and environmental factors on parenting capacity and the child.

Carrying out a CAF assessment aids the formulation of a social work care plan and this early engagement with the family also gives them the opportunity to ask as many questions as they like, such as information about the unit, treatment plan, likely timescales, and so on. It can be useful to have an information pack on the admission facility available giving all the practical information they require. More important, it gives them a link or point of contact. If you can allow parents and carers to vent their feelings at this stage, this tends to create an opportunity to build a positive working relationship with them later on.

The primary role of the social worker in this setting is to act as an interface between the clinical team and the families. Often it is the social worker who is the front line professional that many family members have the most contact with. This is particularly relevant when there are issues relating to the treatment of their child and the sometimes necessary restrictions on the degree and/or type of contact the young person has with the family throughout the admission period. Some parents can have very limited understanding or lack of insight into the nature or degree of their child's illness or disability and they can feel that the clinical team are overreacting or are being punitive when certain limitations are imposed, particularly to manage risk. It is this lack of understanding that can cause the most friction. The social worker has to ensure that a sufficient amount of time is allowed to go through these issues with them if a complete breakdown of the working relationship is to be avoided. Communication is paramount in dealing with families in this setting. Many of the complaints they raise are that 'nobody talks to us'. This tends to be a criticism usually directed at nursing teams on the unit when they are not able to respond immediately to family requests or when perceived unreasonable demands are made.

It is worth noting at this point that the term 'family' can mean many things and should be seen as a loose generic term. The parent or parents of the young person may not be the key individual/s in that person's life and may not have been the predominant figure involved in parenting or a primary relationship. These families can be very complex; the existence of multiple family units can include stepparents, stepsiblings, grandparents, brothers, sisters, aunts, uncles, foster parents, foster siblings and even local authorities if they are the subject of a Care Order. It is important to have a good understanding of the dynamics of each individual family group. Very often the set-up of each family and the predominance of individuals within each group dictate the type and quality of the interaction(s) that take place between the professional and the family members.

All of the young people receiving treatment at Malcolm Arnold House Medium Secure Adolescent Unit are subject to detention under the Mental Health Act (1983) (amended 2007) depending on the nature and degree of their illness and/or disability. In many instances, involvement with the judicial system results in a hospital treatment order being given as opposed to a custodial sentence. However, in all circumstances we have a duty to involve/consult with a family member if he or she is classified as the Nearest Relative under the Mental Health Act.

In certain circumstances, there is a need to withhold or restrict the amount of contact a young person has with their family. There can be many reasons for having to do this, but most usually it tends to be in relation to the serious adverse effect that the contact is having on the behaviour of the young person and the emotional distress caused. In turn, both can be directly related to potential risk issues. The decision to limit contact can never be taken lightly and must be done in consultation with the multidisciplinary team, the young person and the families and with any other external professionals/agencies involved in the young person's care. Consideration also needs to be given to the legality of restricting contact especially with regards to Article 8 of the Human Rights Act (1998) in relation to the right to family life, and the Mental Health Act (1983), where you need to link a particular form of contact to a negative or detrimental effect on the mental health of the young person and balance that with the Children Act (1989), where the main duty is to promote contact with the family.

It should be clear that you have done everything possible before embarking on this course of action. However, the primary responsibility has to be in connection with the treatment, safety and well-being of the young person in the care of the service (in loco parentis) and this can sometimes be where difficulties arise when working with the families.

The term medium secure unit can be a description or a definition of a facility that many families are unclear about. The operational policies of a medium secure unit necessitate varying degrees of security, restriction and compliance and sometimes families will blame the staff for being over-controlling and punitive. Sometimes individual family members can seek to split the team by attempting to find minor differences in feedback from individual team members. In certain situations it can escalate to the point where consistent complaints are made which have to be dealt with formally via the organisations' formal complaints procedure. Quite often the social worker can be dealing with a series of complaints of a very similar nature from one individual and even when they have been investigated, further complaints ensue. There can be significant pressure to vary risk management procedures from particular families. In these circumstances, the social worker has to make every effort to engage with the families to enable dialogue to try to resolve the issues and explain the reasons for procedures, with the intent of continuing to build a therapeutic relationship.

From a practical perspective, social workers have lead responsibility for all family related issues. Facilitating contact is an important element of this role and forms part of the young person's care plan. An approved visitors list is compiled at the time of admission and only those placed on the list are allowed visiting access, with no exceptions. The list is compiled following consultation with the young person and the family and involves detailed discussion with external professionals concerned in the case. This is carried out especially if the young person is subject to a Care Order (Children Act 1989), as there may already be current restrictions in place regarding contact and access. The unit social worker is the only person authorised to make changes to this list, and they are reviewed on a regular basis.

Home safety assessments are also carried out by the social worker prior to the young person having a home visit. Part of this process involves discussion with the family regarding setting conditions such as the duration of each visit, who will be present, whether the young person can go for a walk outside of the home with the family, and so on. It also assesses any areas of potential risk that could compromise the young person, the family, people in the home area or the escorting staff's safety. If the family refuses to agree to the conditions or the risk factors are considered to be too high, then the social worker will not recommend a visit. Other factors may also be relevant. For example the responsible clinician (usually the consultant psychiatrist) will need to seek the permission and agreement of the Ministry of Justice if the young person is subject to a section 41 Restriction Order (Mental Health Act 1983). Consultation with victim liaison officers and local Multi-Agency Public Protection Arrangements (MAPPA) teams is coordinated by the social worker. MAPPA (National MAPPA Team 2009) in the UK support the assessment and management of the most serious sexual and violent offenders.

If it is not possible to facilitate a home visit, then we will try to support the family to visit the unit instead. There can be a number of practical steps to help families visit if financial hardship is involved, such as the unit paying the travelling expenses of families to visit the unit. If individual family members receive income support, a claim from the Social Fund will be supported by the social worker and sometimes negotiation with the young person's local authority can also secure some financial support. In the UK low income families are financially supported to visit young people in prison via the Assisted Prison Visits Scheme, but inexplicably there is no specific fund to support families of young people who are detained in secure psychiatric facilities.

Family-friendly visiting areas have also been developed in recent years within our organisation to make visiting a more positive experience. We have a duty of care to ensure the safety of child visitors, and these visiting areas are closely monitored to ensure that happens.

Social workers also take the lead in safeguarding and child protection issues. Very often a young person may report or disclose incidents of past and/or present abuse. In a number of cases these allegations concern family members and these need to be dealt with as a matter of urgency and with sensitivity. There is a statutory duty on key people and bodies to make arrangements to safeguard and promote the welfare of children. *Working Together to Safeguard Children* (DCSF 2010) is statutory guidance for practitioners and agencies in the UK to promote the welfare of children and young people in accordance with the Children Act (1989) and the Children Act (2004). Sometimes the investigation process that follows can be lengthy and steps will need to be taken to restrict the contact the young person has with those he/she has accused. In some cases these allegations are proven to be correct, but in some instances, the allegation(s) may be unfounded. The damaging effect of these allegations both on the family and the young person can be immense, with long-term consequences regarding the relationship they have with each other. The social worker will endeavour to offer support to the family in these circumstances.

Case description

Peter was a 15-year-old male admitted under section 37 of the Mental Health Act. He had received the hospital order as a disposal at court for offences of assault against a police officer. Peter had a repeated history of antisocial behaviours from the age of five years with reports first noting difficulties settling into primary school.

Peter was an only child and had been brought up by his mother, Jane. His biological father was not on the scene at the time of his birth as he and his mother had split up in the first trimester of her pregnancy; he had been unaware of the pregnancy. His mother had worked throughout Peter's childhood and early adolescence and she was supported in her care of Peter by her own mother.

Peter and his mother had had extensive involvement with community childcare services since he was six years old and it had been noted by various workers that Jane had not always worked proactively with social services. At times she refused to take advice and guidance in relation to parenting techniques with Peter. Although there were no noted worries about obvious abuse of Peter by Jane there were muted concerns about her ability to parent Peter appropriately.

Peter had been excluded from two primary schools due to aggressive behaviour towards other pupils and he was reported to have had significant difficulty in making and sustaining relationships with his peers at school. Jane had also noted that he had never been invited to any parties or anyone's house for tea when he had been at primary school. Although she herself had been upset by this Peter had not seemed to be bothered by these exclusions.

Peter went to a mainstream secondary school and within four weeks was excluded for assaulting a teacher. Professionals from both education and social services arranged a meeting which identified Peter as having special educational needs. It was agreed that Peter attend a secondary school which specialised in supporting children with similar difficulties.

Peter struggled to settle into the routines of the school even with one-to-one support and was noted to be both disruptive in lessons and aggressive in his manner to other pupils as well as teachers. He was not identified as having any particular friendships and indeed some of the more vulnerable pupils appeared frightened of him. Peter was often late for school and at times left the premises without permission to go home. A referral was sent to the local child and adolescent mental health service (CAMHS) by the school. There was a significant wait before an assessment by the CAMHS psychiatrist. Peter was eventually diagnosed as having an autistic spectrum disorder as well as a conduct disorder. The CAMHS team offered specific support to both Peter and Jane and it is noted that Jane was inconsistent with her attendance at meetings as well as being resistive to support and ideas offered by the team.

Following an incident when he was 12 years old, Peter was reported as hitting Jane and she requested social service support once again. Peter was accommodated by the local authority in a children's residential unit. Reports note that Peter attempted to be disruptive within the unit but did in fact respond well to the boundaries and routines of the placement. Over time his negative behaviours decreased in regularity to the point where he was having regular home leave. It was agreed that he would return home to live with Jane when he was 13 years old.

When Peter was 14 years old, he asked Jane for information about his biological father, which she provided for him. Peter made contact with his father who was surprised at finding out that he had a son and they arranged to meet. It was reported that Peter's father had a drug and alcohol problem and that Peter was readily influenced by his father's 'bohemian' lifestyle. Jane noted that Peter's behaviour changed radically and he became aggressive towards her as well as sexually inappropriate. She believed that Peter had started experimenting with illicit substances, but he had denied this. Contact with his father was erratic due to his 'nomadic' existence and Peter struggled to contain his emotions when his father did not turn up for visits arranged with him. Jane once again contacted social services to ask for help and support and CAMHS became involved again. Peter was reluctant to attend booked appointments and the CAMHS team did not offer a community outreach service. Peter's relationship with Jane deteriorated very quickly and following an incident where Peter held Jane hostage in the family home and threatened to kill her, the police were called and Peter was arrested for resisting arrest and threatening a police officer.

Whilst waiting for his court appearance Peter was accommodated in a residential unit, an assessment was requested and following this assessment he was admitted to the medium secure unit.

It was evident through looking at Jane's past involvement with services that her engagement with formal 'therapy' was at its best ad hoc in its commitment. Jane was regularly aggressive in her manner with staff and often undermined the work that the inpatient multidisciplinary team were trying to do with Peter, suggesting to him that he did not need to do what staff asked him to do and that she would arrange for him to be discharged from hospital. Contact with Jane was made on a very regular basis but its focus tended to be based on negative incidents or interactions. Jane requested to make various complaints about individual staff members, structures within the unit as well as concerns about Peter being bullied by other young people on the ward. As a result of staff's concerns about Jane's aggressive manner, it was agreed that contact with Jane would be made by a consistent individual – the ward social worker.

It was decided that the best way to try to get Jane proactively and positively involved in the care and treatment of her son was to offer her regular slots with key individuals from the team in order to vent her feelings and concerns about Peter and his care. Jane was initially dismissive of the idea but times were arranged nonetheless to suit her availability. Social Work took the lead and attended every meeting with Jane. She was asked to identify on a rolling basis which other members of staff she wished to meet with in order to clarify issues that may have arisen for her in relation to the care of Peter.

Despite her initial resistance to the plan Jane attended every meeting. Her manner was at times aggressive but through consistent attendance by the ward social worker Jane's interactions became more positive and she started to work more positively with the team. She in turn encouraged Peter to engage with the therapeutic input offered to him. Jane had always felt intimidated by services telling her how to act and, in her mind, how to be a 'better' mother; by acting in a proactive rather than reactive way Jane was given back the responsibility and the information she needed in order to make the best decisions for her and Peter.

CONCLUSIONS

There is a dearth of research in the area of support for parents and families of young people detained in secure inpatient CAMHS units. Families that come into contact with our service have generally either been dismissive of services in the past or struggled to negotiate the appropriate support for their child. As such they can be wary of asking for or relying on support from the hospital multidisciplinary team (MDT). A family's support needs can easily be overlooked when the young person's needs can be so overt, particularly with accumulated forensic history. The inpatient MDT is very clear that family work and support are an intrinsic part of the holistic and therapeutic network identified for the young person from the point of admission.

It is important that formal time is built into the social worker's duties in order for families to be completely involved in their child's care and treatment as well as receiving specific support for their own individual needs. As a national service such levels of time can be hard to find but the positive outcomes of family work and interventions far outweigh the difficulties and challenges social workers can face.

Future research needs to focus on the needs of families as well as the needs of adolescents detained in inpatient psychiatric units in order that professionals can learn and develop new ways of involving families with their child's care. Often simple offers of support such as regular phone calls from the social worker to the family can have a huge impact on their engagement with the treatment and future care plans for their child. However, more difficult to resolve issues need to be identified at an early stage with families and networks of support and advice researched and identified by the social worker, ideally in conjunction with local services.

REFERENCES

Bailey, S. (1999) 'The interface between mental health, criminal justice and forensic mental health services for children and adolescents.' *Current Opinion in Psychiatry 12*, 4, 425–432.

Child Health Support Group: Inpatient Working Group (2005) *Psychiatric Inpatient Services for Children and Young People in Scotland: A Way Forward.* Available at www.Scotland.gov.uk/Publications/2005/01/20523/49976, accessed on 19 May 2011.

Children Act (1989) London: HMSO. Available at www.legislation.gov.uk/ukpga/2004/31/contents, accessed on 19 May 2011.

Children Act (2004) London: HMSO. Available at www.legislation.gov.uk/ukpga/2004/31/contents, accessed on 19 May 2011.

Chitsabesan, P., Kroll, L., Bailey, S., Kenning, C. *et al.* (2006) 'Mental health needs of young offenders in custody and in the community.' *British Journal of Psychiatry 188*, 534–540.

Department for Children, Schools and Families (DCSF) (2010) *Working Together to Safeguard Children.* Nottingham: DCSF Publications. Available at http://publications.education.gov.uk/eOrderingDownload/00305-2010DOM-EN.pdf, accessed on 19 May 2011.

Department of Health, Department for Education and Employment and Home Office (2000) *Framework for the Assessment of Children in Need and their Families.* London: The Stationery Office.

Emerson, E. and Hatton, C. (2007) 'Mental health of children and adolescents with intellectual disabilities in Britain.' *British Journal of Psychiatry 191*, 6, 493–499.

Heiman, T. and Berger, O. (2008) 'Parents of children with Asperger syndrome or with learning disabilities: Family environment and social support.' *Research in Developmental Disabilities 29*, 4, 289–300.

Holt, S., Buckley, H. and Whelan, S. (2008) 'The impact of exposure to domestic violence on children and young people: A review of the literature.' *Child Abuse and Neglect 32*, 8, 797–810.

Human Rights Act (1998) London: HMSO. Available at www.legislation.gov.uk/ukpga/1998/42/contents, accessed on 25 December 2010.

Mental Health Act (1983) London: HMSO. Available at www.dh.gov.uk/en/Publicationsandstatistics/Legislation/Actsandbills/DH_4002034, accessed on 8 July 2011.

Mental Health Act (2007) London: HMSO. Available at www.legislation.gov.uk/ukpga/2007/12/contents, accessed on 21 March 2011.

Mitchell, D.B. and Hauser-Cram, P. (2008) 'The well-being of mothers of adolescents with developmental disabilities in relation to medical care utilization and satisfaction with health care.' *Research in Developmental Disabilities 29*, 2, 97–112.

Mugno, D., Ruta, L., D'Arrigo, V.G. and Mazzone, L. (2007) 'Impairment of quality of life in parents of children and adolescents with pervasive developmental disorder.' *Health and Quality of Life Outcomes 5*, 22.

National MAPPA Team (2009) MAPPA Guidance 2009. Available at www.lbhf.gov.uk/Images/MAPPA%20Guidance%20%282009%29%20Version%203%200%20_tcm21-120559.pdf, accessed on 8 July 2011.

Novaco, R.W. and Taylor, J.L. (2008) 'Anger and assaultiveness of male forensic patients with developmental disabilities: Links to volatile parents.' *Aggressive Behavior 34*, 4, 380–393.

Plant, M.A., Orford, J. and Grant, M. (1989) 'The effects on children and adolescents of parents' excessive drinking: An international review.' *Public Health Reports 104*, 5, 433–442.

Power, L., Morgan, S., Byrne, S., Boylan, C. *et al.* (2009) 'A pilot study evaluating a support programme for parents of young people with suicidal behaviour.' *Child and Adolescent Psychiatry and Mental Health Journal 3*, 1, 20.

Sin, C., Francis, R. and Cook, C. (2010) 'Access to and experience of child and adolescent mental health services: Barriers to children and young people with learning disabilities and their families.' *Mental Health Review Journal 15*, 1, 20–28.

Tarkka, M., Paavilainen, E. and Lehti, K. (2003) 'In hospital social support for families of heart patients.' *Journal of Clinical Nursing 12*, 5, 736–743.

Ungar, M. (2004) 'The importance of parents and other caregivers to the resilience of high-risk adolescents.' *Family Process 43*, 1, 23–41.

Wright, B., Williams, C. and Richardson, G. (2008) 'Services for children with learning disabilities.' *The Psychiatrist 32*, 3, 81–84.

Chapter 6

EDUCATION IN ADOLESCENTS WITH DEVELOPMENTAL DISABILITIES IN SECURE SETTINGS

Cheryl Smith and Melanie Dixon

INTRODUCTION

In 2003 the UK Government published a Green Paper called *Every Child Matters* (DfES 2003) following the death of Victoria Climbié who tragically died of abuse and neglect. The aim is for all children, whatever their background or their circumstances, to have the support they need to:

- be healthy

- stay safe

- enjoy and achieve

- make a positive contribution

- achieve economic well-being.

Adolescents with developmental disabilities and a forensic history who are admitted to secure services have often had negative experiences within the education system. Family life has often been chaotic, which has had a detrimental impact upon their learning and social development. They frequently come from dysfunctional backgrounds, where they may have suffered emotional, physical or sexual abuse or neglect. Disruptive behaviour has often led to extended periods of absence from school due to suspensions, exclusions or general truancy. The ideals of *Every Child Matters* have unfortunately in some respects failed this group of young people; they have found themselves in secure care, having offended or engaged in high risk behaviour.

It is at this point that the opportunities to be healthy, stay safe, and enjoy and achieve may become possible for these individuals for the first time in their lives. The education teams working with this group of youngsters have an important role to play.

The challenge for teachers educating this complex and challenging group of young people is to re-engage and inspire them to 'enjoy and achieve', in a safe and nurturing environment, whilst equipping them with the valuable tools needed to be successful in life, including goals for lifelong learning.

RESEARCH EVIDENCE

It would be safe to assume that the development of educational skills can do nothing but improve the prospects of young people with developmental disorders and forensic histories; however, there is still limited data within this area.

Stephenson (2007) has highlighted the relatively small amount of good quality research into the impact that educational programmes have had on young offenders in the UK. However, research by the Youth Justice Board (YJB) (2004) suggests that there is a strong link between engaging offenders in an education programme and a reduction in reoffending. Research commissioned by the YJB into Education, Training and Employment (DCSF 2009) found that where students improved their literacy skills, gained qualifications or went on to further training or employment, their reoffending rates were lower than the rates of their less successful peers. There is a clear and significant economic benefit in investing in education for disadvantaged young people who are more likely to commit crime (Heckman and Masterov 2007).

It is therefore essential to ensure that full access to an education programme is available to all young people who have been admitted to a secure provision to enable them to have the opportunity to develop their skills and gain qualifications. This is the starting point, but having access to education itself is not enough. The teacher must also have the necessary skills to overcome some of the challenges presented by the students in order to enable them to benefit from the teaching and learning relationship.

One of the main hurdles to achieving this is the willingness of the young people to engage in education, as more often than not they enter secure psychiatric setting disillusioned and 'switched off'. The challenge for teachers working in these settings is to provide opportunities for educational participation and progression and to find the individual's unique switch to re-engagement.

It is important to look at this issue from two perspectives: first, addressing the problem of how to engage this challenging population; and second, ensuring that the provisions and systems in place meet the needs of young people who have offended.

The YJB in the UK commissioned a project entitled 'Barriers to Engagement' (2006) which found that there are numerous obstacles to engaging these adolescents. The obstacles include shortage of suitable provisions, lack of specialist help for young people with special educational needs, low expectations of students' achievements and providing the appropriate learning environments with one-to-one support being in short supply. This project suggests that a holistic provision with a strong multidisciplinary approach that is child centred and meets their individual needs will provide the best outcomes for this group of young people. The research evidence from this project suggests that engagement in education and training is one of the most important factors in reducing offending and reoffending.

The quality of care offered within secure environments varies greatly, as does the students' experience of education within these settings. The YJB research clearly demonstrates that access to specialised placements which can meet the social, educational, emotional and medical needs of young people who have offended are likely to have the best rehabilitation results.

The YJB (DCSF 2009) found that overall there was a 25 per cent reduction in the rate of offending in the year following enrolment on an education, training and employment project, compared with offending in the year before enrolment. This data is very promising and highlights the importance of specially trained and experienced teachers to deliver an accessible education and the possibility of a 'future' free of antisocial behaviour and offending.

There is a need for more outcome studies to be completed in the area of access to quality education and a reduction in offending. Most current research appears to point to the fact that education is of primary importance when rehabilitating young offenders so that they are equipped with the skills, knowledge and confidence they need to break the cycle of social exclusion and to build a positive future (Youth Justice Board 2004).

PRACTICE ISSUES

Assessment

On admission it is important that students have access to a full educational assessment using nationally recognised tests to ascertain levels of functioning, strengths and deficit areas. This is especially important for students with learning disability or for those who have been out of the education system for large periods of time as they are likely to be functioning well below what is expected for their chronological age. The most common assessments used include the British Picture Vocabulary Scale (BPVS) (Dunn *et al.* 1997) and the Aston Index Vocabulary Scale (Newton, Newton and Thomson 1994) which measure receptive and expressive vocabulary respectively. Alongside these the NFER–NELSON New Group Reading Test (NGRT) (Hagues and Burley 2000) and British Spelling Test Series (BSTS) (Vincent and Crumpler 1997) provide an indication of a young person's reading and spelling ability. For assessing numerical skills the NFER-NELSON Progress in Maths test (PiM) (Clausen-May, Vappula and Ruddock 2004) is used and a coding system can be used in order to ascertain specific areas of strength or concern. Where required, further diagnostic tests are undertaken which can provide additional information pertinent to the young person's deficits, such as Dyslexia Portfolio (Turner 2008), Dyscalculia Screener (Butterworth and Yeo 2004) and the Phonological Assessment Battery (PhAB) (Frederickson, Frith and Reason 1997). The Connors Rating Scales Revised CRS-R (Connors 1997) can be used to assess attention deficit hyperactivity disorder (ADHD).

Students who have been diagnosed with autistic spectrum disorders (ASD) will benefit from further observational assessments looking at their communication, social interaction and flexibility of thought and may also require formal diagnostic testing through the Diagnostic Interview for Social and Communication Disorders (DISCO) (Wing *et al.* 2002), Autism Diagnostic Interview – Revised (ADI-R) (Rutter, Le Couteur and Lord 2001) or Autism Diagnostic Observation Schedule (ADOS) (Lord *et al.* 2002) if their developmental disability has failed to be recognised. National MAPPA Team (2009) MAPPA Guidance 2009. These diagnostic tests must be administered by an appropriately qualified and trained practitioner.

The assessment period can be a particularly valuable opportunity to build a therapeutic rapport with young people and learn about interest areas and future goals. However, it is essential to be aware that formal assessments can be extremely stressful for students with low self-esteem and high levels of anxiety and can lead to under-performance. Following completion of appropriate assessments the need for an individually tailored educational programme is paramount to ensure that specific diagnostic issues and learning styles are catered for. This education plan must take into account all aspects of a young person's development. It must also provide a framework for meeting his or her learning needs including being aware of group sizes and social expectations that are appropriate for each individual.

The appropriate level of support can be highly staff intensive and specialised, and the curriculum chosen may be focused on key skills or deficit areas. However, the end result should be an individual programme which fully addresses the needs of the young person.

Individual education plans

Individual education plans are a crucial tool in the planning and delivery of an appropriate curriculum for young people who present big challenges with regards to engagement and progress. They form the skeleton of the assessment and review process which can provide a measure of the success young people experience as they progress through the education system within secure settings.

It is imperative when working with students who present as disaffected and challenging to work collaboratively, setting short-term targets and long-term goals, so that they are aware of their own learning objectives and have a voice in the direction of their education. The presentation of these individual education plans should reflect the student's level of comprehension and they may be presented in a variety of visual or text based formats depending on the individual. Students with identified learning disabilities or ASD may require a more visual presentation of the individual education plan, with carefully adapted targets that demonstrate to the students exactly what is expected of them and where they are heading in the longer term. It is important to include information for the students as to exactly what they have to do, how to do it, and who can support them for each target. Targets must be achievable but with high enough expectations of the students to ensure that they are achieving their educational potential.

A regular review of these individual education plans with the students enables them to measure their progress and value even the smallest of achievements. They are often able to witness their own progress as the targets get updated and progress is acknowledged. This process in turn can begin their journey towards self-acceptance and belief in their capabilities which can often be their first positive experience within an education setting.

Teaching

When teaching students with developmental disabilities who are in secure psychiatric settings due to their offending behaviour, it is vital to adopt a range of flexible strategies to meet their ever evolving needs. The teaching and learning styles which are selected to suit pupils' needs will depend greatly on their diagnosis and individual presentation. For example, students with a diagnosis of attention deficit hyperactivity disorder (ADHD), autistic spectrum disorder (ASD) and post-traumatic stress disorder (PTSD) all require carefully planned interventions specific to their individual learning needs.

Initially all these adolescents can benefit hugely from individual teaching. This allows them to feel safe and supported enough to develop the confidence to tackle new skills without the fear of failure and rejection, which in many cases has been their experience in previous education settings. A safe and nurturing starting point which promotes success and provides individuals some choices regarding their learning can provide a solid foundation for integration and inclusion into group settings and eventually community-based education programmes.

The curriculum offered to young people needs careful consideration to ensure that the best outcomes can be achieved for the students. In many circumstances students have had such erratic and poor engagement with the education system, or have had unsuccessful support for their special educational needs, that they have substantially fallen behind their peers. The priority for teachers when given a short amount of time to work with young people who have a lot of ground to make up with regards to educational achievement, is to try to develop students' functional skills, such as reading, writing and Information and Computer Technology (ICT). They should strive to develop other areas which may prove beneficial in everyday life as well. In addition to this there needs to be an emphasis on addressing other issues that could be potentially critical to success such as aspects of personal social health education and the development of appropriate social skills. The Youth Justice Board, Ministry of Justice and Department for Children, Schools and Families jointly prescribe that all young people in juvenile custody receive full-time education based on the mainstream National Curriculum. Flexibilities should be put in place to take account of prior learning, specific learning needs and other needs which young people may have, such as substance misuse and behaviour management. A clear focus should be placed on the development of literacy and numeracy skills (DCSF 2003).

Small group teaching can be extremely valuable when wishing to integrate the students with an appropriate peer group where they can practise turn taking and more complex social skills, all crucial to developing them as well-rounded members of the community. The students may also perceive that they are making progress and are viewed as able to accept the next step in their learning journey. Sharing achievements with other young people is another aspect of the learning process which can have very beneficial results as far as self-esteem and self-confidence is concerned and small group teaching with only two or three peers is a great way to achieve this.

Successful outcomes with this challenging population of young people rely heavily upon developing appropriate positive and trusting relationships between student and teacher. In the forefront of the teacher's mind has to be that 'failure' is a common word in the student's vocabulary and that the opportunities for replacing this for 'success' are running out. Accessing nationally recognised qualifications such as AQA Entry Level Awards (www.aqa.org.uk) and Edexcel (www.edexcel.com) online examinations is important especially as these are achievable within a short time frame and can kick start a young person's thirst for knowledge.

Teachers must be mindful that students in a forensic setting and in particular those who have a developmental disability are often receiving pharmacological interventions which can affect their concentration or make them particularly drowsy. Regular multidisciplinary meetings are essential for information to be shared and assessments completed to ensure that the students are able to function to the best of their ability whilst symptoms are managed safely, improving the quality of life for the young people concerned. Effective communication within the team caring for young people is key to this happening successfully.

All students within these settings require individualised and specialist teaching and management. However, there are specific strategies which are useful to employ with individuals who have certain developmental disabilities or mental health problems such as ADHD, ASD or PTSD. It is important to note that some of these complex youngsters have a co-morbid presentation with all three.

Attention deficit hyperactivity disorder

As students' academic success is often dependent on their ability to attend to given instructions and teacher expectations with minimal distractions, a student with ADHD may struggle within a learning environment. Activities that involve listening to and retaining given instructions, group work and completing a piece of work in an allotted time frame can be potentially problematic for students with ADHD. There are a number of strategies that can be employed in relation to the learning environment and teaching styles adopted to support students with ADHD. It should be noted that students with ADHD often have good educational capabilities but need support in appropriately accessing them. It can be beneficial for the students if they are given the opportunity in the initial stages of their learning to work on an individual basis, sometimes with shorter tasks. The next stage would be to include them in a small group, but with their own work bay to reduce distractibility, to finally integrating them within a group with one-to-one support when required. These students can be acutely aware of what they should be doing but are unable to gain control over their behaviour, which can often be equally frustrating for them. Appropriate pharmacological treatment can sometimes significantly improve concentration and engagement.

Autistic spectrum disorders

Students with a diagnosis of ASD require highly structured, individualised teaching using an approach such as the TEACCH Treatment and Education of Autistic and Communication related Handicapped Children (Mesibov, Shea and Schopler 2004). This approach provides students with opportunities to develop independence through the use of high levels of environmental and visual structure. Ideally the classroom should be demarcated visually into group areas, one-to-one areas and individual work bays for the students through strategic placing of furniture and floor tape. This provides visual clarity of what the expectations are for each area of the classroom and therefore reduces anxiety and meets students' need for structure and routine. In addition to this some form of visual schedule should be provided for each individual to ensure that he or she again has knowledge of what needs doing and what the expectations are. Visually presenting information to these students reduces the problems associated with misinterpretation and social interaction difficulties and therefore minimises anxiety. Schedules should be individualised to the students' levels of understanding and may vary from the use of objects or pictures through to a written schedule or diary. Work should be visually presented and set within work trays or boxes to add another dimension of structure. A left-to-right orientation should always be adopted for both schedules and work systems to provide the students with a clearly defined start and finish.

The main benefit of this approach is that it minimises the need for too much verbal interaction which can cause anxiety or confusion. Promoting independence for students with ASD is beneficial as it counterbalances some of the difficulties associated with social interaction and being in the company of others.

The issues of sensory processing difficulties must also be taken into account as many students can be oversensitive to noise levels and lighting; this must be taken into account when planning education sessions. A calm environment with minimal distractions is necessary for this group of young people to be able to engage to their potential. There are many other approaches which can be used with young people with ASD but the most successful outcomes rely on similar strategies of incorporating maximal levels of structure and reducing external stimuli.

Post-traumatic stress disorder

Students with PTSD provide different challenges to the education team. They may present with symptoms such as hyper-vigilance, agitated behaviour, emotional numbness, anxiety or depression. The majority of students with this diagnosis will also need support with developing self-esteem and self-confidence.

They can be very distrustful of others and may take an extended period of time to engage in education or indeed allow themselves to take the risk of undertaking any challenges for fear of failure. There are sometimes particular environment triggers that need to be avoided. It may therefore be necessary to accept that the student is only able to cope with work of very low demand, regardless of his or her ability. During this time encouragement and support should be offered to develop the confidence required to undertake more challenging tasks. The decision about how much demand to place on an individual with PTSD, from a teacher's perspective, is very complex as any form of failure can be the cause of further disengagement by the young person concerned whereas low expectations can lead to underachievement. It is a highly important balancing act. The key to working with students suffering with PTSD is to develop a strong trusting relationship between student and teacher that can tolerate a few minor setbacks and absorb the knocks without causing a breakdown of the teaching–learning relationship.

It is important for this group of youngsters to have a stable and familiar learning environment; wherever possible they are to be taught by one key teacher, rather than a team, in order for them to start their journey towards trusting others. These students may have an overriding lack of self-worth and self-confidence which permeates all aspects of their daily lives. This needs to be developed and improved before expectations can be safely raised and obstacles such as qualifications even considered. Being aware of these delicate issues allows teachers to intercede and attempt to break the cycle of failure and in turn empower the students to experience success.

Case description 1

Laura is a 17-year-old young woman who was admitted to a secure forensic learning disability service on section 37/41 (Restriction Order) of the Mental Health Act 1983 through the UK criminal justice system. She was admitted for treatment rather than serving a prison sentence for murder due to her being deemed unfit to plead as a result of her learning disability. She came from a dysfunctional background and had suffered repeated sexual abuse leading to PTSD symptoms alongside her developmental disability, with a measured IQ below 70.

On admission, attempts were made to conduct a full educational assessment. However, this initially proved problematic due to Laura's extremely low self-esteem and self-worth. It was felt it would be in her best interests to delay formal assessment until such time that she was able to cope with the experience. In the meantime she was timetabled for low demand sessions to build her confidence and a therapeutic rapport. This took some considerable time as she was very self-deprecating, claiming she 'was useless and couldn't do it'. This invariably led to her withdrawing from the lesson by storming out of the classroom. This was a common pattern for a number of months until very gradually she could appreciate for herself that she was learning and making progress, which in turn started the very slow process of improving her self-esteem.

When Laura was finally assessed it was apparent that she had islands of knowledge which could in turn be built upon and it was clear she had some potential despite her poor previous academic attainment and psychometric testing. It was decided in collaboration with Laura to start studying towards some externally recognised qualifications.

Laura's first exam was in ICT and was an AQA Entry level qualification. She found the exam conditions extremely stressful and required constant reassurance throughout the allotted time to ensure she did not walk out. She passed the exam with Distinction, the first accreditation that she had ever gained, which was a huge boost to her confidence and a turning point in her learning.

Despite continuing to find exams challenging and struggling to maintain her belief that she could achieve, Laura went on to be an outstanding student and during her three-year stay with us she became our first student to gain a Level 2 qualification in Literacy, which is equivalent to a GCSE grade A* to C. Alongside this she also gained accreditations in Numeracy and ICT.

Laura was discharged from medium secure care to a low secure adult placement where all reports suggest that she is continuing to further her education and developing into a more confident and happy young woman.

Case description 2

John, a 15-year-old young man with ASD and an IQ below 70, was admitted to medium secure care due to high levels of aggression and social isolation. Upon admission he required special nursing in an extra care facility within the unit, to manage his extreme aggression to others due to high levels of social anxiety which had led to complete social withdrawal. John had not been able to attend his special school for the previous two years due to his problematic behaviour and had received limited educational input at home.

Observational assessments were carried out by the specialist ASD teacher to ascertain his suitability for the TEACCH approach and develop a therapeutic rapport. He remained in extra care for a period of three months. During this time he received one-to-one education sessions within the extra care facility. Following this, John was given an individual session in the TEACCH classroom each day to begin to develop his confidence with familiar adults and access more regular structured education sessions. He was escorted by two male nurses whose role was to provide constant observation at all times to manage John's aggression. He responded well to the structure and his interest in LEGO® Bionicles was incorporated into the majority of his work tasks to develop his engagement and interest in learning.

By week four in the TEACCH classroom John's level of observation had been reduced to one constant escort and he was being managed in the main ward environment rather than extra care. At this point the specialist ASC teacher introduced another young person into the classroom alongside John and closely monitored any interactions to ensure that John's levels of anxiety were manageable and that the classroom remained a positive focus of his day. Over a period of three months two further students were integrated into the classroom; by then John was able to participate in a full day of schooling without escorts.

John remained in the TEACCH classroom until his discharge two years later, by which point he had achieved nationally recognised qualifications in ICT and Numeracy. Alongside these fantastic achievements, John's social interaction, communication and social skills had vastly improved and his levels of social anxiety had reduced dramatically. This opened up opportunities for John to access the community safely and test out his new skills and confidence within a wider range of settings.

John was discharged to a low secure specialist ASD placement in his home area, where he enrolled on a functional skills course at a local further education college. Reports to date suggest that he is continuing to make progress both educationally and socially. He regularly keeps in touch with members of the team who worked with him to update them on his progress and more importantly to thank them for helping him to move on with his life.

CONCLUSIONS

The *Every Child Matters* Green paper (DfES 2003) seeks to address the issues of all young people including those who have been involved in offending behaviour, acknowledging the difficulties faced by young people who have found themselves in the criminal justice system.

The Green paper is clear that preventing young people from engaging in crime is critical to ensuring positive life chances and successful pathways to adulthood. Education and training can help young people develop skills for life and work, and help prevent them from falling into cycles of crime. Many young people in the youth justice system face multiple disadvantages; they have complex needs, and often face barriers to engaging in education, training and employment (DfES 2003).

The UK Government have also addressed the issue of the need for the provision of education for young people detained in youth accommodation in the Apprenticeships, Skills, Children and Learning Bill (UK Parliament 2009). It is clear that young people who are detained must have enough suitable education provided to meet their reasonable needs and a relevant curriculum that considers their aptitudes, abilities and special needs.

This reinforces the statutory role that education plays in the rehabilitation of young people who offend and supporting them back into the community with improved skills and the tools required to make a positive contribution to society and achieve economic well-being. This, coupled with the research findings, shows that participation in education, training and employment is a key protective factor in preventing offending and reoffending behaviour (DfES 2003). Education gives these challenging and disadvantaged young people a genuine chance of a crime-free future with positive outcomes.

REFERENCES

Butterworth, B. and Yeo, D. (eds) (2004) *Dyscalculia Guidance: Helping Pupils with Specific Learning Difficulties in Maths*. London: David Fulton.

Clausen-May, T., Vappula, H. and Ruddock, G. (eds) (2004) *Progress in Maths 5*. London: NFER Nelson.

Connors, C.K. (ed.) (1997) *Connors Rating Scales – Revised*. New York, NY: Multi-Health Systems Inc.

Department for Children, Schools and Families (DCSF) (2009) *Education for Young Offenders*. Available at www.education.gov.uk/childrenandyoungpeople/sen/earlysupport/esinpractice/a0067409/every-child-matters, accessed on 8 July 2011.

Department for Education and Skills (DfES) (2003) *Every Child Matters: Change for Children*. Nottingham: Department for Education and Skills (DfES) Publications.

Dunn, L.M., Dunn, D.N., Styles, D. and Sewell, J. (eds) (1997) *British Picture Vocabulary Scale II*. Slough: NFER.

Frederickson, N., Frith, U. and Reason, R. (eds) (1997) *Phonological Assessment Battery*. Windsor: NFER Nelson.

Hagues, N. and Burley, J. (eds) (2000) *Group Reading Test II (6–14)*. Windsor: NFER Nelson.

Heckman, J. and Masterov, D. (2007) 'The productivity argument for investing in young children.' *Applied Economic Perspectives and Policy 29*, 3, 446.

Lord, C., Rutter, M., DiLavore, P. and Risi, S. (2002) *Autism Diagnostic Observation Schedule*. Los Angeles, CA: Western Psychological Services.

Mesibov, G.B., Shea, V. and Schopler, E. (eds) (2004) *The TEACCH Approach to Autism Spectrum Disorders*. New York, NY: Plenum Publishing.

Newton, M.A.T., Newton, M. and Thomson, M.E. (eds) (1994) *Aston Index Revised*. Wisbech: LDA.

Rutter, M., Le Couteur, A. and Lord, C. (2001) *Autism Diagnostic Scale – Revised*. Los Angeles, CA: Western Psychological Services.

Stephenson, M. (2007) *Young People and Offending: Education, Youth Justice and Social Inclusion*. Cullompton: Willan Publishing.

Turner, M. (2008) *Dyslexia Portfolio*. London: GL Assessment.

UK Parliament (2009) *Apprenticeships, Skills, Children and Learning Bill 2008–09*. Available at http://services.parliament.uk/bills/2008-09/apprenticeshipsskillschildrenandlearning.html, accessed on 9 September 2010.

Vincent, D. and Crumpler, M. (eds) (1997) *British Spelling Test Series*. Windsor: NFER Nelson.

Wing, L., Leekam, S.R., Libby, S.J., Gould, J. and Larcombe, M. (2002) 'Diagnostic Interview for Social and Communication Disorders: Background, inter-rater reliability and clinical use.' *Journal of Child Psychology and Psychiatry 43*, 307–325.

Youth Justice Board (2004) *Education, Training and Employment Projects*. Available at www.yjb.gov.uk/publications/scripts/prodView.asp?idproduct=163&eP=, accessed on 27 April 2010.

Youth Justice Board (2006) *Barriers to Engagement*. Available at www.yjb.gov.uk/publications/scripts/prodView.asp?idProduct=291&eP=, accessed on 27 June 2010.

Chapter 7

AUTISTIC SPECTRUM DISORDERS IN ADOLESCENTS WHO REQUIRE SECURE CARE

Ernest Gralton

INTRODUCTION

Over the last 20 years more young people in populations with behavioural disturbance and offending are recognised as having autistic spectrum disorders (ASD). This is probably because of the increased recognition of higher functioning adolescents with autistic disorder in populations of young people with offending behaviour. A number of deficits in adolescents with ASD can lead to aggression and offending behaviour. Recognition of the disorder is essential in addressing and reducing offending. Complex co-morbidity may make the disorder more difficult to recognise as ASD can exacerbate and alter the presentation of other developmental disorders and mental illness.

RESEARCH EVIDENCE

There is unfortunately limited epidemiological evidence for adolescents with ASD and offending; most of the studies relate to adults. The numbers of young people diagnosed with autistic spectrum disorders has significantly increased in the last 20 years and a prevalence in the UK of 1 per cent is probably still an underestimate (Baird *et al.* 2006). The symptoms of higher functioning autistic spectrum disorders may only become obvious with the social and functional demands of adolescence (Berney 2004).

There has been concern about the possible links between autism and offending in adults since the 1980s (Baron-Cohen 1988; Mawson, Grounds and Tantam 1985; Tantam 1988). There is evidence that there is an over representation of individuals with autistic spectrum disorders in English high secure special hospitals (Hare *et al.* 2000). There was a surprisingly low rate of recognition (less than one-fifth of cases); in some cases a diagnosis had been made, only to be subsequently lost. Diagnosis was recognised as being more difficult in female patients, and there was often confusion with schizophrenia.

It has been argued that ASD is an additional vulnerability factor for delinquent or criminal behaviour which is increased by the presence of other co-morbid disorders and social factors (Palermo 2004). An understanding of the Scandanavian concept of DAMP (Deficits in Attention, Motor control and Perception) is important, particularly in severe DAMP where there are strong links with ASD. DAMP is linked with poor outcomes and offending behaviour (Gillberg 2003).

Comparisons between offenders admitted to a learning disability forensic hospital with and without autism demonstrated that autistic offenders were significantly less likely to have an obvious gain from their offence or appear overtly instrumental, and the offences were less likely to involve drugs or alcohol and less commonly occurred at night (O'Brien and Bell 2004). However, co-morbid substance misuse and psychotic illness has been found to be associated with serious offending in hospitalised adults with autistic spectrum disorders (Langstrom *et al.* 2009). Individuals with autistic spectrum disorders are more likely to adopt either a consistently conforming or non-conforming strategy (Bowler and Worley 1994) and lack adaptive flexibility.

It has been recognised for some time that children who become persistently antisocial do have neuropsychological deficits particularly in verbal ability and executive function (Moffitt 1993). Both these areas can be significantly adversely affected in individuals with ASD. Executive function impairment, although not limited to patients with ASD, is often a significant feature (Gillberg 2002). Weak central coherence or a tendency to focus on details rather than the whole picture is a feature of ASD. It can impair individuals' ability to understand the consequence of their actions (Gomez de la Cuesta 2010). It is also possible that individuals with high functioning ASD are less able to recognise fear in others; this could be a factor in some types of offending (Woodbury-Smith *et al.* 2005).

There is also the issue of overlap between high functioning autism and personality disorder (Tantam 1988b). However, the severity of ASD does not appear to be related to severity of ASD or to core cognitive deficits in adolescent boys with ASD. This may suggest that young people with autism who commit overtly callous and psychopathic acts may have additional deficits that are unrelated to their core autism (Rogers *et al.* 2006). Families often bear the brunt of violence and disruptive behaviour and often do so without reporting it to support agencies or the police (O'Brien and Bell 2004). Co-morbid psychiatric disorders are not common in offenders with ASD and require appropriate recognition and treatment (Newman and Ghaziuddin 2008). Certain types of offences may raise the suspicion of an ASD. Berney (2004) has highlighted particularly obsessive harassment (stalking), inexplicable violence, computer crime and offences arising out of misjudged social relationships. There is concern from the National Autistic Society that it is difficult to substantiate an increased risk from the current literature due to small sample sizes. Large-scale longitudinal prospective studies are required (Gomez de la Cuesta 2010).

There have been concerns about the treatability of people with ASD, particularly those with histories of sexual offending (Milton *et al.* 2002). In terms of pharmacological treatment risperidone in combination with methylphenidate has been shown to be effective in attention deficit hyperactivity disorder (ADHD) and co-morbid disorders (Aman *et al.* 2004) and alone for disruptive behaviour disorders in cognitively impaired young people (van Bellinghen and de Troch 2001).

PRACTICE ISSUES

It may be difficult to obtain a full developmental history from adolescents who present to forensic services. This may be because they have entered the care system at an early age and have had multiple placements and fragmented contact with child health services. Mainstream forensic psychiatric services have traditionally struggled to manage and meet the needs of patients with ASD (Murphy 2010).

Most diagnostic instruments for ASD are dependent on a comprehensive developmental history from a consistent carer including the Autism Diagnostic Instrument Revised (ADI-R) (Lord, Rutter and Le Couteur 1994) and the Diagnostic Interview for Social and Communication Disorders (DISCO) (Wing *et al.* 2002), with the child's behaviour around the age of four years being particularly critical. The ADI in particular concentrates on core autism and will miss more subtle presentations of ASD, particularly in higher functioning individuals (Charman and Baird 2002).

The Autism Diagnostic Observation Schedule–Generic (ADOS-G) is a semistructured assessment of social interaction, communication, play and imaginative use of materials for individuals who may have autism or other pervasive developmental disorders (Lord *et al.* 2000). There are four modules depending on the chronological age and developmental ability of the person; adolescents are usually appropriate for modules 3 or 4. The advantage of the ADOS-G is that it is not reliant on a detailed developmental history.

Adolescent transitions are particularly problematic for young people with ASD and can lead to significant decompensation. The most common in our experience is the transition from primary to secondary school. Relatively high functioning adolescents with ASD may be coping with whole class teaching from a single teacher and a relatively stable peer group, but may not be able to manage the combined stress of navigating around a complex new environment with multiple teaching staff. They are also vulnerable to bullying and manipulation by more able peers. This can lead to a variety of disruptive aggressive and antisocial behaviours in these settings including school refusal and truancy.

Practitioners need to be aware that adolescents who present to forensic services may require specific assessment for ASD, including assessment of social and communication needs, in order to appropriately address and manage risk behaviour (Tiffin, Shah and Le Couteur 2007). Young people with ASD have difficulty adjusting and coping in custodial environments where change can be rapid and without warning, environments are noisy, and rules are unyielding. In custodial settings adolescents with ASD are even more vulnerable to bullying and exploitation by antisocial peers. They are more likely to spend significant periods in isolation or segregation (Cashin and Newman 2009) and are at risk to engage in self-harm.

There is increasing concern about adolescents accessing sexual material on the internet (McColgan and Giardino 2005). Many young people with ASD are highly interested in and motivated by computers (Oberleitner and Laxminarayan 2004) and can spend significant periods of time on the internet where they are exposed to sexual material. Unsurprisingly young people with ASD and other developmental disorders appear more vulnerable to misinterpreting sexual material and misapplying it in real life. They can fail to contextualise sexual behaviour, misinterpret behavioural cues and often have an impaired understanding of issues around consent and legality. They can develop paraphilias including sexual attraction to younger children. Studies of adolescents and young adults with ASD in community group homes have shown a significant need for interventions to address sexual development and behaviour (Hellemans *et al.* 2007). Adolescents with histories of sexual offending referred to our secure service almost always have very significant deficits in sexual knowledge and understanding. They have usually been exposed to a variety of harmful sexual experiences both in real life and virtually via images from the internet. Images and films downloaded from mobile phones appear to be a source that is particularly difficult for parents or carers to regulate or control.

Complex co-morbidities can clearly further impair young people's ability in a range of different areas and further impact their social ability and understanding, bringing them into conflict with other people. Sensory sensitivities and hyposensitivities can occur in the range of sensory modalities and are common features of ASD (Bogdashina 2003). Environmental stimuli in relevant areas can lead to an elevation in arousal and an increased likelihood of physical aggression. Some of the most bizarre and inexplicable offences perpetrated by adolescents with ASD can have their roots in a previously unrecognised sensory issue.

Reasons for offending

The reasons for offending have been modified for adolescents from Berney (2004) and Wing (1997):

- Aggression resulting from the disruption of routines. This includes a lack of motivation to change or adapt behaviour.

- Crimes resulting from social naivety (including various types of sexual offending).

- Pursuit of a special interest, e.g. weapons, militaria, poisons, fire, sadistic interests.

- Experiences of bullying, teasing, rejection and a desire for revenge. This may lead to an assault on the perpetrator or displacement onto another, often completely innocent, person.

- Hostility towards family members (often parents), representing longstanding complex dynamics due to the dependency of the individual with ASD.

- Sensory sensitivities leading to high levels of arousal and violent behaviour.

- Passively following the lead of a stronger personality and committing an offence under that person's direction. More commonly in adolescents this takes the form of wanting to maintain membership of an antisocial peer group and being prepared to do anything to achieve this.

- A 'cry for help', in which violence is seen as the only way to obtain appropriate intervention.

- A lack of awareness of wrongdoing, or an assumption that the individual's own needs supersede all other considerations.

- Deficits in empathy or lack of recognition of fearful emotions in others may lead to indifference to the wider consequences of actions on others.

- An inability to see the consequences of actions due to poor central coherence or executive function impairment.

- Co-morbid mental illness, including affective and psychotic illness.

- Any combinations of the above.

For individuals with ASD who come in contact with the criminal justice system it is important to recognise the potential impact of the disorder on issues like fitness to plead and criminal responsibility (Dein and Woodbury-Smith 2010). Unfortunately there is limited research evidence on this issue and clinicians have to take this into account on a case-by-case basis. Issues that commonly arise are the misinterpretation of social cues as permission to engage in sexual activity and impaired executive function with reduced understanding of the consequences of the behaviour and the impact on the other person.

Treatment

The most important part of treatment is recognition of the disorder and the complex co-morbidities that are frequently present. An offence that may appear 'motiveless' or 'psychopathic' may be explicable once the young person's disabilities are understood in the context of the environment where the offence occurred. The treatment programme needs to be adapted for each individual because of their unique patterns of strengths and deficits. In terms of day-to-day management the National Autistic Society SPELL principles – Structure, a Positive approach, Empathy, Low arousal, and Links with other professionals – are helpful (Murphy 2010). The recognition and treatment of co-morbid mental illness is particularly important. The individual may require areas of skill building or remedial education in specific areas around arousal control, sexual understanding and social skills training. Sometimes an obsessional interest in a high risk area like weapons or poisons can be adapted and focused onto a less harmful interest.

Managing arousal is a key task for many young people with ASD, as high levels of physiological arousal can lead to physical aggression. Strategies to teach arousal control using progressive muscular relaxation augmented by biofeedback or sensory tools can be extremely helpful. Other strategies like the use of structured eastern traditions such as Tai Chi and yoga can also prove useful. Pharmacotherapy using low dose risperidone and/or propranolol may be helpful, but benzodiazepines are less useful due to issues around tolerance and dependence. Group offence-related work may not be possible in some individuals who are unable to maintain confidentiality. Seeking significant changes in empathy in some individuals may be unrealistic. Small gains in a range of areas can make a significant difference overall to the adolescent's ability to function in a structured supported setting in the community. Much of the management on return to the community centres around careful environmental management, ensuring that issues like social skills deficits and sensory sensitivities are not exacerbated, thus leading to decompensation. It is also important that the staff supporting a person with ASD who has seriously offended fully understand the risk issues and the exacerbating factors and do not become complacent.

Case description

Alex is a 17-year-old boy who lives at home with his mother; his elder sister has recently left to go to university. His parents separated when he was six. He attends a mainstream secondary school. He had some behavioural problems starting around the age of three years around change intolerance, noise sensitivity and insistence on routines. Initially these problems were attributed to marital conflict at home. A formal diagnosis of an ASD was made at age nine, although his IQ is in the normal range (Performance 100, Verbal 80).

He managed to cope in primary school but found the transition to secondary school difficult. He was extensively bullied at first and found it difficult to make friends because of his social impairment. He subsequently moved to a school slightly farther away from the family home where he has a special needs assistant in school. He is better at maths and science and weaker in English. His mother drops him off on the way to work and he catches a taxi back home most days. He spends most of his spare time playing online computer games and interacting with others in a virtual world as a role play character. Alex has been watching pornographic films on the internet but he has been concealing his internet history. Some of the films contain significant sexual aggression.

Alex was invited to a birthday party by a female classmate named Naomi, at her parent's home. Alex has not been to a social event like this since he was a child. He found it difficult at that time to cope with the rules of social party games so he was invited to very few. Alex is desperate for social acceptance and tells his mother he wants to go the birthday party. She drops him off and gives him the money for a taxi home.

Alex attends the party which has no adult supervision. There is free access to alcohol. Alex has very little experience with alcohol. He downs several alcopops and quite quickly becomes intoxicated. He is finding the loud music difficult to tolerate and goes upstairs to the toilet. Alex opens a bedroom door thinking it is the toilet and sees a young couple having sex on the bed. Alex observes them for a few seconds and recognises the girl as someone in his class who he has found attractive and in the past has been nice to him. Her name is Stephanie and she is 16. Alex is sexually aroused by what he sees.

Alex goes to the toilet and comes back past the room, where the door is still ajar. The boy has gone but Stephanie is still lying on the bed. Alex goes in and lies on the bed next to her. Stephanie smells strongly of alcohol and she turns over and puts her head on his shoulder. Alex takes down his pants and starts to have sex with her. She wakes up and tells him to stop. He ignores her (like the guys do in the films) and continues to have sex. He thinks she is excited by having sex with him and that was why she was moving her body around under him instead of struggling. Then he pulls up his pants and abruptly leaves the room without saying anything.

The party is still very noisy when Alex goes downstairs and he finds this difficult to cope with. He rings a taxi and leaves without saying goodbye to any guests. Alex arrives home, is let into the house by his mother and goes straight to bed.

The following day there is a knock at the door; the police are there. The girl has made an accusation that Alex raped her on the night of the party. She says she told him to stop and she struggled but he held her down and continued to have sex with her.

CONCLUSIONS

The assessment and treatment of adolescents with ASD begins with recognition of the disorder and associated co-morbidities. An understanding of the unique impairments of each individual with ASD can help significantly in understanding complex offence related issues. Treatment needs to focus on education and skill building across the whole range of domains and adapting the environment to reduce the impact on deficits, particularly in areas of social and sensory impairment. Pharmacotherapy has a limited role, mainly in the modulation of excessive anxiety and the treatment of co-morbid disorders.

REFERENCES

Aman, M.G., Binder, C. and Turgay, A. (2004) 'Risperidone effects in the presence/absence of psychostimulant medicine in children with ADHD, other disruptive behaviour disorders, and subaverage IQ.' *Journal of Child and Adolescent Psychopharmacology 14*, 2, 243–254.

Baird, G., Simonoff, E., Pickles, A., Chandler, S., Loucas, T., Meldrum, D. and Charman, T. (2006) 'Prevalence of disorders of the autism spectrum in a population cohort of children in South Thames: The Special Needs and Autism Project (SNAP).' *Lancet 368*, 210–15.

Baron-Cohen, S. (1988) 'An assessment of violence in a young man with Asperger's syndrome.' *Journal of Child Psychology and Psychiatry 29*, 3, 351–360.

Berney, T. (2004) 'Asperger syndrome from childhood into adulthood.' *Advances in Psychiatric Treatment 10*, 341–351.

Bogdashina, O. (2003) *Sensory Perception Issues in Autism and Asperger Syndrome.* London: Jessica Kingsley Publishers.

Bowler, M.D. and Worley, K. (1994) 'Susceptibility to social influence in adults with Asperger's syndrome: A research note.' *Journal of Child Psychology and Psychiatry 35*, 4, 689–697.

Cashin, A. and Newman, C. (2009) 'Autism in the criminal justice detention system: A review of the literature.' *Journal of Forensic Nursing 5*, 70–75.

Charman, T. and Baird, G. (2002) 'Practitioner review: Diagnosis of autism spectrum disorder in 2- and 3-year-old children.' *Child Psychology and Psychiatry 43*, 3, 289–305.

Dein, K. and Woodbury-Smith, M. (2010) 'Asperger syndrome and criminal behaviour.' *Advances in Psychiatric Treatment 16*, 37–43.

Gillberg, C. (2002) *A Guide to Asperger Syndrome.* Cambridge: Cambridge University Press.

Gillberg, C. (2003) 'Deficits in attention, motor control, and perception: A brief review.' *Archives of Disease in Childhood 88*, 904–910.

Gomez de la Cuesta, G. (2010) 'A selective review of offending behaviour in individuals with autism spectrum disorders.' *Journal of Learning Disabilities and Offending Behaviour 1*, 2, 47–58.

Hare, D.J., Gould, J., Mills, R. and Wing, L.A. (2000) *A Preliminary Study of Individuals with Autistic Spectrum Disorders in Three Special Hospitals in England.* London: National Autistic Society.

Hellemans, H., Colson, K., Verbraeken, C., Vermeiren, R. and Deboutte, D. (2007) 'Sexual behavior in high-functioning male adolescents and young adults with autism spectrum disorder.' *Journal of Autism and Developmental Disorders 37*, 2, 260–269.

Langstrom, N., Grann, M., Ruchkin, V., Sjostedt, G. and Fazel, S. (2009) 'Risk factors for violent offending in autism spectrum disorder.' *Journal of Interpersonal Violence 24*, 8, 1358–1370.

Lord, C., Risi, S., Lambrecht, L., Cook, E.H. *et al.* (2000) 'The Autism Diagnostic Observation Schedule – Generic: A standard measure of social and communication deficits associated with the spectrum of autism.' *Journal of Autism and Developmental Disorders 30*, 3, 205–233.

Lord, C., Rutter, M. and Le Couteur, A. (1994) 'Autism diagnostic interview – revised.' *Journal of Autism and Developmental Disorders 24*, 659–686.

Mawson, D., Grounds, A. and Tantam, D. (1985) 'Violence and Asperger's syndrome: A case study.' *British Journal of Psychiatry 147*, 566–569.

McColgan, M.D. and Giardino, A.P. (2005) 'Internet poses multiple risks to children and adolescents.' *Pediatric Annals 34*, 5, 505–14.

Milton, J., Duggan, C., Latham, A., Egan, V. and Tantam, D. (2002) 'Case history of co-morbid Asperger's syndrome and paraphilic behaviour.' *Medicine Science and the Law 42*, 3, 237–244.

Moffitt, T. (1993) 'Adolescent-limited and life-course-persistent antisocial behaviour: A developmental taxonomy.' *Psychological Review 100*, 4, 674–701.

Murphy, D. (2010) 'Understanding offenders with autism-spectrum disorders: What can forensic services do?' *Advances in Psychiatric Treatment 16*, 1, 44.

Newman, S.S. and Ghaziuddin, M. (2008) 'Violent crime in Asperger syndrome: The role of psychiatric comorbidity.' *Journal of Autism and Developmental Disorders 38*, 10, 1848–1852.

Oberleitner, R. and Laxminarayan, S. (2004) 'Information technology and behavioural medicine: Impact on autism treatment and research.' In L. Bos, S. Laxminarayan and A. Marsh (eds) *Medical and Care Compunetics 1*. Amsterdam: IOS Press.

O'Brien, G. and Bell, G. (2004) 'Learning disability, autism and offending behaviour.' In S. Bailey and M. Dolan (eds) *Adolescent Forensic Psychiatry*. London: Arnold.

Palermo, M. (2004) 'Pervasive developmental disorders, psychiatric comorbidities and the law.' *International Journal of Offender Therapy and Comparative Criminology 48*, 1, 40–48.

Rogers, J., Viding, E., Blair, R.J., Frith, U. and Happe, F. (2006) 'Autism spectrum disorder and psychopathy: Shared cognitive underpinnings or double hit?' *Psychological Medicine 36*, 1789–1798.

Tantam, D. (1988a) 'Lifelong eccentricity and social isolation I: Psychiatric social and forensic aspects.' *British Journal of Psychiatry 153*, 777–782.

Tantam, D. (1988b) 'Lifelong eccentricity and social isolation II: Asperger's syndrome or schizoid personality disorder?' *British Journal of Psychiatry 153*, 783–791.

Tiffin, P., Shah, P. and Le Couteur, A. (2007) 'Diagnosing pervasive developmental disorders in a forensic adolescent mental health setting.' *British Journal of Forensic Practice 9*, 3, 31–40.

Van Bellinghen, M. and de Troch, C. (2001) 'Risperidone in the treatment of behavioural disturbance in children and adolescents with borderline intellectual functioning: A double blind, placebo-controlled pilot trial.' *Journal of Child and Adolescent Psychopharmacology 11*, 1, 5–13.

Wing, L. (1997) 'Asperger's syndrome: Management requires diagnosis.' *Journal of Forensic Psychiatry 8*, 253–257.

Wing, L., Leekam, S.R., Libby, S.J., Gould, J. and Larcombe, M. (2002) 'The diagnostic interview for social and communication disorders: Background, inter-rater reliability and clinical use.' *Journal of Child Psychology and Psychiatry 43*, 3, 307–325.

Woodbury-Smith, M., Clare, I., Holland, A., Kearns, A., Staufenberg, E. and Watson, P. (2005) 'A case-control study of offenders with high functioning autistic spectrum disorders.' *Journal of Forensic Psychiatry and Psychology 16*, 4, 747–763.

Chapter 8

OCCUPATIONAL THERAPY INPUT FOR ADOLESCENTS WITH DEVELOPMENTAL DISABILITIES IN SECURE SETTINGS

Belafonte Hosier, Jackie O'Connell and Lesley Tebbutt

INTRODUCTION

Adolescence can be a challenging and difficult time for many young people. Over a century ago Hall (1904) suggested that normal adolescence was characterised by emotional upheavals and extensive stress and turmoil, with exaggerated emotional swings from being exuberant and euphoric to suddenly becoming indifferent and melancholy.

It is certainly a period of growth and transition. Adolescents are faced with physical, cognitive, emotional, spiritual and social changes that may have repercussions for their future physical and mental well-being (Arnett 1997). With this in mind it is clear that young people with a developmental disability and forensic needs start this transition toward adulthood at a distinct disadvantage.

In this chapter the authors will describe the range of assessments used in our Occupational Therapy (OT) service, and explain a graded skills programme and the range of interventions used to motivate and engage our young people in the process of becoming more functional and productive members of society. Occupational Therapy is a holistic, problem solving process which involves the therapeutic use of activities to enable individuals to perform their daily occupations to a satisfying and effective level.

RESEARCH EVIDENCE

Currently there is a limited amount of research geared primarily at the adolescent population, particularly those with complex and multiple diagnoses; often these may be included in child or adult services. As highlighted, adolescence is a time of change when a person moves from being a child to becoming an adult. In people without multiple diagnoses this is a difficult and emotional time. Add to this a complex range of learning disabilities, forensic histories and mental illness, and it can be very challenging to determine which interventions may help people make a successful transition. Research has highlighted that people with learning disabilities are more likely to experience mental illness and sensory dysfunction (DOH 2001). Therefore many of our young people have many complex problems to cope with. Recently an increased interest has been shown in the area of sensory needs and young people's sensory tolerances (Brown *et al.* 2006; Champagne and Stromberg 2004).

Within our OT service, the majority of our young people complete a range of assessments to determine their functional level of ability. They will then be offered sessions in line with their functional skills, following a graded skills pathway and utilising the principles of the Vona du Toit Model of Creative Ability (VdT MoCA), to enhance and build their skills. The VdT MoCA (Du Toit 2009) has gained much popularity in recent years among many countries. This model focuses on a detailed assessment and gives treatment guidelines to use in line with it. It gives detailed examples of the functional skills the young people need to build, and ideas of how to offer the 'just right' challenge, to provide people with enough support whilst still stretching their abilities. This model gives a structure and a framework to the interventions already offered by the OTs in the adolescent service. When considering appropriate interventions for adolescents, it is necessary to incorporate activities appropriate for their interests, age, culture and functional abilities (College of Occupational Therapists 2003, 2006b).

OTs are experts in 'doing', thus playing an integral role in building people's skills and helping them to explore and develop their own interests to enable them to build satisfying lifestyles. OTs believe in the value of purposeful activity or occupation to enhance their well-being (College of Occupational Therapists 2003, 2006b, 2007, 2008; Hocking 2007). 'Being deprived of or having limited access to occupation can affect physical and psychological health' (College of Occupational Therapists 2009, p.1). Our interventions aim to use the young people's existing interests to build the skills they need, providing these in a graded manner and allowing lots of opportunities for them to succeed. The young people respond well to these successes and the positive reinforcement they engender.

'Within a unique knowledge base on occupation and with their distinctive skills, occupational therapy staff have a pivotal role in providing rehabilitation, in aiding the recovery of people with mental health problems' (College of College of Occupational Therapists 2007, p.5).

We work in collaboration with the young people to offer a diverse range of interventions as detailed in the graded skills pathway, to increase motivation and stimulate the desire to change, including offering opportunities to access activities that their peers in the community may take for granted (College of Occupational Therapists 2003, 2006b; DOH 2001, 2004). OTs consider not only the difficulties young people may experience but also the effect this has on their lifestyle and quality of life (College of Occupational Therapists 2003). 'Occupation is complex and multifaceted, incorporating physical, social, psychological, emotional and spiritual dimensions' (College of Occupational Therapists 2003, p.32).

Another important aspect which has often been overlooked until recent years is spirituality; in the true sense this is not necessarily about particular religions, but can relate to cultural influences and strong interests (College of Occupational Therapists 2003). It is important to remember that cultural influences will affect the treatment offered, and interventions needed to respect people's cultural and spiritual backgrounds (College of Occupational Therapists 2003, 2009; Cotton *et al.* 2006). This may encompass dietary needs or access to particular activities or arenas for religious expression. In adolescence this is often an area that we have to consider and discuss more openly with the young person as they may be unable to identify these needs initially. In our service the young individuals have access to spiritual leaders and groups to provide them with the opportunity to learn about and explore spirituality in a broad sense. Spirituality may encompass caring for animals (in our animal unit) (Tebbutt 2009), being able to express their identity through fashion, music (joining the unit band or drum circle) or supporting their local football team. All of our interventions have an evidence based rationale.

By providing young people with the necessary skills and interests, we are empowering them to take control of their lives and build a fulfilling future (College of Occupational Therapists 2006b; Inclusion Institute 2009). Research has shown that involving people in occupation can have a positive effect on their mental health (College of Occupational Therapists 2006b, 2007; Inclusion Institute 2009). People have an innate drive to be involved in occupation (College of Occupational Therapists 2007). OTs are ideally placed to look at enhancing and enabling people to achieve this, using activity-based sessions to build a diverse range of skills to enhance independence and functional abilities, focusing on people's interests and cultural needs.

Initially our young people benefit from a structured environment, through timetabled sessions and expectations regarding engagement and behaviour. These mirror societal rules which enhance our feelings of being safe and secure. This is often something which our young people have not experienced previously, and although challenging, provides boundaries and a framework within which the young people can develop life skills.

A variety of different interventions are utilised to teach and enhance the young people's skills, including social and daily living skills groups, and practical interventions in the community. In addition, current legislation, including social inclusion and the national service framework, are incorporated into treatment aims (College of Occupational Therapists 2003). For young people to be fully functioning members of society, they need to be able to understand and follow social norms. This includes an awareness of how to behave in particular situations, and having the social skills to initiate, maintain and terminate social interaction in an appropriate way (College of Occupational Therapists 2003; DOH 2001; Whitehouse, Chamberlain and O'Brien 2001). Many of the young people struggle to generalise skills from one situation to another. Therefore a multimodal approach is necessary to enable the young people to build and utilise these skills, including role modelling, activity-based skills building and community-based interventions. Research has shown that teaching, practising and supporting young people with skills-building activities is a successful way of ensuring that they are able to retain, remember and use these skills (College of Occupational Therapists 2003, 2006b; Erikson 1968; Passmore and French 2003). It is important to remember that social inclusion is not simply about access to community-based activities, but about providing people with the skills to participate actively in them (DOH 2004).

Current legislation highlights issues regarding social inclusion and emphasises the need to offer community-based activities (DOH 2001; Inclusion Institute 2009; O'Connell and Farnworth 2007), to enable young people to build the skills necessary to function as members of a community (DOH 2001, 2004). It is important that young people have as much access to community-based activities as possible. This will reduce institutionalisation, as well as fears and anxieties. The interventions will enable young people to build appropriate skills in terms of behaviour and expectations when out, plus help to build social and interaction skills. They will also enable young people to find more appropriate and prosocial ways to occupy their time, and engage in other activities. When considering patient interventions, therapists endeavour to look towards future goals, which can be agreed with the young person, ensuring that these are realistic and achievable (College of Occupational Therapists 2003, 2007).

Voluntary work can offer our young people a sense of belonging and responsibility. 'In the eyes of the world and in our own eyes we are largely what we do' (College of Occupational Therapists 2006b, p.3). All our young people are offered the opportunity to enrol in the Duke of Edinburgh's Award scheme. This allows them to build a vast array of skills including a sense of identity, respect and understanding of others and social skills, along with giving them the opportunity to develop roles and responsibilities (dofe.org). This award can help them to build valuable skills which may enhance their ability to find future employment (dofe. org). In research carried out by the United Learning Trust (Duke of Edinburgh's Award 2007), a variety of employers were asked what skills and characteristics they felt were important when recruiting new staff. They rated 'leadership, teamwork, self-motivation, communication, confidence, consideration and ability to learn' as skills which are the most important, and which are developed and enhanced through people engaging in the Duke of Edinburgh's Award scheme. Coupled with this is the satisfaction and sense of achievement our young people get from earning this award. The Duke of Edinburgh's Award has now been recognised as appropriate for young people in other secure settings (Dubberley and Parry 2010).

Historically, people with learning disabilities have found it difficult to find paid employment; figures suggest that less than 10 per cent of people with a learning disability have a job (DOH 2001). This has no doubt been compounded by recent economic circumstances. In the current climate, when unemployment rates are high, people with forensic histories, mental health issues, learning disabilities and challenging behaviours are likely to struggle to find satisfying paid employment with an appropriate level of support (College of Occupational Therapists 2007, 2008; Inclusion Institute 2009). Research completed by a national mental health membership charity, found that less than 40 per cent of companies would consider employing people with mental health problems (Rethink 2009). In addition to this there may be limited opportunities for work placements, due to pared down work forces in many companies. However, the government has a number of schemes which are designed to support these individuals to find employment (College of Occupational Therapists 2007; DOH 2001; Inclusion Institute 2009). We offer young people voluntary work and supported work placements, such as Workbridge, which is a supported work environment based within the grounds. They offer young people the opportunity to build work skills, social networks, a sense of purpose and experience of a work environment, which may improve their ability to find a future job or work placement (College of Occupational Therapists 2007; DOH 2001; Inclusion Institute 2009).

Leisure pursuits are a valuable tool; these may compensate for a lack of paid employment for some of our young people. 'Not everyone wants to be employed, but almost all want to "work", that is to be engaged in some kind of valued activity that uses their skills and facilitates social inclusion' (College of Occupational Therapists 2007, p.9). Exploring and developing leisure skills is an important tool in helping to avoid a return to the maladaptive use of free time they may have made in the past. Leisure activities help to tackle social exclusion and encourage healthy lifestyles. Some articles have linked engagement in fulfilling and enjoyable leisure activities to motivation and quality of life (DOH 2001; Passmore and French 2003). This is imperative to consider when dealing with adolescents who may have low levels of motivation and expectation. 'Participation in play and sporting activities can help build self-esteem and social skills' (DOH 2001).

PRACTICE ISSUES

Challenges in interventions

The ongoing challenge for the OT service is to ensure that our range of interventions meets the identified needs of our young people. This includes offering interventions that reflect individuals' interests, culture, skills, sensory needs, level of motivation and level of risk. Different interventions need to be prioritised according to the most appropriate needs at the current time.

Figure 8.1 illustrates how the FAIR (facilitates allows inhibits restricts) process (Cavendish 2007), creative ability assessment (De Witt 2005) and the graded skills programme (Helbig 2005) support a structured OT service. The Model of Human Occupation Screening Tool (MoHOST) (Parkinson *et al.* 2006) is first used to cluster young people into various therapeutic groups, using the scoring criteria. The FAIR process produces average scores for each domain (volition, habituation, skills and environment) for each young person; they can then be clustered into groups (Cavendish 2007). Young people can then be further clustered by establishing the strength of motivation alongside their performance skills using the creative ability assessment (De Witt 2005). The graded skills programme enables the therapist to select appropriate interventions based on the outcome of the FAIR process and the creative ability assessment.

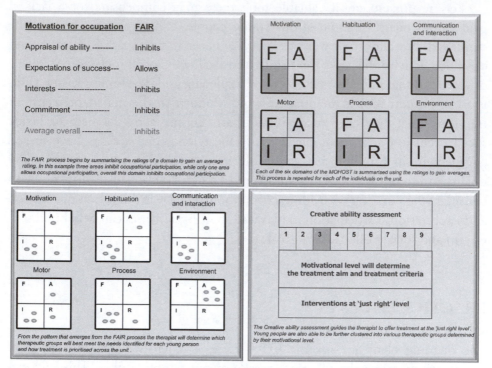

Figure 8.1 Integrating the FAIR process with the VdT MoCA (adapted from Parkinson et al. *2006 and De Witt 2005)*

Helbig (2005) describes a graded skills development programme consisting of hierarchical levels of groups which have been graded to meet the occupational performance and development needs of individuals. The development programme draws on principles from the Model of Human Occupation (MoHO) (Kielhofner 2008) and development theory (Mosey 1986). The graded skills development programme (see Figure 8.2) consists of five stages: assessment, engagement, task-based groups, life skills groups and advanced groups. As a young person makes progress he or she will be referred to the next stage of the programme where the demands of the activities are more challenging. The engagement primarily focuses on maintaining motivation and rapport with the young person. Task-based groups continue to maintain motivation whilst establishing a more meaningful routine and developing basic skills. As the young person continues to progress he or she will develop more meaningful roles that afford a range of responsibilities. The advanced groups enable the young people to generalise and practise the skills in a variety of environments.

Ongoing assessment is vital to the process; the risk level system and performance skills are indicators of readiness for more challenging tasks as well a person's motivation and commitment to therapy. The graded skills development programme takes account of allowing the young person to access all appropriate levels. Often at the engagement stage sensory integration will be offered to provide a foundation for further skills development. Young people are able to access these groups shortly after admission.

The advantages of using such a programme can aid understanding for young people and the multidisciplinary team regarding OT intervention. Figure 8.2 demonstrates the range of interventions available, grouping similar ones together based on their demands within a hierarchical format.

Risk issues

It has been well documented that health care professionals working within forensic settings need to consider risk before intervention (Cordingley and Ryan 2009; Garrett and Rowe 2004; Kettles, Robinson and Moody 2003). Over recent years attention has been given to risk assessment concerned primarily with violence and sexual offending (Monahan *et al.* 2000). Within OT determining access to various resources and environments is primarily based on risk; other influencing factors include skill capacity (Helbig 2005), motivation (De Witt 2005) and the preference for activities of the individual (King *et al.* 2004).

It is proposed that people with learning disabilities be given more choice and control over their lives (DOH 2001); however, the challenge for OT is balancing client-centred practice with risk management. Client-centred practice is the essence of occupational therapy practice. The College of Occupational Therapists (COT) (2003) describe it as an approach which places the client at the centre of therapy. The COT (2003) acknowledge the challenges faced by the OT with clients who have intellectual or emotional disabilities which may impact on their ability to rationalise decisions. Thus, the therapist may have to take responsibility on their behalf.

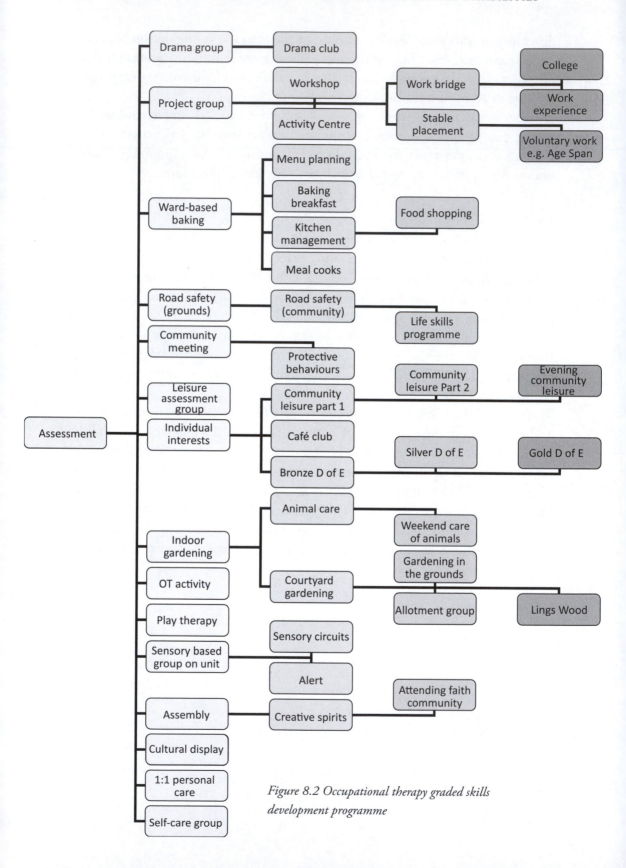

Figure 8.2 Occupational therapy graded skills development programme

The COT provides guidelines for OT risk management which also includes risk assessment (College of Occupational Therapists 2006a). Cordingley and Ryan (2009) identified no specific occupational therapy model for risk assessment and suggested 'risk assessment could be mapped using the concepts of person, environment, occupation and performance (PEOP) from models of practice' (p.532). The multidisciplinary team constantly assesses and manages risk in relation to access to various environments and other resources. The VdT MoCA (De Witt 2005) and the Model of Human Occupation (Kielhofner 2008) can support the risk assessment process, although they are not specifically designed to establish and manage risk. These do enable the therapist to understand better individuals' performance in the areas of adaptability and responsibility, communication and interaction with others, environmental factors influencing performance and the strength of motivation.

Extra care unit

When young people are unable to be safely managed within the open unit environment, they are admitted to extra care unit. This is a purpose built environment where a young person can be segregated from his or her peers for significant periods, with additional staff support. Once there, the challenges are multifaceted, including: the prevention and management of aggression and violence; sustaining/recovering the young person's motivation; maintaining/ establishing a meaningful routine and maintaining/establishing a balance of activities. A planned approach that is flexible can support the young person's recovery and ensure a prompt reintegration back into the open unit. The VdT MoCA (De Witt 2005) is an appropriate framework in which to work with the young person whilst in extra care; this model supports the team to work in a systematic and consistent manner whilst guiding intervention suitable to the young person's needs. By identifying an individual's level of motivation the therapist can then present an intervention package to meet the young person's needs and facilitate growth towards further levels of motivation and skill development.

Whilst in extra care unit it is important that young people continue to access a range of tools and materials that support engagement. The establishment of an activity resource cabinet (see Figure 8.3) allows for a range of low level activities to be facilitated within extra care. The resource cabinet contains materials and worksheets for sensory-based, educational, art and craft, and goal-setting games and activities. The tools and materials within the activity resource cabinet will have been risk assessed as to their suitability for the environment. The resources are organised according to levels outlined in the VdT MoCA.

Figure 8.3 Extra care resource cabinet

The COT (2003) informs that therapists need to be familiar and experiment with different assessment tools so that the most appropriate tool can be selected in a particular situation. Kielhofner (2008) explains that in order for OTs to fully understand a person's situation, the assessment process should be dynamic and holistic, taking into consideration volition, habituation, performance capacity and environmental factors. Due to the complex occupational needs of the young people with co-morbidities and with developmental disabilities a range of assessments are required to understand the extent of dysfunction on the individual's overall performance and the difficulties that are experienced when engaged in meaningful activity. Furthermore, no one assessment alone is able to capture overall functioning. Prentice and Wilson (2003) describe the assessment process as complex with individuals who have a mild or borderline learning disability who have offended and may also have a mental illness. Both Kielhofner's (2008) Model of Human Occupation (MoHO) and Du Toit's (2009) VdT MoCA are used as frameworks to guide the occupational therapy process. MoHO is the primary model used because it covers all domains of occupational functioning. The VdT MoCA has been crucial to the service as it has been able to give clinicians a better understanding of how to engage young people at an appropriate level. The following case example demonstrates the need for a range of assessments to guide intervention; whilst this is fictional it is representative.

Case description

David, a 16-year-old male with a diagnosis of autism and biopolar disorder, has shown that he struggles to attend to task. He has a poor attention span and is resistant to joining activities, particularly with his peers. When encouraged to attend he is prone to displaying challenging and inappropriate behaviours. David's responses would suggest that he is sensory defensive, meaning that he has a disorganised response to sensory input. As a result of this David may perceive sensory input that others feel is harmless as threatening, resulting in the flight or fight reaction highlighted above. David needs specific sensory input which is calming and organising, such as deep pressure, vestibular activities (e.g. rocking, spinning) or proprioceptive (heavy muscle work) input. The occupational therapist would assess to decide upon the specific intervention necessary and this would be dependent upon David's particular needs and sensory preferences.

Regular supervision is needed to complete basic activities of daily living (ADLs) such as self-care. If left to complete ADLs independently he is likely to not initiate the task, have an undesirable outcome or make lots of mistakes which could lead to injury. His range of interests is narrow, having a strong preference for drawing, and he will habitually overreact if encouraged to undertake an alternative activity. These activities have become a dominant feature of his day, leading to an imbalance of ADLs. In terms of his social skills David requires staff to compensate for his deficits. He is vulnerable to being bullied by other peers and in a wider context is limited in terms of task accomplishment within a community setting. David is regularly observed to spend considerable time on his own. However, he does have infrequent interactions with peers. These social exchanges are often brief.

The Model of Human Occupation Screening Tool (MoHOST) (Parkinson *et al.* 2006) indicated that further, more detailed assessments were needed. Those chosen were:

- assessment of motor and process skills (Fisher 2006)

- evaluation of social Interaction (Fisher and Griswold 2009)

- children's Assessment of Participation and Enjoyment and the Preferences for Activities of Children questionnaire (King *et al.* 2004)

- sensory profile questionnaire (Brown and Dunn 2002)

- creative ability assessment (from the Model of Creative ability) (De Witt 2005).

CONCLUSION

'Recovery is about building a meaningful and satisfying life, as defined by the person themselves, whether or not there are any ongoing or recurring symptoms or problems' (Shepherd, Boardman and Slade 2008, p.ii). In our service we recognise that the key issue in getting our young people engaged is to uncover what interests and motivates them by using careful observation and assessment and offering a wide variety of evidence based, appropriately graded, interventions. As practitioners working with these very challenging young people we do need a willingness 'to go the extra mile' (Shepherd *et al.* 2008, p.9) and to put 'hope-inspiring relationships' (Perkins 2006) at the heart of our practice.

REFERENCES

Arnett, J.J. (1997) 'Young people's conceptions of the transition to adulthood.' *Youth and Society* *29*, 1, 3–23.

Brown, C. and Dunn, W. (2002) *Adolescent/Adult Sensory Profile User's Manual.* San Antonio, TX: The Psychological Corporation.

Brown, S., Shankar, R., Smith, K., Turner, A. and Wyndham-Smith, T. (2006) 'Sensory processing disorder in mental health.' *Occupational Therapy News*, May, 28–29.

Cavendish, S. (2007) *The Fair Process, as defined by/produced by Cavendish.* Coventry: Coventry University.

Champagne, T. and Stromberg, N. (2004) 'Sensory approaches in inpatient psychiatric settings: Innovative alternatives to seclusion and restraint.' *Journal of Psychosocial Nursing 42*, 9, 34–44.

College of Occupational Therapists (2003) *Occupational Therapy Defined as a Complex Intervention.* London: College of Occupational Therapists.

College of Occupational Therapists (2006a) *Risk Management Guidance 1.* London: College of Occupational Therapists.

College of Occupational Therapists (2006b) *Recovering Ordinary Lives: The Strategy for Occupational Therapy in Mental Health Services 2007–2017: A Vision for the Next Ten Years.* London: College of Occupational Therapists.

College of Occupational Therapists (2007) *Work Matters: Vocational Navigation for Occupational Therapy Staff.* London: College of Occupational Therapists.

College of Occupational Therapists (2008) *Valuing People Now 2008–2011. Response from the College of Occupational Therapists.* London: College of Occupational Therapists.

College of Occupational Therapists (2009) *New Horizons: Towards a shared vision for mental health. Response from the College of Occupational Therapists.* London: College of Occupational Therapists.

Cordingley, K. and Ryan, S. (2009) 'Occupational therapy risk assessment in forensic mental health practice: An exploration.' *British Journal of Occupational Therapy 72*, 12, 531–538.

Cotton, S., Zebracki, K., Rosenthal, S.L., Tsevat, J. and Drotar, D. (2006) 'Religion/spirituality and adolescent health outcome: A review.' *Journal of Adolescent Health 39*, 4, 617.

Department of Health (2001) *Valuing People: A New Strategy for Learning Disabilities for the 21st Century, A White Paper.* London: Department of Health.

Department of Health (2004) *Executive Summary, National Service Framework for Children, Young People and Maternity Services: Every Child Matters.* London: Department Of Health.

De Witt, P. (2005) 'Creative ability: A model for psychosocial occupational therapy.' In R. Crouch and V. Alers (eds) *Occupational Therapy in Psychiatry and Mental Health.* London: Whurr Publishers Limited.

Dubberley, S. and Parry, O. (2010) '"Something we don't normally do": A qualitative study of the Duke of Edinburgh's award in the secure estate.' *Journal of the Social Service Research Group 27,* 3, 151–162.

Duke of Edinburgh's Award (2007) *Putting It All in Perspective: The Value of the DofE to Employers.* Available at www.dofe.org/media/viewfile.ashx?filetype=4&filepath=resourcezone/Research/value%20of%20theDofE%20to%20employers.pdf, accessed on 8 July 2011.

Du Toit, V. (ed.) (2009) *Patient Volition and Action in Occupational Therapy.* Pretoria: Vona and Marie du Toit Foundation.

Erikson, E.H. (1968) *Identity: Youth and Crisis.* Baltimore, MD: Mosby. Cited in Passmore, A. and French, D. (2003) 'The nature of leisure in adolescence: A focus study.' *British Journal of Occupational Therapy 66,* 9, 419–426.

Fisher, A. (2006) *Assessment of Motor and Process Skills.* Sixth edition. Fort Collins, CO: Three Star Press.

Fisher, A.G. and Griswold, L.A. (2009) *Evaluation of Social Interaction.* Fort Collins, CO: Three Star Press.

Garrett, T. and Rowe, R. (2004) 'Violence risk assessment training for local mental health services.' *British Journal of Forensic Practice 6,* 3, 13–17.

Hall, G.S. (ed.) (1904) *Adolescence: Its Psychology and Its Relations to Physiology, Anthropology, Sociology, Sex, Crime, and Religion.* Upper Saddle River, NJ: Prentice Hall.

Helbig, K. (2005) 'The graded skills development programme.' *Mental Health Occupational Therapy 10,* 2, 51–53.

Hocking, C. (2007) 'Early perspectives of patients, practice and the profession.' *British Journal of Occupational Therapy 70,* 7, 284–291.

Inclusion Institute (2009) *Vision and Progress: Social Inclusion and Mental Health.* Preston: Inclusion Institute. Available at www.socialinclusion.org.uk/publications/NSIP_Vision_and_Progress.pdf, accessed on 11 July 2011.

Kettles, A.M., Robinson, D. and Moody, E. (2003) 'A review of clinical risk and related assessments in forensic psychiatric units.' *British Journal of Forensic Practice 5,* 3, 3–11.

Kielhofner, G. (2008) 'The dynamics of human occupation.' In Kielfhofner, G. (ed.) *Model of Human Occupation Theory and Application.* Fourth edition. Baltimore, MD: Lippincott, Williams and Wilkins.

King, G., Law, M., King, S., Hurley, P. *et al.* (2004) *Children's Assessment of Participation and Enjoyment (CAPE) and Preferences for Activities of Children (PAC).* San Antonio, TX: Harcourt Assessment.

Monahan, J., Steadman, H.J., Robbins, P.C., Silver, E. *et al.* (2000) 'Developing a useful actuarial tool for assessing violence risk.' *British Journal of Psychiatry 176,* 166–70.

Mosey, A.C. (ed.) (1986) *Psychosocial Components of Occupational Therapy.* New York, NY: Raven Press.

O'Connell, M. and Farnworth, L. (2007) 'Occupational therapy in forensic psychiatry: A review of the literature and a call for a united and international response.' *British Journal of Occupational Therapy 70*, 5, 184–191.

Parkinson, S., Chester, A., Cratchley, S. and Rowbottom, J. (2006) 'Application of the model of human occupation screening tool in an acute psychiatric setting.' *Occupational Therapy in Health Care 22*, 2–3, 63–75.

Passmore, A. and French, D. (2003) 'The nature of leisure in adolescence: A focus study.' *British Journal of Occupational Therapy 66*, 9, 419–426.

Perkins, R. (2006) 'First person: "You need hope to cope."' In G. Roberts, S. Davenport, F. Holloway and T. Tattan (eds) *Enabling Recovery: Principles and Practice of Rehabilitation Psychiatry*. London: Gaskell.

Prentice, R. and Wilson, K. (2003) 'Forensic occupational therapy within learning disability services.' In L. Couldrick and A. Deborah (eds) *Forensic Occupational Therapy*. London: Whurr Publishers.

Rethink (2009) *Briefing – Mental Health, Stigma and Employment*. London: Rethink. Available at www.rethink.org/how_we_can_help/news_and_media/briefing_notes/briefing_mental_he.html, accessed on 14 January 2010.

Shepherd, G., Boardman, J. and Slade, M. (2008) *Making Recovery a Reality*. London: The Sainsbury Centre for Mental Health. Available at www.centreformentalhealth.org.uk/publications/making_recovery_a_reality.aspx?ID=578, accessed on 25 December 2010.

Tebbutt, L. (2009) 'Never work with animals or children…work with both.' *Occupational Therapy News 1*, 25.

Whitehouse, R., Chamberlain, P. and O'Brien, A. (2001) 'Increasing social interactions for people with more severe learning disabilities who have difficulty developing personal relationships.' *Journal of Learning Disabilities 5*, 3, 209–220.

Chapter 9

PHYSIOTHERAPY IN ADOLESCENTS WITH DEVELOPMENTAL DISABILITIES WHO REQUIRE SECURE CARE

Hilary Haynes

INTRODUCTION

The majority of young people admitted to our service have physical difficulties which have not been addressed, or even recognised, because of the overwhelming need to manage their emotional and behavioural problems and presenting risks. For this reason all admissions have physiotherapy screening assessments for sensory-motor and musculoskeletal problems and fitness. Those with the more severe and complex presentations are given priority for individual treatment, particularly if the effects of their developmental disabilities are causing distress and damaging their self-esteem. The rest are included in weekly physical activity, balance and coordination and rebound therapy groups.

This chapter will describe difficulties commonly encountered in this population, assessments used, physiotherapy approaches which have been found useful and examples of interdisciplinary working. Dyspraxia and developmental coordination disorder (DCD) for the purpose of this chapter are used interchangeably.

RESEARCH EVIDENCE

The benefits of physical activity and exercise on both physical and mental health are well known and there is a growing literature to suggest that exercise and physical activity interventions have beneficial effects across several physical and mental health outcomes for all age groups including adolescents (Biddle, Fox and Boutcher 2000; Donaghy 2007; Penedo and Dahn 2005). Exercise can also alleviate symptoms of low self-esteem and social withdrawal in adults with mental illness (Richardson *et al.* 2005). A wide-ranging review of physical activity and sedentary behaviour in children and adolescents found that a substantial number are not adequately active for health benefits and current trends in juvenile obesity are a cause for concern (Biddle, Gorely and Steusel 2004). The challenge lies in putting the convincing evidence into effective practice in the face of barriers such as low mood, hopelessness, withdrawal, sedentary lifestyle and lack of motivation (Seime and Vickers 2006). Young people with developmental disabilities typically are less physically able than their normally developing peers, leading to early experience of failure and aversion to exercise.

Physiotherapy has a particular interest in dyspraxia/DCD because the difficulties with movement control, coordination and quality are amenable to intervention. Physiotherapists have been successfully treating 'clumsy children' since the 1970s (Addy 1996; Baker 1981; Gordon and Grimley 1974; Lee and Smith 1998; Sherborne 2001). These approaches were initially developed empirically, but research on brain plasticity, such as synaptic pruning in adolescence, would seem to provide a rationale for their effectiveness (Blakemore and Choudhury 2006).

Physical fitness tends to be poor in children with movement difficulties (Haga 2008) and this can be exacerbated by lack of opportunities for physical activity, avoidance of exercise, unhealthy food choices and medication. As well as addressing motor learning and motor control issues, physiotherapists should consider deconditioning and loss of strength and flexibility, and promote access to recreational facilities.

In a forensic learning disability service physiotherapists are unlikely to be dealing with dyspraxia on its own. The Leeds Consensus Statement (Sugden 2006) recognised that while 'pure' DCD does exist, the reality is that it is more often co-occurring with other developmental disorders, as described in the introductory chapter of this book. Dyspraxia seems to be best addressed by a combination of 'top-down', such as problem-solving or cognitive-behavioural, and 'bottom-up', such as sensory-motor, repeated practice and functional task approaches (Miller *et al.* 2001). Practical problems in applying these approaches are compounded by the attention and executive function deficits of attention deficit hyperactivity disorder (ADHD), or the communication and sensory dysfunction or hypersensitivity of autistic spectrum disorders (ASD). Young people with abuse/trauma histories often present with dyspraxic features as well as emotional dysregulation due to the effects of chronic stress on the developing brain.

Dyspraxia is not a benign condition and children do not 'grow out of it' (Christiansen 2000; Gillberg, Gillberg and Groth 1989; Losse *et al.* 1991; Polatajko, Fox and Missiuna 1995). Sensory motor problems may contribute to the social difficulties experienced by DCD and ASD children (Piek and Dyck 2004). Physical appearance and physical ability are important determinants of young people's sense of self-worth and social support may be not be enough to compensate a child with DCD (Piek *et al.* 2000). Children as young as six or seven will start to discriminate against peers of lesser physical ability, exacerbating their social and emotional problems (Schoemaker and Kalverboer 1994). This could be alleviated by a whole-school approach to motor difficulties as in the Balance Education and Movement (BEAM) (Finlayson and Rickard 2003) programme where classroom assistants are trained by physiotherapists to deliver physical activities, and only those children who fail to progress satisfactorily are referred for specialist physiotherapy assessment and treatment. Unfortunately early diagnosis and intervention are not the norm and the majority of children with these difficulties are not identified in time to prevent serious behavioural problems developing.

The Disorders of Attention, Motor Processing and Perception (DAMP) syndrome is strongly associated with classroom dysfunction (Kadesjö and Gillberg 1998) and DCD has been shown to be associated with poor socialisation and the expression of deviant behaviours (Kanioglou, Tsorbatzoudis and Barkoukis 2005). Portwood (1999) stated that 'clumsy kids' suffer from an accumulating social handicap. In her survey of 140 young offenders, about 50 per cent were dyspraxic. Our experience in forensic adolescent learning disability (LD) services presents a similar picture. Any physiotherapy intervention therefore has to take communication, relationship and behavioural factors into account, work within the risk management strategies and use any opportunity to reinforce the psychological approaches appropriate to the individual.

An American study (Jones *et al.* 2006) found that a 16-week exercise programme for a group of women with intellectual disability and challenging behaviour improved goal attainment in areas of health and physical competence, behaviour and access to community-based experiences. The programme included exercise, walking, swimming, hydrotherapy, team games and rebound therapy. The authors conclude that continuing care settings should provide similar routines continuing exercise programmes.

PRACTICE ISSUES

Assessments

The Quick Neurological Screening Test (QNST) II (1998 edition) (Mutti *et al.* 1998) was designed by an educational psychologist and a paediatrician to be administered by teachers of reception class children to identify those who may need additional classroom support. It screens for sensory, perceptual and motor difficulties and picks up 'soft' neurological signs. A higher score indicates more difficulties. Scores are categorised into Normal Range (NR 0–25), Moderate Discrepancy (MD 26–50) and Severe Discrepancy (SD > 50).

Most of our young people fall in the MD category, although scoring within NR does not mean they have not got a learning disability as soft signs tend to decrease over time and are more significant if they persist into adolescence. Those in the SD category usually have a definite neurological condition: acquired brain injury, mild cerebral palsy or a genetic syndrome; however, patients who are mentally unwell may also score poorly.

The QNST requires minimal equipment and is quick and easy to administer, taking 20–30 minutes. It is non-threatening and can even be fun. Some people have difficulty closing their eyes and others dislike being touched so it is not always possible to complete every sub-test but a good deal of information is gleaned from the young person's attitude and behaviour in the assessment situation. For those with extremely short attention spans the test splits easily into tasks assessed in sitting or standing positions and can be completed in two sessions.

The Movement Assessment Battery for Children (MABC) (Henderson and Sugden 1992) is commonly used to screen for dyspraxia/DCD, with higher scores indicating more difficulties. A normal score is between 0–10, 11–15 is borderline and 16–40 is indicative of DCD.

In a series of 20 full tests completed with our clinical population some years ago, only one young person scored in the normal range. The average score was 27, showing that most of our young people with a mild learning disability meet the criteria for DCD. The complete battery was found to be too time-consuming and frustrating for this client group. In particular the manual dexterity task, 'cutting out the elephant', may involve the risk of handing scissors to someone you don't know well, who has a history of aggression and who cannot handle failure.

Two sub-tests of the MABC, the Peg Test and Jump and Clap, are informative. The Peg Test requires turning 12 short matchstick pieces over and replacing them in the board one-handed. It is a timed test and has population norms so can be used as an outcome measure. Jump and Clap requires a standing jump over a length of wool strung at just below knee height between two uprights and clapping hands as many times as possible while in the air. It picks up motor planning and sequencing difficulties.

The Three-Minute Step Test was adapted from the original one described by Brouha, Health and Graybiel (1943). Most subseqent step tests were developed in American colleges using bleachers as the standard height (17 inches). We use a Reebok™ step on its highest setting (12 inches). A resting pulse is taken with the young person lying down. He or she then steps up and down the step at a prescribed steady rate (96 beats per minute or 24 completed step-ups for boys and 88 beats per minute or 22 completed steps for girls) for three minutes. After this he or she lies down for another three minutes. Heart rate and oxygen saturation are monitored using a pulse oxymeter. This is not a maximal fitness test but gives a rough indication of fitness level and screens that the young person is able to participate in normal physical activities.

Observation during the step test provides further useful information: Do individuals have difficulty lying still and not talking? Have they sufficient muscle power and balance to step up unaided? Can they keep to the timing and maintain the reciprocal stepping sequence? If they give up before the three minutes is it due to genuine lack of stamina or is perceived exertion higher than actual? Can they be motivated to keep going with sufficient encouragement? Young people with the common combination of ADHD and DCD often find this test quite challenging but are usually interested in the results and motivated to improve their fitness when the results are explained to them.

Musculoskeletal screening

Due to the prevalence of low muscle tone, delayed development, poor posture and lack of opportunities for exercise, various postural pain syndromes are common: shoulder impingement, neck and back pain, clicking hips, anterior knee pain, unstable ankles or painful flat feet. Lack of core and shoulder girdle stability is very evident, with some young people affected by hypermobility syndrome, where the lack of stability is accompanied by multiple joint aches and pains and possible autonomic dysregulation (Keer and Grahame 2003). Adolescent boys generally are at risk of tight hamstrings and those with ASDs more so, with a tendency to stiff and rigid quality of movement and lack of flexibility and agility. Minor congenital abnormalities are quite common. The young people often mention operations or injuries that have not been recorded in their histories.

Self-harm and psychosomatic complaints also present themselves. While full-blown conversion syndromes are rarely seen, it is not unusual to find temporary dissociation from a part of the body, such as a complete inability to produce active movement after an apparently trivial injury. There may also be abnormal sensation, either numbness or reports of burning pain with light touch, raising the possibility of risk for complex regional pain syndrome. Generally these symptoms respond well to reassurance, ultrasound or TENS set to produce muscle twitching and resolve within a few hours or a couple of weeks. The physiotherapist has a role in determining what conditions can be dealt with in-house and what needs referring to Accident and Emergency or for an orthopaedic opinion.

Treatment approaches

Based on the needs identified at assessment, intervention may be directed towards neurodevelopmental or musculoskeletal problems, or towards improving fitness and promoting physical and mental health.

Physical activity/balance and coordination sessions are held as either group or individual. These are often sports skills based, breaking down tasks into manageable steps and adapting games to the levels of ability within the group. The approach is similar to lower primary school PE or remedial gymnastics for neurological patients. The aim is to teach basic physical skills and build confidence while at the same time encouraging team work, social skills, competition without aggression, and the ability to cope with failure. Alternatively, balance and coordination groups make use of equipment such as the parachute, Swiss balls, rocker boards, step and mini-trampolines. Activities encourage organising and sequencing abilities as well as balance, coordination and general fitness. Adapted Tai Chi/Qigong exercises improve balance and posture and encourage the development of normal efficient movement patterns.

Many of our young people with social and communication difficulties find it very hard to cope in a group and present with challenging behaviour if they cannot understand what is expected, feel humiliated when they make minor mistakes, have problematic relations with their peers or become overloaded by too much sensory information. They may not have learned to play as young children and PE sessions may have been an ordeal. They are best treated individually in the first instance to improve basic motor skills, build trust and confidence and overcome fears of being laughed at or hurt by the ball. The young person can then be included in his or her own small group consisting of trusted staff and get accustomed to simple games and sequencing activities and taking turns. Once these sessions are experienced as fun and enjoyable, it is then possible to integrate the young person into the larger peer group, at first with one-to-one staff support. Dropping in and out of the group is tolerated, the young person being encouraged to re-join but not put under any pressure. The expectation is that participation will gradually improve. This structured and graded approach has been very successful with young people with combined autistic spectrum disorder and developmental coordination disorder.

Mat work/floor work is difficult to implement in a group as so much individual facilitation is required, both to keep people working and to get accurate performance of an exercise. Self-conscious teenagers can find the exercises too embarrassing. However, on an individual basis, flexibility, strengthening and stabilisation exercises are acceptable and effective. Challenging balance and core stability in different positions with rhythmic stabilisations, modified yoga or Pilates is useful. Providing increased sensory feedback through wall exercises, beanbags, prickle balls and medicine balls is helpful for people with poor joint position sense. Graded step exercises help to develop hip, knee and ankle control particularly for eccentric muscle work. A general stretching programme develops body awareness as well as flexibility.

Simple passing and throwing games can develop left/right discrimination, midline crossing ability, spatial concepts and basic mathematical skills such as counting on and telling the time. *Take Time*, written by a speech and language therapist and a Eurythmist, contains many examples (Nash-Wortham and Hunt 1997).

Rebound – therapeutic use of the trampoline

The trampoline holds a lot of potential for individuals who have a poor movement vocabulary. Use of the equipment gives wider movement experience and the opportunity for individuals to gain control over their own bodies and improve their quality of movement. Being on the trampoline is a change of physical environment comparable to hydrotherapy or horse riding and is a fun activity which is valued by others (Smith and Cook 2001).

Movement in space with acceleration and deceleration and joint compression forces on contacting the bed provides enormous proprioceptive input. It is possible to influence all three of the body's balance systems – visual, vestibular and kinaesthetic. This provides a total sensory integration experience. Improvements in balance, coordination and body and spatial awareness can be observed, sometimes within a single session. Rebound has been used successfully as part of a school exercise programme for children with DCD (Addy 1996).

The physiological effects of physical activity on mood and arousal levels can also be exploited. Benefits of 'letting off steam' have to be balanced against the risk of getting over-excited. Some of the young people with ADHD and conduct disorders are sensation-seeking and like to take risks, jumping too high and going out of control. Firm boundaries have to be maintained for safety but it is usually possible to reach a compromise where the young person is allowed his or her request to 'just jump' provided that he or she stays in the centre of the bed.

For the rest of the group acting as spotters around the sides, there is the potential for vicarious learning and demands on their attention and concentration. They need to stay at the sides and not wander off, to be quiet while the jumper is listening to instructions, to take turns and to be responsible for their own and each other's safety. Usually the group members become very supportive of each other, giving verbal encouragement and cheering when a peer succeeds at a new task. As in any group there are possibilities to prompt or ignore inappropriate behaviour and to reinforce improving social skills.

Basic Body Awareness Therapy (BBAT)

There are various whole-body approaches available to the physiotherapist, including traditional systems like yoga and Tai Chi and specific work with mirrors to address distorted body image, for example, in eating disorders. In North America body-oriented psychotherapy recognises the importance of working with the body before addressing emotional and cognitive-behavioural issues, particularly for people with trauma histories (Ogden, Minton and Pain 2006).

BBAT developed in Scandinavia in the 1970s and 1980s and has accumulated evidence of effectiveness with a variety of clinical populations but predominantly with psychiatric, psychosomatic and stress-related conditions (Mattsson *et al.* 1998; Roxendal 1990). BBAT uses simple everyday movements in lying, sitting or standing but tries to elicit recognition from the person of how he or she is experiencing the movement, to experiment with exercises to find ways of moving with ease and comfort, and in the long term, to cope better with the demands of daily life. Training in BBAM is currently a two-year post-graduate course based in Bergen, Norway.

Assessments have been developed with both quantitative and qualitative aspects: the Body Awareness Rating Scale (BARS) (Skatteboe 2005) and the Body Awareness Scale Interview (BAS-I) (Gyllensten, Ekdahl and Hansson 2009; Roxendal 1985).

BARS scores quality of movement on a seven point scale but is process-oriented, allowing for guidance and coaching from the physiotherapist and recording any comments by the patient about his or her experience. The BAS-I is a semi-structured psychiatric interview with 26 items covering psychological and physiological symptoms, as well as attitudes to the body and to exercise. It is a 'snapshot' of the last three days; items are rated on a 0–3 scale where 0 indicates no problem and 3 indicates a serious problem. Anecdotally, physiotherapists use BBAT with children and adolescents, but at this point there is nothing about working with adolescents published in English language journals. Our young people have limited ability to verbalise their experiences, or to focus on the here-and-now for any length of time; sessions are relatively short and concentrate on finding a secure balance and being able to move around the midline. If able to maintain engagement with the process they generally report feeling calm and relaxed after a session.

Working with small groups makes it possible to incorporate massage, voice work and partner exercises, which help to build trust and improve interpersonal relationships. Body awareness sessions have been run in tandem with psycho-educational groups led by psychology, to promote understanding and management of emotions by first recognising the physical and physiological feelings associated with different emotional states.

Health promotion

The health risks associated with obesity are increasingly prevalent in the general population, but present in even greater proportion in those with mental health problems or learning disabilities. The weight management programme described here was developed in this secure hospital setting at Malcolm Arnold House by a working party led by physiotherapy and dietetics. Physiotherapy interventions to encourage more physical activity include morning walks, simple circuit training, swimming and hydrotherapy and treadmill training. Dance mats and the Wii Fit™ are very popular. Physiotherapy is also involved in delivering the weight management programme with nursing or occupational (OT) colleagues. It has been planned as a number of educational and motivational sessions emphasising the benefits of healthy eating and increased physical activity. For young people with a learning disability the programme has been simplified, with information delivered in manageable chunks with plenty of visual reinforcement, repetition and revision. Each session includes about 10–15 minutes of physical activity which not only helps the young people to concentrate for the rest of the session but also reinforces messages that exercise can be fun and physical activity can be incorporated into a daily routine.

Drama

A study of children with developmental disabilities showed that they had major difficulties with social information processing and understanding complex emotions (Bauminger, Schorr Edelzstein and Morash 2005). The authors recommended that social skills training should include understanding of emotions, verbal and nonverbal cues, social contexts and role-taking abilities.

Drama is the ideal medium for developing these skills within an action-oriented approach. The drama group is co-facilitated by OT and physiotherapy and uses several short activities within a 45 minute session to accommodate short attention spans and different learning styles. The activities are selected from drama warm-ups and improvisations, party games and ice breakers. The focus is on understanding and portraying emotions through expression and body language, using imagination and creativity and developing observational, social and communication skills. Although role-playing is part of the programme the facilitators are clear that this is drama, not Drama Therapy, for which specialised qualifications are required. Graduates from the drama group and more able peers participate in an evening Drama Club supported by volunteers. They practise more advanced exercises, go on theatre visits and have developed in-house productions which have been very well received by both peers and staff members.

Case description 1

Eric is a 16-year-old young man with a diagnosis of autism, visual problems that probably result from a traumatic brain injury in early childhood, oppositional-defiant disorder and attachment difficulties due to rejection by biological and foster parents. On admission his named nurse recognised the features of dyspraxia and referred him for a physiotherapy assessment. Eric was not easy to assess or treat as he had a number of persistent antisocial habits including nose-picking and attempting to smear other people with semen or faeces. His attention span was very short and he used argument as a tactic to delay doing anything he was asked. He was puzzled when this didn't work, repeatedly asking 'Why don't you just give up?'

Eric's QNST score was 62, category SD, with difficulties in most areas. He was allocated a half-hour session once a week, initially cooperating with treatment for about ten minutes altogether and spending the rest of the time arguing that he didn't need treatment, that it wouldn't do any good anyway, or doing the opposite of what was asked, such as moving an arm instead of a leg. Gradually more of the time was used constructively and improvements in global stability, postural control and balance could be seen. Eric could now keep up with his peers and was less likely to stumble when walking outside. His progress seemed to have plateaued after a year so his individual treatment was discontinued and attendance at a Rebound group substituted.

Eric initially needed help to get on the trampoline and was very insecure on the unstable surface, being reluctant to stand up and wanting to get off almost immediately. He sometimes refused to participate and sat by the wall. After a while his confidence improved, and he was able to get on unaided and perform basic skills, albeit very uncoordinated. A year later, with repeated practice and encouragement from his peers, Eric was able to demonstrate front drop/seat drop/back drop combinations. The improvement in his personal hygiene, social skills and behaviour were the result of hard work by Eric and the whole multidisciplinary team (MDT), but his increased physical competence had considerably boosted his self-esteem. A repeat QNST showed a ten point improvement but the score of 52, still in the SD range, suggests that Eric's severe perceptual-motor difficulties will always impact on his ability to cope independently. After 30 months' treatment Eric was discharged at the age of 19 to a placement specialising in autism.

Case description 2

Sean, a 19-year-old man, came from an abusive background and had become a danger to other young people. When admitted he had long-standing neck and shoulder pain which responded within three months to postural correction, shoulder setting and shoulder girdle stabilisation exercises. Over the next couple of years, Sean had several episodes of neck, shoulder, back or leg pains which resolved with a few weeks' treatment but would recur after two or three months. Sean also developed a disabling level of health anxiety with complaints of chest or stomach pains, nausea, constipation and frequent requests for doctors' appointments and for his pulse and blood pressure to be checked as he was terrified of dropping dead with a heart attack.

When discharge to another placement was getting closer, it was suggested to Sean that he may not find it easy to get instant access to physiotherapy, so it may be worth his while to try a whole-body approach that would help him self-manage his symptoms. It was explained to him that his habitual posture and walking pattern were perpetuating his problems and although they might occur in a different part of his body, the underlying mechanism was the same. Sean was more than willing to try something different and engaged very well in therapy.

On initial assessment, Sean reported numerous painful or strange symptoms when doing the exercises: muscle shaking, numbness, feeling paralysed and so on. He was very guarded in his movement and complained of tiredness after a few repetitions.

However, he was motivated, almost obsessively, doing all the exercises twice a day in his room. Most of our young people will only exercise under direct supervision so this came as something of a surprise to the therapist.

After two months, Sean's posture, balance and walking pattern were much improved. His BARS scores were around 4–5, much closer to normal.

He still had a slight chin poke and was a little heavy on his heels, but was moving with much more ease and confidence. Sean's BAS-I had improved from 41 to 12 with no somatic complaints. Sean was still dissatisfied with his body and his looks but he was no longer anxious about his health, saying, 'I know I've got to die sometime, so I'm not going to worry about it.'

CONCLUSION

Physiotherapy aims to promote physical and mental health, using a range of physical approaches to optimise an individual's quality of movement, body awareness, confidence and self-esteem. Most interventions are exercise-based, often delivered in the form of games and fun activities to maintain motivation to participate. Whether treatment is individual or in groups depends on assessed needs, priorities and resources, taking individual preferences into account.

Exercise and physical activities may be delivered by other professionals but physiotherapy intervention can be crucial to building up the basic skills and confidence to participate. Willingness to engage in physical activity may be affected by poor posture and quality of movement, painful musculoskeletal conditions, difficulties with body and spatial awareness and early experiences of failure and exclusion.

Regarding musculoskeletal conditions, access to generic community based physiotherapy is problematic. Young people are better treated in-house by a therapist who knows them well and understands their communication and behavioural difficulties and can adapt treatment accordingly. It is easier to make the connections between stress and psychosomatic symptoms when familiar with the environment and contributing psychosocial factors.

While the physiotherapy approach may vary in order to address neurodevelopmental, musculoskeletal, psychosomatic presentations or health promotion, the underlying need is to improve the young person's self-acceptance, self-efficacy and sense of self-worth to be able to move on in his or her life.

REFERENCES

Addy, L.M. (1996) 'A multiprofessional approach to the treatment of developmental coordination disorder.' *British Journal of Therapy and Rehabilitation 3*, 11, 593–99.

Baker, J. (1981) 'A psycho-motor approach to the assessment and treatment of clumsy children.' *Physiotherapy 67*, 12, 356–63.

Bauminger, N., Schorr Edelzstein, H. and Morash, J. (2005) 'Social information processing and emotional understanding in children with learning disabilities.' *Journal of Learning Disabilities* *38*, 1, 45–61.

Biddle, S.J.H., Fox, K. and Boutcher, S. (eds) (2000) *Physical Activity and Psychological Wellbeing*. London: Routledge.

Biddle, S.J.H., Gorely, T. and Stensel, D.J. (2004) 'Health-enhancing physical activity and sedentary behaviour in children and adolescents.' *Journal of Sports Sciences 22*, 8, 679–701.

Blakemore, S.J. and Choudhury, S. (2006) 'Development of the adolescent brain: Implications for executive function and social cognition.' *Journal of Child Psychology and Psychiatry 47*, 3/4, 296–312.

Brouha, L., Health, C.W. and Graybiel, A. (1943) 'The step test: A simple method of measuring physical fitness for hard muscular work in adult men.' *Reviews of Canadian Biology 2*, 86.

Christiansen, A. (2000) 'Persisting motor control problems in 11–12 year old boys previously diagnosed with deficits in attention motor control and perception (DAMP).' *Developmental Medicine and Child Neurology 42*, 4–7.

Donaghy, M. (2007) 'Exercise can seriously improve your mental health: Fact or fiction?' *Advances in Physiotherapy 9*, 2, 76–88.

Finlayson, A. and Rickard, D. (2003) 'Development of Beam: A screening package for schools aiding identification of children with co-ordination difficulties.' *Dyspraxia Foundation Professional Journal 2*. Available at www.dyspraxiafoundation.org.uk/downloads/Professional_Journal_Issue_2.pdf

Gillberg, I.C., Gillberg, C. and Groth, J. (1989) 'Children with preschool minor neurodevelopmental disorders V: Neurodevelopmental profiles at age 13.' *Developmental Medicine and Child Neurology 89*, 31, 14–24.

Gordon, N. and Grimley, A. (1974) 'Clumsiness and perceptuo-motor disorders in children.' *Physiotherapy 60*, 10, 311–314.

Gyllensten, A.L., Ekdahl, C. and Hansson, L. (2009) 'Long-term effectiveness of basic body awareness therapy in psychiatric outpatient care: A randomised controlled study.' *Advances in Physiotherapy 11*, 1, 2–12.

Haga, M. (2008) 'Physical fitness in children with movement difficulties.' *Physiotherapy 94*, 253–259.

Henderson, S. and Sugden, D. (1992) *The Movement Assessment Battery for Children*. London: The Psychological Corporation.

Jones, M.C., Walley, R.M., Leech, A., Paterson, M., Common, S. and Metcalf, C. (2006) 'Using goal attainment scaling to evaluate a needs-led exercise programme for people with severe and profound intellectual disabilities.' *Journal of Intellectual Disabilities 10*, 4, 317–335.

Kadesjö, B. and Gillberg, C. (1998) 'Attention deficits and clumsiness in Swedish 7-year-old children.' *Developmental Medicine and Child Neurology 40*, 12, 796–804.

Kanioglou, A., Tsorbatzoudis, H. and Barkoukis, V. (2005) 'Socialization and behavioral problems of elementary school pupils with developmental coordination disorder.' *Perceptual and Motor Skills 101*, 163–73.

Keer, R.J. and Grahame, R. (2003) *Hypermobility Syndrome: Recognition and Management for Physiotherapists*. Oxford: Butterworth Heinemann.

Lee, M.G. and Smith, G.N. (1998) 'The effectiveness of physiotherapy for dyspraxia.' *Physiotherapy 84*, 6, 276–84.

Losse, A., Henderson, S.E., Elliman, D., Hall, D., Knight, E. and Jongmans, M. (1991) 'Clumsiness in children – do they grow out of it? A 10-year follow-up study.' *Developmental Medicine and Child Neurology 91*, 33, 55–68.

Mattsson, M., Wikman, M., Dahlgren, L., Mattasson, B. and Armelius, K. (1998) 'Body awareness therapy with sexually abused women. Part 2: Evaluation of body awareness in a group setting.' *Journal of Bodywork and Movement Therapies 2*, 38–45.

Miller, L.T., Polatajko, H.J., Missiuna, C., Mandich, A.D. and Macnab, J.J. (2001) 'A pilot trial of a cognitive treatment for children with developmental coordination disorder.' *Human Movement Science 20*, 1–2, 183–210.

Mutti, M., Martin, N., Sterling, H. and Spaulding, N. (1998) *QNST-II Quick Neurological Screening Test 2nd Revised Edition Manual*. Novato, CA: Academic Therapy Publications.

Nash-Wortham, M. and Hunt, J. (2000) *Take Time: Movement Exercises for Parents, Teachers and Therapists of Children with Difficulties in Speaking, Reading, Writing and Spelling*. Fourth revised and updated edition. Stourbridge: Robinswood Press.

Ogden, P., Minton, K. and Pain, C. (2006) *Trauma and the Body: A Sensorimotor Approach to Psychotherapy*. New York, NY: WW Norton.

Penedo, F.J. and Dahn, J.R. (2005) 'Exercise and well-being: A review of mental and physical health benefits associated with physical activity.' *Current Opinion in Psychiatry 18*, 2, 189–193.

Piek, J.P., Dworcan, M., Barrett, N.C. and Coleman, R. (2000) 'Determinants of self-worth in children with and without DCD.' *International Journal of Disability, Development and Education 47*, 3, 259–272.

Piek, J.P. and Dyck, M.J. (2004) 'Sensory-motor deficits in children with developmental coordination disorder, attention deficit hyperactivity disorder and autistic disorder.' *Human Movement Science 23*, 475–488.

Polatajko, H., Fox, M. and Missiuna, C. (1995) 'An international consensus on children with developmental coordination disorder.' *Canadian Journal of Occupational Therapy 62*, 1, 3–6.

Portwood, M. (1999) *Developmental Dyspraxia: Identification and Intervention*. Second edition. London: David Fulton.

Richardson, C.R., Faulkner, G., McDevitt, J., Skrinar, G.S., Hutchinson, D.S. and Piette, J.D. (2005) 'Integrating physical activity into mental health services for persons with serious mental illness.' *Psychiatric Services 56*, 3, 324–331.

Roxendal, G. (1985) *Body Awareness Therapy and the Body Awareness Scale: Treatment and Evaluation in Psychiatric Physiotherapy*. Doctoral dissertation, Dept. of Rehabilitation Medicine, Gotesborg, Sweden.

Roxendal, G. (1990) 'Physiotherapy as an approach in psychiatric care with emphasis on body awareness therapy.' In T. Hegna and M. Sveram (eds) *Psychological and Psychosomatic Problems*. Edinburgh: Livingstone Publishers.

Schoemaker, M.M. and Kalverboer, A.F. (1994) 'Social and affective problems of children who are clumsy: How early do they begin?' *Adapted Physical Activity Quarterly 11*, 130–140.

Seime, R. and Vickers, K.S. (2006) 'The challenges of treating depression with exercise: From evidence to practice.' *Clinical Psychology: Science and Practice 13*, 2, 194–197.

Sherborne, V. (2001) *Developmental Movement for Children: Mainstream, Special Needs and Pre-school*. Second edition. London: Worth.

Skatteboe, U.B. (2005) *Basic Body Awareness and Movement Harmony: Development of the Assessment Method Body Awareness Rating Scale BARS – Movement Harmony*. HiO-report, 2005, 31. Oslo University College, Oslo, Norway.

Smith, S. and Cook, D. (2001) 'Rebound therapy.' In J. Rennie (ed.) *Learning Disability: Physical Therapy, Treatment and Management – A Collaborative Approach*. London: Whurr Publishers.

Sugden, D.A. (2006) *ESRC Research Seminar Series 2004–2005: Leeds Consensus Statement. Developmental Coordination Disorder as a Specific Learning Difficulty*. Swindon: Economic and Social Research Council (ESRC).

FURTHER READING

Chartered Society of Physiotherapy (CSP) (2007) *Safe Practice in Rebound Therapy*. Practice and Development Information Paper, ref. PA69. London: CSP.

Chapter 10

RISK ASSESSMENT IN ADOLESCENTS WITH DEVELOPMENTAL DISABILITIES

Lucy Adamson, Anne McLean and Marilyn Sher

INTRODUCTION

The aim of this chapter is to provide the reader with an overview of risk assessment in adolescents with developmental disabilities (DD). For the purpose of this chapter, the umbrella term developmental disabilities (DD) is employed over learning disabilities, as it incorporates those individuals who struggle to function adaptively yet whose IQ score may or may not be above 70 (Hassiotis and Hall 2004). To date there has been very little research in the area of risk assessment in adolescents with DD. This poses significant challenges to professionals working with this client group who all too often are left to rely on using adult and/or adolescent measures not designed for young people with DD, or simply rely on unstructured clinical opinion. However, research on risk assessment in the general population has moved on considerably in recent years, and there appears to be a general shift towards acknowledging risk assessment as a crucial part of the assessment and treatment process. The value of Structured Clinical Assessment Guides/Structured Professional Judgement (SPJ) tools within this process is readily becoming accepted. This is exemplified in the Department of Health's *Best Practice in Managing Risk* guidelines (2007) which suggest that SPJ tools are the most effective approach to violence risk management.

This chapter will summarise some of the preliminary literature relevant to adults with DD, and will then make some suggestions as to how we might advance the field with regards to risk assessment in adolescents with DD. An anonymised case study will be used to demonstrate the practical application of some of these recommendations. Emphasis is placed on some of the better known risk assessment tools, as this seems to be the most logical starting point.

In the adult literature, the Historical Clinical Risk-20 (HCR-20) (Webster *et al.* 1997) for violence and the Sexual Violence Risk-20 (SVR-20) (Boer *et al.* 1997) for sexual violence are widely known. In the adolescent literature the Structured Assessment of Violence Risk in Youth (SAVRY; Borum, Bartel and Forth 2003) for violence and the Estimate of Risk of Adolescent Sexual Offense Recidivism (ERASOR) (Worling and Curwen 2001) and Juvenile Sex Offender Assessment Protocol-II (J-SOAP-II) (Prentky and Righthand 2003) for sexual violence are commonly used tools.

STRUCTURED PROFESSIONAL JUDGEMENT TOOLS

Structured Professional Judgement tools aim to use structured assessment approaches based upon research to inform, rather than replace, clinical decision making. Whilst still common practice in some settings, it is now considered unacceptable and unethical to base opinions and decisions on risk purely upon subjective clinical assessment (Mills 2005). This is primarily due to the disconcerting findings of the research literature on clinical prediction, where clinicians' unstructured violence risk assessments have repeatedly been shown to be only modestly more accurate than chance (Lidz, Mulvey and Gardner 1993).

SPJ tools are composed of a set of risk factors (generated through an analysis of the research) that are designed to be used as a guide to considering risk. In some instances, some of these factors may not be relevant; in others, additional risk factors can be added. It is hoped that this chapter will highlight those risk factors which might be more relevant to adolescents with DD. We should highlight here that the issue of adapting assessments to meet the requirements of individuals with DD has been contentious. Lindsay and Taylor (2005) suggest that on one hand we run the risk of declaring that persons with DD are homogenous with non-DD offenders; or, on the other hand, suggesting that they present in ways grossly divergent from persons without DD. Similar issues apply in adapting tools developed for adults to an adolescent population. Adolescent offenders are not necessarily 'younger versions' of adult offenders (Rich 2009).

Recent literature has highlighted the paucity of research studies focusing on offenders with DD and offered tentative suggestions of how best to move forward in terms of identifying what the specific needs of these client groups are. For instance, see Lindsay and Taylor (2005) for a systematic review into assessment and treatment of adult offenders with DD; Matson, Dixon and Matson (2005) for a review of assessment and treatment of aggression in adolescents with DD; Timms and Goreczny (2002) for a review on the assessment of adolescent sex offenders, including those with learning disabilities; Mikkelsen (2004) for an overview of the assessment of individuals with developmental disabilities who commit criminal offences and Lindsay *et al.* (2008) on some specific adult risk assessment tools and their ability to predict risk in offenders with intellectual disability across three levels of security. In addition, more specific recommendations are beginning to emerge in the adult literature. For instance Boer *et al.* (2010a) provide a detailed description of adaptations that could be made to an existing adult SPJ tool (the HCR-20) in order to make it more applicable to assessing risk in adults with DD.

RESEARCH EVIDENCE

Assessing violence risk: in adults

The most widely used risk assessment tool is the HCR-20 (Webster *et al.* 1997). Composed of three sections (ten historical items, five clinical items and five risk items), the HCR-20 has been investigated extensively within the general adult offending population. However, whilst the HCR-20 was designed for adults without DD, there is preliminary evidence to suggest that the HCR-20 is also valid for male violent offenders with DD (Lindsay *et al.* 2008). There is also some limited evidence of the applicability of the HCR-20 to female offenders with DD (Gray *et al.* 2007).

Boer *et al.* (2010a) suggest that the HCR-20 should not be used with adults with DD under the age of 21. This concurs with the guidance from the Royal College of Psychiatrists (2001) who suggest that diagnoses of personality disorder should not be made in people with DD under the age of 21. Both these suggestions are based on the understanding that individuals with DD have delayed development and maturation. Boer *et al.* (2010a) also suggest that the HCR-20 should not be used in individuals with DD whose IQ has been assessed as being below 55. The reasoning for this is based on limitations in the assessment of personality disorder, and more specifically psychopathy, in individuals with lower functioning (Morrissey *et al.* 2007). Boer *et al.* (2010a) additionally provide detailed description of how item ratings may be interpreted for use with individuals with a DD. They note, however, that these recommendations are not approved by the authors of the HCR-20 and should be read in conjunction with the manual, and not as a replacement.

Assessing violence risk: in adolescents

The evidence base supporting the use of adolescent tools is still developing. Currently the SAVRY (Borum *et al.* 2003) is probably one of the better known violence risk assessment tools for adolescents. The SAVRY consists of ten historical, six social, eight clinical and six protective factors and is used for adolescents aged between 12 and 18 years to assess violence risk. Similar to the HCR-20 and other SPJ tools, the SAVRY does allow for additional items to be added to it; to account, for instance, for difficulties relating to learning disability or autism spectrum disorders. Soothill, Rogers and Dolan (2008, p.262), state that 'to date there is limited UK psychometric data on the SAVRY' although in that year, Dolan herself published one of the first UK studies (Dolan and Rennie 2008). The article showed that the SAVRY has moderate predictive accuracy for violent and general recidivism. Additionally it demonstrated that the protective subscale was actually predictive of non-offending.

As far as the authors are aware, there are no published validation studies of the SAVRY's utility in predicting risk for adolescents with DD. However, in a very small inpatient sample of adolescents with DD, Adamson, Dixon and McLean (unpublished; 2010) recently found that the SAVRY was a strong predictor of risk of violence in adolescents with DD. This is clearly an area requiring further research.

In a similar vein to the suggested adaptations of the HCR-20 for adults with DD (Boer *et al.* 2010a), we would suggest adaptations to the SAVRY to make it more applicable to adolescents with DD. As with Boer *et al.*'s recommendations regarding the HCR-20, we would concur with their cautions and highlight that the following suggestions have not been approved by the authors of the SAVRY. Primary amongst our suggestions would be extending the upper age limit of the SAVRY to include all individuals with DD under the age of 21. This is justified by the delayed development and maturation of individuals with DD, whereby adolescence as a developmental stage is extended. There is already some research that the SAVRY continues to have good predictive validity for individuals without a DD subsequent to their 18th birthday (McEachran 2001) which provides further tentative support for this suggestion. Additionally we would also recommend extreme caution in using the SAVRY with individuals with an assessed IQ below 55 given the lack of evidence base for any SPJ tool with individuals with this degree of DD (Boer *et al.* 2010a; Morrissey *et al.* 2007).

With regard to adapted SAVRY item definitions for use with individuals with DD, as yet there are none published. However, as Boer *et al.* (2010a) comment, if all users of these tools make their own adaptations there will be 'greater variability and lack of precision' (p.179) in DD risk assessment. This highlights the need for guidelines to be developed for use with adolescents with DD.

Assessing sexual risk: in adults

Despite advances in other areas within the DD sex offender literature, specific research on the assessment of risk in sex offenders with DD is only recently beginning to emerge. In terms of established risk assessments, the Sexual Violence Risk-20 (Boer *et al.* 1997) has been reported to have been of use with intellectually disabled sex offenders (Lambrick and Glaser 2004). Additionally Blacker *et al.* (2010) found that the SVR-20 performed well for an adult DD sample. Again Boer *et al.* (2010b) have produced a set of guidelines regarding how this tool could be adapted for use in the DD population, similar to those produced for the HCR-20.

More recently Boer *et al.* (2009) developed the Assessment of Risk Manageability for Intellectually Disabled Individuals who Offend (ARMIDILO), containing 30 stable and acute dynamic risk factors for the assessment of risk of sexual violence in adults with DD. Haaven (2005) recommended that environmental factors need to be added to the assessment of risk for this particular population of sexual offender and these are incorporated into the ARMIDILO. There is to date, however, a paucity of research regarding the predictive validity of the ARMIDILO. According to the authors, the ARMIDILO is still in its construction phase and lacks any empirical validation. Blacker *et al.* (2010) provide some preliminary data using only the client subscales of the ARMIDILO, as information required to complete the environmental subscales was not available. The ARMIDILO was found to have good predictive validity for DD adult offenders.

Assessing sexual risk: in adolescents

There are a number of risk assessment tools for assessing risk of sexually harmful behaviour in adolescents. The most widely used of these are the ERASOR (Worling and Curwen 2001) and the J-SOAP II (Prentky and Righthand 2003). A body of research regarding the predictive validity of both of these tools in adolescents without DD is beginning to emerge. Initial results were inconsistent. For example Martinez, Flores and Rosenfeld (2007) found that the J-SOAP-II had good predictive validity, whilst McCoy (2007) found that the J-SOAP-II did not predict sexual reoffending. Skowron (2004) found that the ERASOR significantly predicted sexual recidivism while McCoy (2007) found that it was not predictive. More recently, Viljoen *et al.* (2009) found that the ERASOR 'nearly reached' predictive validity. Rajlic and Gretton (2010) offer a plausible explanation for these results in their study which compared the ERASOR and the J-SOAP-II across different 'offender types'. Whilst they found that both tools had good predictive validity for young people with a previous history of solely sexually harmful behaviour, neither was a useful tool with individuals whose sexually harmful behaviour occurred within a more general pattern of delinquency. To the authors' knowledge there is to date no research published regarding the use of these tools with adolescents with DD who are at risk of displaying further sexually harmful behaviour.

As can be seen from the above brief review of literature there is some evidence that these tools are useful with adults with DD, particularly in the field of violence risk prediction. Research is beginning to emerge regarding prediction of sexual violence within this group. However, as Craig and Hutchinson (2005) concluded, there remains a pressing need for further research in this area. When considering risk assessment for adolescents with DD there is to date no published research in this area highlighting a significant gap in the professional literature.

PRACTICE ISSUES

There are a variety of different guidelines and advice to facilitate the completion of thorough risk assessments including the Department of Health's *Best Practice in Managing Risk* guidelines (2007). Before completing any risk assessment, we would recommend that the administrator is familiar with these guidelines. In addition, we would also suggest that professionals are mindful of the following common principles:

- In order to complete an SPJ risk assessment tool, there is a professional requirement to have a grasp of the general literature regarding risk assessment, as well as specific training in conducting risk assessments in the area in which one is assessing.

- With particular reference to working with adolescents, it is imperative that clinicians are aware of the challenges with assessing this population. Of paramount importance should be awareness that adolescence is a time of great change, and consequently the risk assessment should be regularly updated. In practice, this suggests the need for up-to-date assessments that take account of current functioning and needs.

- A number of factors contribute to the difficulties in accurately predicting risk for adolescents. These include developmental trajectories and an understanding that most offending which occurs in adolescence is time-limited, and will spontaneously cease over time. Additionally sexual offending has a low base rate, and it is hard to accurately predict events that have a low likelihood of occurring. In the Rajlic and Gretton (2010) study, for example, only 9.4 per cent of the young people were charged with another sex offence during the follow-up period.

- Conversely there are some risk factors which will have high base rates for this client group such as poor school achievement on the SAVRY. This calls into question the ability of this risk factor to discriminate between those adolescents with DD who go on to recidivate and those who do not. Similarly, substance misuse has been shown to be significantly less prevalent in adults with DD who offend (Lunsky *et al.* 2010), emphasising the importance of being aware of the literature in the area of individuals with DD.

- There also needs to be consideration of the specific issues involved in the assessment of people with DD, such as the lack of standardised assessment tools. Assessment questionnaires developed for offenders without DD are largely unsuitable because of complicated language (Broxholme and Lindsay 2003). Some specialist psychometric assessments adapted for adult sexual offenders with learning disabilities are available, including the Questionnaire on Attitudes Consistent with Sex Offences (QACSO) (Lindsay, Whitefield and Carson 2007) and the Sex Offender's Self Appraisal Scale (Bray and Forshaw 1996). However, there are no tools developed specifically for assessing adolescents with DD.

- The importance of identifying protective factors which might mitigate against the risk cannot be over-emphasised. There is a growing body of research which shows that the presence of protective factors predicts non-reoffending (Dolan and Rennie 2008).

- The completion of an SPJ risk assessment tool requires the collaboration of the range of professionals involved with the young person. Equally important is the communication of the risk management plan to the range of clinicians and services involved in the young person's care.

- There needs to be an awareness that the outcome of completing an SPJ tool should be the development of a plausible theory as to how risk factors combine and feed into the risk. It should be clear how risk factors link to risk management strategies, specifically, what factors in what combinations increase risk and how suggested interventions are expected to reduce that defined risk. The most appropriate way to do this is in the production of 'risk scenarios' or risk formulations.

Risk scenarios

Hart *et al.* (2003, p.28) define a risk scenario for sexual offending as 'a story about sexual violence which the person might commit' and their purpose as facilitating the development of appropriate risk reduction plans. Historically the task of risk assessment used to be, 'to determine whether or not an individual was or was not a dangerous person, whereas now the task is to determine the nature and degree of risk a given individual may pose for certain kinds of behaviours, in light of anticipated conditions and contexts' (Borum 2000, p.1264). Mikkelsen (2004, p.121) takes this concept further and states 'the purpose of a thorough assessment of risk is to provide the offender with a therapeutic environment that is sufficient to provide safety to themselves and the community at large, whilst also providing them with as normal a life as possible'.

Risk scenarios allow the clinician to communicate exactly what circumstances heighten that individual's risk, and thus allow the logical formation of recommendations for the optimum therapeutic environment, given the concerns outlined in the risk scenarios. With certain procedures and environmental control in place, optimal therapeutic environments can be produced and risk can be successfully managed. For example, Mikkelsen (2004) puts forward a case for positive risk taking using 'auxiliary egos' for those individuals with DD who require a person to supervise them when out in the community, the mere presence of whom deters them from offending. In our experience, this is often the case with adolescents with DD who have sexually offended. They report that having a member of staff nearby provides the control that they lack internally. The absence of such a person/external control may thus prove to be a risk factor for certain individuals with DD and one perhaps worthy of inclusion in risk assessments with this population.

Case description

Peter is a 16-year-old young man who was arrested following two allegations of rape of males under the age of 10. He has a current diagnosis of Learning Disability, with a Full Scale IQ of 62 as assessed by the Wechsler Intelligence Scale for Children-IV (Wechsler 2003). At the time of the offences Peter was living at home with his mother and elder sister and attending a school for children with learning disabilities. He had been the victim of severe sexual abuse as well as witnessing domestic violence perpetrated by his mother's previous partner. Lunsky *et al.* (2010) report on the high rates of abuse and neglect experienced by individuals with DD and forensic involvement in a study which sought to examine how these individuals may differ from other service users within a psychiatric hospital setting.

Both offences occurred when Peter's mother had friends visiting who brought their young sons. On both occasions Peter invited the boys upstairs to play computer games with him and proceeded to rape them. He was convicted of the offences and detained under section 37/41 of the Mental Health Act (1983, amended 2007). He was placed in a medium secure unit for young people with DD and forensic issues. This was his first placement away from home.

One of the first tasks in our work with Peter was to develop an appropriate risk management and intervention plan. In keeping with best practice guidelines, an appropriate SPJ tool formed the basis. Notwithstanding the current lack of empirical evidence regarding its use specifically with a young person with DD, the ERASOR was used in Peter's case. We were mindful that the results needed to be interpreted with caution. In order to complete the ERASOR, information was gathered from a variety of sources. Initially all reports prepared for court were obtained as were witness statements; Peter's mother was a valuable source of information and she provided school reports to help us gain a full picture of Peter's past difficulties and strengths. During initial assessments, Peter was reluctant to discuss his sexually harmful behaviour at all. As with all adolescents, significant periods of time were spent building rapport with Peter and engaging him in fun and interesting activities in an effort to help him become more comfortable with the assessor, thus more at ease in discussing issues surrounding his offences. Due to the limitations of self-report information, particularly with this client group, information should always be gleaned from a variety of sources, including observational data, file information and family/carer interviews.

As part of the assessment process with Peter the QACSO (Lindsay *et al.* 2007) was used. This assesses attitudes around a number of areas, including rape and sex offences against children, and was designed to be used with offenders with DD, though not specifically adolescents. It is essential to make the reader of the risk assessment aware if the tools you are using have not been specifically developed for the adolescent DD population. We find that rather than comparing scores to inappropriate norms, the tools provide valuable information when used qualitatively, and also aid the assessment process when the young person is encouraged to elaborate on and give examples for his or her answers on particular questions pertinent to the risk assessment.

Lambrick and Glaser (2004) state that another important initial step in the risk assessment process is to assess whether the offending behaviour was due to an educational or other deficit in knowledge or understanding leading to inappropriate behaviour, or was due to more serious underlying criminogenic processes such as sexual deviance or antisocial attitudes and beliefs. Consequently the Sexual Knowledge and Behaviour Assessment Tool for use with young people with learning disabilities (Fraser 2010) was used to assess Peter's current knowledge and plan to address any deficits.

Other members of the clinical team caring for Peter were involved in the risk assessment process in a variety of ways. First, in team meetings Peter's presentation was regularly discussed and valuable information regarding his ratings on a number of risk items was gathered. Second, all staff were involved in completing the Overt Aggression Scale Modified for Neuro-Rehabilitation (OAS-MNR) (Alderman, Knight and Morgan 1997) which was used to record incidents of Peter acting in such a way as to be at risk to himself or others, to identify immediate antecedents and evaluate methods of management. Additionally all staff completed the St Andrew's Sexual Behaviour Assessment scale (SASBA) (Knight *et al.* 2008). The SASBA, which has evolved from, and can work with, the OAS-MNR, was used to record incidents of Peter acting in a sexualised manner. Information from both scales was used to inform the risk assessment process. Finally there were a number of meetings in which all staff working with Peter were involved in devising possible risk scenarios and plans to manage his risk. This was particularly helpful as some staff were previously unaware of Peter's risk history, and as he was generally very compliant and settled on the unit there was a tendency to underestimate his risk. These meetings also highlighted erroneous stereotypes about Peter's sexuality, for example a tendency for some team members to view Peter as a 'big child' and to deny his sexual urges and development. These meetings provided an opportunity to challenge these attitudes in staff.

Through the careful assessment process outlined above, a thorough risk assessment was completed, collating information from a wide variety of sources. This enabled the development of risk management plans to ensure Peter's safety, as well as that of potential victims. The multidisciplinary nature of this undertaking ensured that all staff working with Peter were aware of his risks, strengths and vulnerabilities and the plans in place to manage these effectively. Finally, through the risk assessment process, treatment goals for Peter were identified and appropriate interventions developed to address these.

CONCLUSION

In conclusion, it is now widely accepted that SPJ tools are 'best practice' for assessing risk. There is a small but growing evidence base for the predictive validity of existing SPJ tools for use with adults with DD. In addition, the development of new tools for this population such as the ARMIDILO, as well as recommendations for adaptations to existing tools, are positive steps towards establishing whether there are certain risk factors more pertinent to individuals with DD. The importance of environmental factors within this client group is particularly emphasised. Despite the recent advances in the adult literature, however, there remains a clear lack of evidence base to date for adolescents with DD. Notwithstanding this, SPJ should still form the basis of risk assessment within this client group, with a strong onus on the coordinator of the risk assessment to make him- or herself aware of the relevant research in the area. It is hoped that in the coming years more research will emerge to further guide and inform the risk assessment process for adolescents with DD.

REFERENCES

Adamson, L.G, Dixon, L. and McLean, A. (2010) 'Measuring and predicting institutional violence in adolescents with and without Developmental Disabilities in a forensic inpatient service.' In L.G. Adamson *Investigating the Assessment and Treatment of Violence in Adolescents with Developmental Disabilities* (pp.39–60). Unpublished Doctor of Forensic Psychology thesis, University of Birmingham.

Alderman, N., Knight, C. and Morgan, C. (1997) 'Use of a modified version of the overt aggression scale in the measurement and assessment of aggressive behaviours following brain injury.' *Brain Injury 11*, 503–523.

Blacker, J., Beech, A., Wilcox, D.T. and Boer, D.P. (2010) 'The assessment of dynamic risk and recidivism in a sample of special needs sexual offenders.' *Psychology, Crime and Law 1*, 1–18.

Boer, D.P., Frize, M., Pappas, R., Morrissey, C. and Lindsay, W.R. (2010a) 'Suggested adaptations to the HCR-20 for offenders with intellectual disabilities.' In L.A. Craig, W.R. Lindsay and K.D. Browne (eds) *Assessment and Treatment of Sexual Offenders with Intellectual Disabilities: A Handbook*. Chichester: John Wiley and Sons.

Boer, D.P., Frize, M., Pappas, R., Morrissey, C. and Lindsay, W.R. (2010b) 'Suggested adaptations to the SVR-20 for offenders with intellectual disabilities.' In L.A. Craig, W.R. Lindsay and K.D. Browne (eds) *Assessment and Treatment of Sexual Offenders with Intellectual Disabilities: A Handbook*. Chichester: John Wiley and Sons.

Boer, D., Haaven, J., Lindsay, W., McVilly, K.R. and Sakdalan, J. (2009) *The Manual for the Assessment of Risk and Manageability of Intellectual Disabled Individuals who Offend – Sexually (The ARMIDILO-S)*. Personal communication.

Boer, D.P., Hart, S.D., Kropp, P.R. and Webster, C.D. (1997) *Manual for the Sexual Violence Risk – 20: Professional Guidelines for Assessing Risk of Sexual Violence*. Vancouver, BC: The Mental Health, Law, and Policy Institute.

Borum, R. (2000) 'Assessing violence risk among youth.' *Journal of Clinical Psychology 56*, 1263–1288.

Borum, R., Bartel, P. and Forth, A. (2003) *Manual for the Structured Risk Assessment of Violence in Youth, Version 1.1*. Lutz, FL: University of South Florida.

Bray, D. and Forshaw, N. (1996) *Sex Offender's Self Appraisal Scale, Version 1.1*. Preston: Lancashire Care NHS Trust and North Warwickshire NHS Trust.

Broxholme, S.L. and Lindsay, W.R. (2003) 'Development and preliminary evaluation of a questionnaire on cognitions related to sex offending for use with individuals who have mild intellectual disabilities.' *Journal of Intellectual Disability Research 47*, 472–482.

Craig, L.A. and Hutchinson, R.B. (2005) 'Sexual offenders with learning disabilities: Risk, recidivism and treatment.' *Journal of Sexual Aggression 11*, 289–304.

Department of Health (2007) *Best Practice in Managing Risk: Principles and Evidence for Best Practice in the Assessment and Management of Risk to Self and Others in Mental Health Services.* London: Department of Health.

Dolan, M.C. and Rennie, C.E. (2008) 'The structured assessment of violence risk in youth (SAVRY) as a predictor of recidivism in a UK cohort of adolescent offenders with conduct disorder.' *Psychological Assessment 20*, 35–46.

Fraser, J. (2010) *Sexual Knowledge and Behaviour Assessment Tool: For Assessing Levels of Sexual Knowledge and Understanding of Someone with a Learning Disability Before and After a Programme of Sex and Relationships Education.* Sedbergh: Me-and-Us.

Gray, N.S., Fitzgerald, S., Taylor, J., MacCulloch, M.J. and Snowden, R.J. (2007) 'Predicting future reconviction in offenders with intellectual disabilities: The predictive efficacy of VRAG, PCL-SV and the HCR-20.' *Psychological Assessment 19*, 474–479.

Haaven, J. (2005) 'Treating intellectually disabled sex offenders allows us to see with "new eyes".' *NOTANews 49*, 2–5.

Hart, S.D., Kropp, P.R., Laws, D.R., Klaver, J., Logan, C. and Watt, K.A. (2003) *The Risk for Sexual Violence Protocol (RSVP).* Victoria: Pacific Psychological Assessment Corporation.

Hassiotis, A. and Hall, I. (2008) 'Behavioural and cognitive-behavioural interventions for outwardly-directed aggressive behaviour in people with learning disabilities.' *Cochrane Database of Systematic Reviews 1*, 3, CD003406.

Knight, C., Alderman, N., Johnson, C., Green, S., Birkett-Swan, L. and Yorstan, G. (2008) 'The St Andrew's sexual behaviour assessment (SASBA): Development of a standardised recording instrument for the measurement and assessment of challenging sexual behaviour in people with progressive and acquired neurological impairment.' *Neuropsychological Rehabilitation 18*, 2, 129–159.

Lambrick, F. and Glaser, W. (2004) 'Sex offenders with an intellectual disability.' *Sex Abuse 16*, 381–392.

Lidz, C., Mulvey, E. and Gardner, W. (1993) 'The accuracy of predictions of violence to others.' *Journal of the American Medical Association 269*, 1007–1011.

Lindsay, W.R., Hogue, T.E., Taylor, J.L., Steptoe, L. *et al.* (2008) 'Risk assessment in offenders with intellectual disability: A comparison across three levels of security.' *International Journal of Offender Therapy and Comparative Criminology 52*, 90–111.

Lindsay, W.R. and Taylor, J.L. (2005) 'A selective review of research on offenders with developmental disabilities: Assessment and treatment.' *Clinical Psychology and Psychotherapy 12*, 201–214.

Lindsay, W.R., Whitefield, E. and Carson, D. (2007) 'The development of a questionnaire to measure cognitive distortions in sex offenders with intellectual disability.' *Legal and Criminological Psychology 11*, 113–130.

Lunsky, Y., Gracey, C., Koegl, C., Bradley, E., Durbin, J. and Raina, P. (2010) 'The clinical profile and service needs of psychiatric inpatients with intellectual disabilities and forensic involvement.' *Psychology, Crime and Law 1*, 1–15.

Martinez, R., Flores, J. and Rosenfeld, B. (2007) 'Validity of the juvenile sex offender assessment protocol II (J-Soap-II) in a sample of urban minority youth.' *Criminal Justice and Behavior 34*, 1284–1295.

Matson, J.L., Dixon, D.R. and Matson, M.L. (2005) 'Assessing and treating aggression in children and adolescents with DD: A 20-year overview.' *Educational Psychology 25*, 2, 151–181.

McCoy, W.K. (2007) *Predicting Treatment Outcome and Recidivism Among Juvenile Sex Offenders: The Utility of the J-SOAP-II and ERASOR in an Outpatient Treatment Program.* Unpublished doctoral dissertation. Huntsville, TX: Sam Houston State University.

McEachran, A. (2001) *The Predictive Validity of the PCL:YV and the SAVRY in a Population of Adolescent Offenders.* Unpublished master's thesis. Burnaby, British Columbia: Simon Fraser University.

Mikkelsen, E.J. (2004) 'The assessment of individuals with developmental disabilities who commit criminal offences.' In W.R. Lindsay, J.L. Taylor and P. Sturmey (eds) *Offenders with Developmental Disabilities.* Chichester: John Wiley and Sons.

Mills, J.F. (2005) 'Advances in the assessment and prediction of interpersonal violence.' *Journal of Interpersonal Violence 20*, 2, 236–241.

Morrissey, C., Hogue, T., Mooney, P., Allen, C. *et al.* (2007) 'Predictive validity of the PCL-R in offenders with intellectual disability in a high secure hospital setting: Institutional aggression.' *Journal of Forensic Psychiatry and Psychology 18*, 1–15.

Prentky, R. and Righthand, S. (2003) *Juvenile Sex Offender Assessment Protocol-II (J-SOAP-II).* Unpublished manuscript, copies available from the Office of Juvenile Justice Clearing House.

Rajlic, G. and Gretton, H.M. (2010) 'An examination of two sexual recidivism risk measures in adolescent offenders: The moderating effect of offender type.' *Criminal Justice and Behavior 37*, 1066–1085.

Rich, P. (2009) 'Understanding the complexities and needs of adolescent sex offenders.' In A.R. Beech, L.A. Craig and K.D. Browne (eds) *Assessment and Treatment of Sex Offenders.* Chichester: John Wiley and Sons.

Royal College of Psychiatrists (2001) *Diagnostic Criteria for Learning Disability* (DC-LD). London: Gaskell.

Skowron, C. (2004) *Differentiation and Predictive Factors in Adolescent Sexual Offending.* Unpublished doctoral dissertation. Ottawa: Carleton University.

Soothill, K., Rogers, P. and Dolan, M. (eds) (2008) *Handbook of Forensic Mental Health.* Devon: Willan Publishing.

Timms, S. and Goreczny, A.J. (2002) 'Adolescent sex offenders with mental retardation: Literature review and assessment considerations.' *Aggression and Violent Behavior 7*, 1, 1–19.

Viljoen, J.L., Elkovitch, N., Scalora, M.J. and Ullman, D. (2009) 'Assessment of reoffense risk in adolescents who have committed sexual offenses: Predictive validity of the ERASOR, PCL:YV, YLS/CMI, and Static-99.' *Criminal Justice and Behavior 36*, 981–1000.

Webster, C.D., Douglas, K.S., Eaves, D. and Hart, S.D. (1997) *HCR-20: Assessing Risk for Violence (Version 2).* Burnaby: The Mental Health Law, and Policy Institute of Simon Fraser University.

Wechsler, D. (2003) *Wechsler Intelligence Scale for Children – Fourth UK Edition (WISC-IV UK).* London: The Psychological Corporation.

Worling, J. and Curwen, M.A. (2001) 'Estimate of risk of adolescent sexual offense recidivism: The ERASOR, version 2.' In M. Calder (ed.) *Juveniles Who Sexually Abuse: Frameworks for Assessment.* Second edition. Lyme Regis: Russell House.

Chapter 11

DEVELOPMENTAL TRAUMATOLOGY
Its Relevance to Secure Settings for Adolescents
with Developmental Disabilities

Ernest Gralton

INTRODUCTION

Recent research, including advances in neuro-imaging, indicates a profound effect on brain development as a result of exposure to abuse and neglect in childhood. This area is called Developmental Traumatology. Areas of the brain that may be particularly affected are important in arousal control and executive function. Many adolescents including those with developmental disabilities presenting to forensic services have histories of neglect and abuse that have contributed to deficits in key brain developmental functions. The management and treatment options for young people with Developmental Trauma and forensic needs are explored.

RESEARCH EVIDENCE

Exposure to abuse and neglect in childhood is a significant problem in Western societies including the UK. Some experts have rated it the most serious preventable public health problem in the Western world today (Van der Kolk 2005). Domestic violence may affect up to 25 per cent of families, and around 20 per cent of all children are subject to regular physical violence (Bradley *et al.* 2002; Richardson and Feder 1996). There is evidence that children in the care system (Bromfield and Higgins 2005) and those with developmental disabilities (O'Brien and Bell 2004; Sullivan and Knutson 2000) are at higher risk of sexual and physical abuse. Domestic violence has been shown to impair children's emotional, behavioural and cognitive development and is associated with anxiety, fear, aggressive and antisocial behaviour, sexual aggression, substance misuse and a failure to acquire social competence (Itzin 2006; Skuse *et al.* 1998) in addition to the more obvious causes of direct brain injury through violence (Frasier 2008). This issue has been recognised as a political priority and new legislation has been introduced in the UK to tackle this serious public health problem (Itzin 2006).

Another related problem with similar impact is childhood neglect. Neglect may be even more prevalent than physical or sexual abuse and is linked with domestic violence in many cases. It appears neglect also has a profoundly negative impact on brain development in children and the biological mechanisms that produce damage are probably similar to other forms of maltreatment (De Bellis 2005). The earlier and more sustained the neglect, the more devastating the developmental damage for the young person (Perry 2002). Both abuse and childhood neglect are independently associated with impaired cognition and academic functioning in adolescence (Mills *et al.* 2010). Why some children appear more seriously affected by abusive and neglectful experiences is likely to be in part due to complex gene–environment interaction that is not fully understood (Caspi *et al.* 2002; Teicher 2010). When abuse and neglect becomes intergenerational then there may also be epigenetic factors at work (Neigh, Gillespie and Nemeroff 2009).

It has long been theorised that the social bond, including physical touch, between mother and child is crucial for normal brain, behavioural and emotional development (Bowlby 1982). This has been repeatedly shown in animal models (Kuhn, Pauk and Shanberg 1990). Primates subjected to laboratory-induced neglect went on to become socially deviant and highly aggressive adults (Harlow and Harlow 1962). This is most likely because maternal interaction including touch causes the release of neurotrophic substances that assist the complex process of neuronal development (Fleming, O'Day and Kraemer 1999).

Paul MacLean at the National Institute of Mental Health in the US originally proposed 50 years ago that the human brain consists of three parts: the archipallidum or reptillian brain, the paleopallidum or intermediate mammalian brain and the neopallidum or rational brain; the last of these is responsible for higher order cognitive functions like speech, writing and abstract thought, which are human characteristics (MacLean 1985). These three biological structures are further lateralised into left and right hemispheres and linked together as part of our evolutionary development.

The human brain is therefore a highly sophisticated organ consisting of 100 billion interconnected neurones. Its myriad systems and activities have been developed primarily in order to promote survival, as is common in all living things (Le Doux 1998). Its growth is a complex biological process involving neurogenesis, neural differentiation, neural migration, neural pruning and mylenation. It appears that this process is vulnerable to disruption by environmental influences including the effects of neglect and abuse

(De Bellis 2005). In addition it appears that there are differential effects on areas of the brain depending on the trauma timing, with early abuse affecting areas of the midbrain like the hippocampus and later abuse having greater effect on the corpus callosum and frontal cortex development (Andersen *et al.* 2008).

The main systems for arousal control, threat perception, attachment and social functioning exist in the two more primitive areas of the brain, the reticular activating system and the limbic system. The amygdala in particular plays an important role in modulating vigilance and generating negative emotional states. If dysregulated it can play an important role in problems with arousal and the disturbance of interpersonal relations (Donegan *et al.* 2003).

The prefrontal cortex, which is important for the development of executive functions crucial for complex social development, problem solving and the development of coping strategies, has the most protracted development. It shows continued growth throughout adolescence and early adulthood (Fuster 1980). Areas of the brain that have to do with arousal control and emotional regulation in the limbic system of the brain also continue to develop well into adolescence (Jernigan and Sowell 1997).

Right brain dysregulation has been suggested as a key problem in young people with histories of neglect and abuse as it produces insecure attachment with problems regulating emotion (Schore 2002). The indications are that the brain is right dominant in very early childhood and that memories of early neglect and abuse are held in somatic (body feeling) rather than verbal form. This has been supported by the results of PET scanning studies of cerebral blood flow (Chiron *et al.* 1997) and by EEG studies showing reduced interhemispheric coherence (Miskovic *et al.* 2010). Memories involving fear are predominantly processed by right sided midbrain systems (Le Doux 1998; Schore 2002). These right brain deficits manifest in a reduced capacity to modulate the intensity and duration of affects, particularly biologically primitive affects like rage, shame, disgust, fear and despair (Shore 2003).

The likely biological mechanisms for the disruption of the process of brain development involve the elevated levels of stress neurohormones (De Bellis *et al.* 1999b). There is significant disruption of the Corticotrophin Releasing Factor (CRF) systems that regulate the stress response (Heim and Nemeroff 2001). Catecholaminergic and steroid hormones are also known to modulate the overall process of neuronal migration, differentiation and synaptic proliferation. Chronically elevated glucocorticoids cause disruption to dentritic growth and neuronal connections in animal models (Sapolski 2003). Children with histories of abuse continue to excrete significantly higher amounts of catecholamine and cortisol than controls (De Bellis *et al.* 1999a) indicating chronic dysregulation of the body's stress and arousal control systems. Maltreated children have smaller intracranial and cerebral volumes, smaller midsaggital areas of the corpus callosum and larger lateral ventricles than controls (De Bellis *et al.* 1999a; Jackowski *et al.* 2008). Both parental and peer verbal abuse (bullying) is associated with adverse neuroanatomical brain changes detected with sophisticated new scanning techniques (Teicher *et al.* 2010).

A key integrating centre is probably the orbital prefrontal area. It processes information from the external environment and integrates it with the internal emotional state and is particularly expanded in the right cortex. This area is activated by tasks such as the mental generation of images of faces, which means it almost certainly takes part in object relations and attachment behaviour. It is the thinking part of the emotional brain responsible for adaptations to the emotional realm. It helps the individual to cope with stress and adapt to a variety of challenges in the environment, including modulating distressing psychobiological states (Schore 2003).

A history of childhood maltreatment is significantly and consistently associated with a variety of developmental and psychiatric disorders including anxiety and affective disorders, schizophrenia and ADHD (Hammersley *et al.* 2003; Heim and Nemeroff 2001; Read *et al.* 2005). It is also associated with violence in delinquent adolescents in recent studies (Lansford *et al.* 2007; Mersky and Reynolds 2007) and with adolescent and adult alcohol and substance misuse (De Bellis 2002). There are also significant alterations in threat perception demonstrated by studies that show physically abused children are more sensitised to facial displays of anger (Pollak and Sinha 2002).

Current nomenclature and classification

Severe and chronic psychological trauma is likely to have significantly more impact on a developing brain than the nervous system of a mature adult and therefore the current diagnostic category of post-traumatic stress disorder (PTSD) is inadequate to describe the condition as it manifests in children and adolescents who are the victims of repeated abuse and neglect (Van der Kolk 2005).

It may be argued that new evidence is leading to a paradigm shift in the way that we view the adolescents with histories of abuse and neglect who present to forensic psychiatric services. For the first time there appears to be unequivocal biological evidence of brain impairment that is likely to be as significant as brain dysfunction in young people with a functional mental illness like schizophrenia or bipolar affective disorder. There also appears to be some significant overlap with the concept of borderline personality disorder (Ball and Links 2009; Herman, Perry and Van der Kolk 1989). There is a strong argument that this disorder is best seen as a form of acquired brain damage that requires the correct conditions for recovery and repair. This view of the difficulties of adolescents with neglect and abuse informed by neuro-imaging evidence will need to be incorporated into the management of treatment of young people in secure forensic services.

PRACTICE ISSUES

Young people with histories of neglect and abuse often present with a complex neurodevelopmental picture with extremes of behavioural disturbance including: hyperactivity, severe aggression and self-harm complicated by severe affective disturbance, eating disorders and substance misuse. In young people with pre-existing neurodevelopmental disorders like autism, developmental trauma further exacerbates deficits in arousal and anxiety control and compromises their ability to cope and manage in their environment. They are diagnostically difficult as many of the symptoms and behavioural manifestations are common to a variety of disorders. In some cases they can go on to manifest serious affective illness and psychotic symptoms. Combinations of developmental disorders and developmental trauma produce the most complex and problematic young people referred to the service.

Attachment has several key elements. It is an enduring emotional relationship with a specific person. The relationship brings safety, comfort, soothing and pleasure. The threat or loss of the relationship can provoke intense distress. Four main types of attachment in children have been described: secure, avoidant, resistant and disorganised. It is likely the maternal–child relationship provides the working framework for all subsequent relationships (Ainsworth 1989).

The conceptual model of Early Maladaptive Schemas (Young, Klosko and Weishaar 2003) is potentially helpful for understanding the impact of developmental trauma on young people. These schemas are broadly pervasive consisting of memories, emotions, cognitions and bodily sensations regarding oneself and one's relationship with others. At any one time some of our schemas are operational and others are inactive or dormant. However, they can be triggered by environmental events, that is, 'triggers' or 'emotional buttons'. They can be activated extremely quickly and lead to significant changes in arousal and a variety of dysphoric cognitions and emotions. These schemas can significantly adversely affect traditional cognitive behavioural therapy approaches as well as complicating risk management by leading to high risk behaviours.

There needs to be a recognition that it is a significant challenge to meet the needs of these highly traumatised young people in a secure setting. They require a model of care that has a long-term developmental perspective seeking to minimise transitions and carefully planning transitions to avoid constant disruption to attachments. The environment should provide the ability to manage young people at high risk in highly aroused states intensively and separately from their peers if required. They will require a variety of interventions to help manage arousal, and teach arousal management skills and self-soothing behaviours.

This group of young people require a robust environment and skilled staff group that can contain and safely manage severe aggression and self-harm. These services need a recruitment process that ensures a staff group are committed and interested in traumatised young people, together with appropriate supervision and a commitment to ongoing staff training. These young people need an environment allowing a range of habilitative activities and experiences of success and mastery within a secure perimeter for those young people who are initially at high risk of absconding. A culture of respect is essential, where care is valued but risk is also managed appropriately. A structured programme needs high levels of consistency between staff. Staff members see themselves as mentors or guides who model appropriate behaviour and avoid where possible confrontational and overly authoritarian relationships. The service needs sophisticated systems to identify triggers for disturbed behaviour and monitor the impact of interventions including behavioural programmes. Family contact is appropriately managed and the young person will need to be supported through (and sometimes protected from) contact that may precipitate dysphoric emotional responses.

Physical contact

The issue of the management of physical contact is one of the most problematic areas for forensic services, particularly forensic adolescent services. Forensic services are likely to have policies that limit physical touch. This is in view of patients who have histories of inappropriate sexual behaviour and also to try to prevent staff from being accused of inappropriate physical contact. However, some individual adolescent patients can engage in a variety of inappropriate behaviours in order to meet their physical touch needs including deliberately precipitating physical restraint, a procedure involving high risk of physical injury to the young person and staff. There is evidence that depressed, anxious and aggressive adolescents can benefit from massage therapy; they have lower saliva cortisol as an index of reduced stress as well as improved immune function (Diego *et al.* 2001, 2002; Field *et al.* 1992). This would imply that regulated types of physical touch like peripheral massage may be beneficial for young people with histories of neglect and abuse and subsequent histories of violence (Field 2002).

Diet

Long chain omega-3 fatty acids are essential building blocks for brain development and can only be obtained from specific dietary sources. The current Western diet is very low in these essential nutrients (Richardson 2006). Mammals fed diets low in omega-3 fatty acids have impaired brain repair (Bourre *et al.* 1989). There is already strong evidence that these essential nutrients can reduce aggression in adolescent offenders (Gesch *et al.* 2002) whose brains are still developing and have the chance of repairing neurological deficits. Adolescents in forensic inpatient settings should therefore be offered a diet high in omega-3 fatty acids and essential nutrients or should have them supplemented (Hibbeln, Furguson and Blasbalg 2006).

There is also longstanding concern about the serious adverse effects of a variety of artificial colours and preservatives on young people with behavioural problems, confirmed by meta analysis (Schab and Trinh 2004). A variety of food additives are known to significantly affect brain function by interfering with neurotransmitter function (Maher and Wurtman 1987) or being directly neurotoxic (Lau *et al.* 2006). It makes sense that these compounds be avoided in the nutrition available to young people with behavioural problems who are in secure settings.

Exercise

Exercise is an effective treatment in disruptive behaviour disorders with few side effects (Allison, Faith and Franklin 1995). Exercise increases neural plasticity and brain repair probably by the up-regulation of Brain Derived Neurotrophic Factor (BDNF) (Vaynman and Gomez Pinilla 2005). Sports and exercise programmes are important for a range of reasons including weight control, teaching leadership and social interaction, reducing overall arousal and promoting brain recovery. It may require modification to de-emphasise some of the overcompetitive aspects. However, exercise and sports should be a key component to any overall programme in a secure setting (Andrews and Andrews 2003).

Right brain therapies

Conventional therapies that rely completely on verbal interaction may be problematic with respect to young people with early neglect and abuse. This is because trauma memories are likely to be right sided and traumatised young people have damaged inter-cerebral communication systems. The case for Art Therapy for young people with trauma histories has been cogently made by O'Brien (2004) and the benefits of Music Therapy for behaviourally disturbed young people have been strongly supported by meta analysis (Gold, Voracek and Wigram 2004). Eye Movement Desensitisation and Reprocessing (EMDR) has been found to be very effective in traumatised young people (Ahmad, Larsson and Sundelin-Wahlsten 2007) and should be available as part of the programme offered to young people with histories of neglect, abuse and aggressive behaviour. The rationale for EMDR has been significantly strengthened by the recent evidence from brain neuro-imaging (Solomon and Heide 2005). However, a significant period of 'resource installation' often needs to take place prior to any trauma specific work; trauma-related therapy has the potential to destabilise a young person and may need to occur relatively late in the therapeutic programme following skill building including arousal management skills.

Rehabilitation systems

Disruption of attachment appears to be a key issue underlying many of the symptoms of young people with conduct disturbance (Holland *et al.* 1993; Moretti, Holland and Peterson 1994). Unsurprisingly interventions by multiple agencies with different personnel can, without careful coordination, worsen outcomes for youth with conduct disorder (Shamsie, Sykes and Hamilton 1994). Conventional rehabilitation systems for adults with mental illness that rely on moving through multiple settings with changes in personnel and progressively reduced security may be problematic for these young people with attachment difficulties who have often already been in multiple care settings prior to admission. Systems that rely on the minimum of disruption with a single well planned structured transition from a secure setting into the community under an appropriate legal framework are preferable. This approach may question the flexibility of some systems of secure care for adolescents and young adults.

Pharmacology

Agents that block the effects of stress neurohormones may be useful adjuncts to the treatment of young people with neglect and abuse who have demonstrated aggressive and other offending behaviour. Perry (1994) has advocated the use of the alpha-adrenergic blocker clonidine for children with histories of trauma and abuse; it affects noradrenergic autoreceptors by inhibiting the firing of cells in the reticular activating system, thus reducing the release of brain noradrenaline. Clonidine has been used to treat severely and chronically abused and neglected children. It improves disturbed behaviour by reducing aggression, impulsivity, emotional outbursts and oppositionality (Harmon and

Riggs 1996). Propranolol has been used for established PTSD in adults (Taylor and Cahill 2002). Propranolol has the best evidence for treatment of aggression post-brain injury both in the short and long term (Fleminger, Greenwood and Oliver 2003). Propranolol has also been successfully used for chronically hospitalised aggressive adults (Silver *et al.* 1999) and aggression in children and adolescents (Kuperman and Stewart 1987; Sims and Galvin 1990).

Case description

Ben was admitted at the age of 14 to a secure setting. His mother was a heroin addict and was engaged in prostitution. Ben's father was unknown but may have been her pimp who was violent toward her. She was hospitalised with a fractured rib on at least one occasion. Ben had memories of his mother lying unconscious and unresponsive on the floor with a needle in her arm. Ben was found at the age of six years by the police alone and naked inside an unheated house during winter after neighbours reported seeing him distressed at the lounge window, and was taken into care. Ben was placed in foster care but he was aggressive toward the other children and he needed to be placed by himself. Ben found it difficult to concentrate and engage in education and was repeatedly excluded from school, but was never formally assessed for a Statement of Special Educational Need. He seriously assaulted his foster mother at the age of 13 and was placed in residential care but repeatedly absconded, using drugs and alcohol. When he was returned by the police he assaulted the residential care staff and he was placed in a secure social services unit where he began to cut himself and placed ligatures around his neck. He also required recurrent restraint. On formal psychometric assessment Ben had a full scale IQ of 59 and was placed in a specialist service.

Initially Ben engaged in behaviours that resulted in staff having to intervene recurrently to restrain him. Staff expressed concern that Ben appeared to enjoy being tightly held as part of the restraint process and that they were reinforcing his behaviour. A functional analysis supported this view. Ben responded particularly well to a sensory programme, particularly using a weighted blanket when distressed and peripheral massage using vibrating equipment. Ben learned to modulate his arousal using biofeedback with Biodots® and was prescribed adjunctive propranolol. Ben also engaged in repetitive drumming activities and sporting activity. He participated in art psychotherapy where he was able to draw and process some of his traumatic memories independent of his verbal ability.

CONCLUSIONS

It is clear that exposure to interfamilial violence and other chronic trauma such as neglect results in pervasive psychological and biological deficits (Streeck-Fischer and Van der Kolk 2000). It is likely that our understanding of the biological links between abuse, neglect and violence will only increase. The advances in neuro-imaging are continuing at a rapid pace and show enormous promise in better understanding violent and high risk behaviour (Hoptman 2003). Brain imaging techniques like functional magnetic resonance imaging (fMRI) and diffusion tensor imaging (DTI) can be used to assist our understanding of brain development, maturation (Durston and Casey 2005) and its response to violence (Tomoda *et al.* 2011). It is important that clinicians who are managing young people with histories of developmental trauma and aggression are aware of this evidence and use it to inform the interventions and programmes that are available to assist this complex and problematic group of young people.

Permission was kindly given to reproduce material previously used in an article by the author in the British Journal of Forensic Practice (2008) 10, 2, 33–39.

REFERENCES

Ahmad, A., Larsson, B. and Sundelin-Wahlsten, V. (2007) 'EMDR treatment for children with PTSD: Results of a randomized controlled trial.' *Nordic Journal of Psychiatry 61*, 5, 349–354.

Ainsworth, M.D. (1989) 'Attachments beyond infancy.' *American Psychologist 44*, 4, 709–716.

Allison, D.B., Faith, M.S. and Franklin, R.D. (1995) 'Antecedent exercise in the treatment of disruptive behaviour: A meta-analytic review.' *Clinical Psychology: Science and Practice 2*, 3, 279–303.

Andersen, S.L., Tomada, A., Vincow, E.S., Valente, E., Polcari, A. and Teicher, M.H. (2008) 'Preliminary evidence for sensitive periods in the effect of childhood sexual abuse on regional brain development.' *Journal of Neuropsychiatry and Clinical Neurosciences 20*, 3, 292–301.

Andrews, J.P. and Andrews, G.J. (2003) 'Life in a secure unit: The rehabilitation of young people through the use of sport.' *Social Science and Medicine 56*, 3, 531–550.

Ball, J.S. and Links, P.S. (2009) 'Borderline personality disorder and childhood trauma: Evidence for a causal relationship.' *Current Psychiatry Reports 11*, 1, 63–68.

Bourre, J.M., Durand, G., Pascal, G. and Youyou, A. (1989) 'Brain cell and tissue recovery in rats made deficient in n-3 fatty acids by alteration of dietary fat.' *Journal of Nutrition 119*, 15–22.

Bowlby, J. (1982) *Attachment: Attachment and Loss.* New York, NY: Basic Books.

Bradley, F., Smith, M., Long, J. and O'Dowd, T. (2002) 'Reported frequency of domestic violence: Cross-sectional survey of women attending general practice.' *British Medical Journal 324*, 271.

Bromfield, L.M. and Higgins, D.J. (2005) 'Chronic and isolated maltreatment in a child protection sample.' *Family Matters 70*, 38–45.

Caspi, A., McClay, J., Moffitt, T.E., Mill, J. *et al.* (2002) 'Role of genotype in the cycle of violence in maltreated children.' *Science 297*, 5582, 851–854.

Chiron, C., Jambaque, I., Nabbout, R., Lounes, R., Syrota, A. and Dulac, O. (1997) 'The right brain hemisphere is dominant in human infants.' *Brain 120*, 6, 1057–1065.

De Bellis, M. (2002) 'Developmental traumatology: A contributory mechanism for alcohol and substance use disorders.' *Psychoneuroendocrinology 27*, 155–170.

De Bellis, M. (2005) 'The psychobiology of neglect.' *Child Maltreatment 10*, 2, 150–172.

De Bellis, M., Keshavan, M.S., Clark, D.B., Casey, B.J. *et al.* (1999a) 'Developmental traumatology, part I: Biological stress systems.' *Biological Psychiatry 45*, 1259–1270.

De Bellis, M., Keshavan, M.S., Clark, D.B., Casey, B.J. *et al.* (1999b) 'Developmental traumatology, part II: Brain development.' *Biological Psychiatry 45*, 1271–1284.

Diego, M.A., Field, T., Hernandez-Reif, M., Shaw, K., Friedman, L. and Ironson, G. (2001) 'HIV adolescents show improved immune function following massage therapy.' *International Journal of Neuroscience 106*, 1–2, 35–45.

Diego, M.A., Field, T., Hernandez-Reif, M., Shaw, J.A. and Rothe, E.M (2002) 'Aggressive adolescents benefit from massage therapy.' *Adolescence 37*, 147, 597–607.

Donegan, N.H., Sanislow, C.A., Blumberg, H.P., Fulbright, R.K. *et al.* (2003) 'Amygdala hyperreactivity in borderline personality disorder: Implications for emotional dysregulation.' *Biological Psychiatry 54*, 1284–1293.

Durston, S. and Casey, B.J. (2005) 'What have we learned about cognitive development from neuroimaging?' *Neuropsychologia 44*, 11, 2149–2157.

Field, T. (2002) 'Violence and touch deprivation in adolescents.' *Adolescence 37*, 148, 735–749.

Field, T., Morrow, C., Valdeon, C., Larson, S., Kuhn, C. and Shanberg, S. (1992) 'Massage reduces anxiety in child and adolescent psychiatric patients.' *Journal of the American Academy of Child and Adolescent Psychiatry 31*, 1, 125–131.

Fleming, A.S., O'Day, D.H. and Kraemer, G.W. (1999) 'Neurobiology of mother-infant interactions: Experience and central nervous system plasticity across development and generations.' *Neuroscience Biobehavioural Review 23*, 5, 673–685.

Fleminger, S., Greenwood, R.J. and Oliver, D.L. (2003) 'Pharmacological management for agitation and aggression in people with acquired brain injury.' *Cochrane Database of Systematic Reviews 1*. Art. No.: CD003299.

Frasier, L.D. (2008) 'Abusive head trauma in infants and young children: A unique contributor to developmental disabilities.' *Pediatric Clinics of North America 55*, 6, 1269–1285.

Fuster, J.M. (1980) *The Prefrontal Cortex: Anatomy, Physiology and Neuropsychology of the Frontal Lobe.* New York, NY: Raven Press.

Gesch, C.B., Hammond, S.M., Hampson, S.E., Eves, A. and Crowder, M.J. (2002) 'Influence of supplementary vitamins, minerals and essential fatty acids on the antisocial behaviour of young adult prisoners: Randomised placebo controlled trial.' *British Journal of Psychiatry 181*, 22–28.

Gold, C., Voracek, M. and Wigram, T. (2004) 'Effects of music therapy for children and adolescents with psychopathology: A meta-analysis.' *Journal of Child Psychology and Psychiatry 45*, 6, 1054–1063.

Hammersley, P., Dias, A., Todd, G., Bowen-Jones, K., Reilly, B. and Bentall, R.P. (2003) 'Childhood trauma and hallucinations in bipolar affective disorder: Preliminary investigation.' *British Journal of Psychiatry 182*, 543–547.

Harlow, H.F. and Harlow, M. (1962) 'Social deprivation in monkeys.' *Scientific American 207*, 136–146.

Harmon, R.J. and Riggs, P. (1996) 'Clonidine for posttraumatic stress disorder in preschool children.' *Journal of the American Academy of Child and Adolescent Psychiatry 35*, 1247–1249.

Heim, C. and Nemeroff, B. (2001) 'The role of childhood trauma in the neurobiology of mood and anxiety disorders: Preclinical and clinical studies.' *Biological Psychiatry 49*, 1023–1039.

Herman, J.L., Perry, J.C. and Van der Kolk, B.A. (1989) 'Childhood trauma in borderline personality disorder.' *American Journal of Psychiatry 146*, 490–495.

Hibbeln, J., Furguson, T. and Blasbalg, T.L. (2006) 'Omega-3 fatty acid deficiencies in neurodevelopment, aggression and autonomic dysregulation: Opportunities for intervention.' *International Review of Psychiatry 18*, 2, 107–118.

Holland, R., Moretti, M.M., Verlaan, V. and Peterson, S. (1993) 'Attachment and conduct disorder: The Response Program.' *Canadian Journal of Psychiatry 38*, 6, 420–431.

Hoptman, M.J. (2003) 'Neuroimaging studies of violence and antisocial behaviour.' *Journal of Psychiatric Practice 9*, 4, 265–278.

Itzin, C. (2006) *Tackling the Health and Mental Health Effects of Domestic and Sexual Violence and Abuse.* London: Home Office and Department of Health.

Jackowski, A.P., Douglas-Palumberi, H., Jackowski, M., Win, L. *et al.* (2008) 'Corpus callosum in maltreated children with posttraumatic stress disorder: A diffusion tensor imaging study.' *Psychiatry Research 162*, 3, 256–261.

Jernigan, T.L. and Sowell, E.R. (1997) 'Magnetic Resonance Imaging Studies of the Developing Brain.' In M.S. Keshavan and R.M. Murray (eds) *Neurodevelopment and Adult Psychopathology.* Cambridge: Cambridge University Press.

Kuhn, C.M., Pauk, J. and Shanberg, S.M. (1990) 'Endocrine response to mother-infant separation in developing rats.' *Developmental Psychobiology 23*, 395–410.

Kuperman, S. and Stewart, M.A. (1987) 'Use of propranolol to decrease aggressive outbursts in younger patients.' *Psychosomatics 28*, 315–319.

Lansford, J.E., Miller-Johnson, S., Berlin, L.J., Dodge, K.A., Bates, J.E. and Pettit, G.S. (2007) 'Early physical abuse and later violent delinquency: A prospective longitudinal study.' *Child Maltreatment 12*, 3, 233–345.

Lau, K., McLean, W.G., Williams, D.P. and Howard, V. (2006) 'Synergistic interactions between commonly used food additives in a developmental neurotoxicity test.' *Toxicological Sciences 90*, 1, 178–187.

Le Doux, J. (1998) *The Emotional Brain.* London: Wiedenfeld and Nicholson.

MacLean, P.D. (1985) 'Evolutionary psychiatry and the triune brain.' *Psychological Medicine 15*, 2, 219–221.

Maher, T.J. and Wurtman, R.J. (1987) 'Possible neurologic effects of aspartame, a widely used food additive.' *Environmental Health Perspectives 75*, 53–57.

Mersky, J.P. and Reynolds, A.J. (2007) 'Child maltreatment and violent delinquency: Disentangling main effects and subgroup effects.' *Child Maltreatment 12*, 3, 246–258.

Mills, R., Alati, R., O'Callaghan, M., Najman, J.M. *et al.* (2010) 'Child abuse and neglect and cognitive function at 14 years of age: Findings from a birth cohort.' *Pediatrics 127*, 1, 4–10.

Miskovic, V., Schmidt, L.A., Georgiades, K., Boyle, M. and Macmillan, H.L. (2010) 'Adolescent females exposed to child maltreatment exhibit atypical EEG coherence and psychiatric impairment: Linking early adversity, the brain, and psychopathology.' *Development and Psychopathology 22*, 2, 419–432.

Moretti, M., Holland, R. and Peterson, S. (1994) 'Long term outcome of an attachment-based program for conduct disorder.' *Canadian Journal of Psychiatry 39*, 6, 360–370.

Neigh, G.N., Gillespie, C.F. and Nemeroff, C.B. (2009) 'The neurobiological toll of child abuse and neglect.' *Trauma Violence Abuse 10*, 4, 389–410.

O'Brien, F. (2004) 'The making of mess in art therapy: Attachment, trauma and the brain.' *Inscape 9*, 1, 2–13.

O'Brien, G. and Bell, G. (2004) 'Learning Disability, Autism and Offending Behaviour.' In S. Bailey and M. Dolan (eds) *Adolescent Forensic Psychiatry*. London: Arnold.

Perry, B. (1994) 'Neurobiological sequelae of childhood trauma: PTSD in children.' In M. Murburg (ed.) *Catecholamine Function in Post-traumatic Stress Disorder: Emerging Concepts*. Arlington, VA: American Psychiatric Press.

Perry, B. (2002) 'Childhood experience and the expression of genetic potential: What childhood neglect tells us about nature and nurture.' *Brain and Mind 3*, 79–100.

Pollak, S.D. and Sinha, P. (2002) 'Effects of early experience on children's recognition of facial displays of emotion.' *Developmental Psychology 38*, 5, 784–791.

Read, J., van Os, J., Morrison, A.P. and Ross, C.A. (2005) 'Childhood trauma, psychosis and schizophrenia: A literature review with theoretical and clinical implications.' *Acta Psychiatrica Scandinavica 112*, 330–350.

Richardson, A.J. (2006) 'Omega 3 fatty acids in ADHD and related neurodevelopmental disorders.' *International Review of Psychiatry 18*, 2, 155–172.

Richardson, J. and Feder, G. (1996) 'Domestic violence: A hidden problem for general practice.' *British Journal of General Practice 46*, 411, 623–624.

Sapolski, R.M. (2003) 'Stress and plasticity in the limbic system.' *Neurochemical Research 28*, 1753–1742.

Schab, D.W. and Trinh, N.H. (2004) 'Do artificial food colors promote hyperactivity in children with hyperactive syndromes? A meta-analysis of double blind placebo controlled trials.' *Journal of Developmental and Behavioural Pediatrics 25*, 6, 423–434.

Schore, A. (2002) 'Dysregulation of the right brain: A fundamental mechanism of traumatic attachment and the psychopathogenesis of posttraumatic stress disorder.' *Australian and New Zealand Journal of Psychiatry 36*, 9–30.

Schore, A. (2003) *Affect Regulation and the Repair of the Self*. New York, NY: WW Norton and Co.

Shamsie, J., Sykes, C. and Hamilton, H. (1994) 'Continuity of care for conduct disordered youth.' *Canadian Journal of Psychiatry 39*, 7, 415–420.

Silver, J.M., Yudofsky, S.C., Slater, J.A., Gold, R.K. *et al.* (1999) 'Propranolol treatment of chronically hospitalized aggressive patients.' *Journal of Neuropsychiatry and Clinical Neurosciences 11*, 328–335.

Sims, J. and Galvin, M.R. (1990) 'Pediatric psychopharmacologic uses of propranolol: Review and case illustrations.' *Journal of Child and Adolescent Psychiatric Nursing 3*, 1, 18–24.

Skuse, D., Bentovim, A., Hodges, J., Stevenson, J. *et al.* (1998) 'Risk factors for the development of sexually abusive behaviour in sexually victimised adolescent boys: Cross sectional study.' *British Medical Journal 317*, 175–179.

Solomon, E.P. and Heide, K.M. (2005) 'The biology of trauma: Implications for treatment.' *Journal of Interpersonal Violence 20*, 1, 51–60.

Streeck-Fischer, A. and Van der Kolk, B.A. (2000) 'Down will come baby, cradle and all: Diagnostic and therapeutic implications of chronic trauma on child development.' *Australian and New Zealand Journal of Psychiatry 34*, 6, 903–918.

Sullivan, P.M. and Knutson, J.F. (2000) 'Maltreatment and disabilities: A population-based epidemiological study.' *Child Abuse and Neglect 24*, 10, 1257–1273.

Taylor, F. and Cahill, L. (2002) 'Propranolol for re-emergent posttraumatic stress disorder following an event of retraumatization: A case study.' *Journal of Traumatic Stress 15*, 5, 433–437.

Teicher, M.H. (2010) 'Commentary: Childhood abuse: New insights into its association with posttraumatic stress, suicidal ideation, and aggression.' *Journal of Pediatric Psychology 35*, 5, 578–580.

Teicher, M.H., Samson, J.A., Sheu, Y.S., Polcari, A. and McGreenery, C.E. (2010) 'Hurtful words: Association of exposure to peer verbal abuse with elevated psychiatric symptom scores and corpus callosum abnormalities.' *American Journal of Psychiatry 167*, 12, 1464–1471.

Tomoda, A., Sheu, Y.S., Rabi, K., Suzuki, H. *et al.* (2011) 'Exposure to parental verbal abuse is associated with increased gray matter volume in superior temporal gyrus.' *Neuroimage 54*, S280–286.

Van der Kolk, B.A. (2005) 'Developmental trauma disorder: Toward a rational diagnosis for children with trauma histories.' *Psychiatric Annals 35*, 5, 401–408.

Vaynman, S. and Gomez Pinilla, F. (2005) 'License to run: Exercise impacts functional plasticity in the intact and injured central nervous system by using neurotrophins.' *Neurorehabilitation and Neural Repair 19*, 4, 283–295.

Young, J.E., Klosko, J.S. and Weishaar, M.E. (2003) *Schema Therapy: A Practitioners' Guide*. New York, NY: The Guilford Press.

Chapter 12

GENETIC INFLUENCES IN FORENSIC ADOLESCENT PSYCHIATRY

Anu Iyer

INTRODUCTION

Historical background

The search for causes of antisocial and aggressive behaviours has a long and chequered history. It has never been limited to a theoretical exercise as the prevalent zeitgeist has substantially influenced the practice of law and mental health.

The traditional school of *utilitarian* ethics has viewed crime as a rational act of choice by an individual and has been a dominant influence on the current legal systems based on punishment for the criminal act. The *positivist* school have postulated that crime is determined by constitutional and heritable factors (*biological positivists*) or by environmental influences (*social positivists*).

The position of the biological positivist thought was best exemplified in the work of Cesare Lombroso, who proposed the theory of *anthropological criminology* which stated that criminality was inherited and that 'born criminals' could be identified by physical defects that delineated them as 'atavistic' (a creature who has *devolved* in distinction to humankind which is evolving). Atavistic stigmata included large jaw, sloping foreheads and handle shaped ears among others which had obvious implications in identifying persons with developmental disabilities, especially those who had physical dysmorphisms associated with genetic disorders (Gibson 2002).

Lombroso himself advocated humane treatment of 'born criminals'. His theories had far reaching implications, particularly in relation to the *eugenics* movement of the late 19th century which proposed the selective breeding of humans with the aim of improving the species by countering *dysgenic dynamics* which included congenital disorders. They proposed the category of 'defective delinquents' to describe persons with genetic disorders who were doomed from birth to commit crime. This led to the creation of 'eugenic institutions' where those deemed congenitally criminalistic could be indefinitely incarcerated to prevent them from reproducing. This resulted in the incarceration of persons with intellectual disabilities (ID) merely on the presumption of criminal tendencies (Hahn Rafter 1997).

The backlashes against this inhumane treatment led to a repudiation of genetics as a cause of crime with increasing emphasis on social causes. Biological theories enjoyed brief resurgence in the 1960s with the work on sex chromosome abnormalities being associated with violent crime (Court Brown 1962). These studies were based in penal and institutional populations and questions were raised regarding the methodologies of these studies. It was highlighted as early as the 1970s that 'the XYY syndrome occurs in 1:700 among consecutive born males and makes it appear likely that there are large number of XYY males whose conforming behaviours permits them to remain unidentified in the population at large' (Baker *et al*. 1970, p.878). This study also stressed the importance of longitudinal population studies and emphasised that males with Klinefelter's syndrome who had antisocial behaviours also had lower IQs than those without. More recent research on young people with XYY reveals that there are particular cognitive phenotypes. Both the XYY and XXY groups performed less well, on average, than the controls on tests of general cognitive ability, achievement, language, verbal memory, some aspects of attention, and executive and motor function. The boys with XYY on average had more severe and pervasive language impairment, at both simple and complex levels, and the boys with XXY on average had greater motor impairment in gross motor function and coordination (Ross *et al*. 2009). Boys with XYY, even those with average intelligence, have a greater risk of psychosocial problems and psychiatric disorders and have a greater requirement for special education (Geerts, Steyaert and Fryns 2003). Their problems therefore are likely to be secondary to cognitive impairments and psychiatric co-morbidities rather than a specific manifestation of the chromosomal disorder.

The deterministic biological theories suggesting 'crime as genetic destiny' received a further blow in examples such as phenylketonuria (PKU). PKU is a genetic condition involving a single gene defect which had been traditionally associated with significant and enduring behaviour difficulties. It was demonstrated that the aggressive phenotype mediated by genetic defect was solely ameliorated by modifying an environmental factor, namely diet (Scrivner *et al*. 1995).

The field of behavioural genetics evolved as a reasoned stance in favour of genetic influences. It does not seek to identify genes or sets of genes leading to particular crimes committed by a particular individual. Instead, it seeks to elucidate the influences of multiple genes which confer varying degrees of genetic predispositions to criminal behaviours within the population. However, behaviour genetic research in forensic populations has been bedevilled by difficulties in defining the phenotype, heterogeneity within populations being studied as well as methodological issues.

Challenges within behavioural genetics of aggression

Behaviour geneticists have often had the difficult task of defining the phenotype pertinent to their research. They have had to examine a wide range of phenomena, from criminal acts (which are essentially a legal and social construct) to various types of aggression (which can be complex situation-dependent behaviours). They have then sought to identify those maladaptive clusters that may have clinical significance.

Research has also focused on defined clusters of traits such as psychopathy which increase risks of criminal behaviours and at specific personality traits such as callous and unemotional traits which are particular risk factors for criminal behaviours (Blair *et al.* 2006).

There have been efforts to define genetic influences on clinically defined syndromes such as antisocial personality disorders and conduct disorder in childhood, of which aggression forms a major manifestation and which are associated with criminal behaviours. However, studies looking at the nosological validity of childhood disruptive disorders including attention deficit hyperactivity disorder (ADHD), oppositional defiant disorder, conduct disorder (CD) and hyperkinetic conduct disorder (HKCD) have failed to delineate 'zones of rarity' separating these disorders from each other and from normal variation (Hofvander *et al.* 2009). Moreover, multivariate genetic research suggests that the genetic structure of common disorders differs substantially from current diagnostic classifications based on symptoms and level of intellectual disability (Plomin and Davis 2009).

There have been paradigms which have made the distinctions between aggressive versus non-aggressive delinquent behaviours (Loeber and Hay 1997). Antisocial behaviours have also been defined on the basis of developmental trajectories. Moffit (1993) has described two categories: first, the *life course persistent individuals* who are characterised by early onset, presence of multiple risk factors including neuropsychological deficits, hyperactivity and perinatal complications, whose trajectory is associated with poorer prognosis across all domains in adulthood, and, second, *adolescent limited* antisocial behaviour, which is predicated by influence of delinquent peers and lack of parental supervision, and has a later onset and relatively better prognosis.

More recent studies have identified gender differences in there being additional trajectories into antisocial behaviour in females including a late onset persistent subtype which has antecedents. Prognosis is similar to life course persistent trajectory in males (Fontaine *et al.* 2009).

Antisocial behaviour associated with early onset hyperactivity has emerged as another clinical cluster of importance to genetic research. It is associated with cognitive impairments and difficulties with peer relatedness. The genetic liability associated with this cluster seems to encompass a range of behaviours that extends beyond orthodox diagnostic categories (Rutter *et al.* 1999b).

Whole population studies have been deemed gold standard (Baker *et al.* 1970) but many studies have looked at populations within penal systems, mental health institutions and institutions for the developmentally disabled. Objections have been raised that study within these populations are fraught by scientific biases of various kinds and are a legal minefield in their implications for criminal responsibility and predicating crime (Appelbaum 2005).

The heterogeneity of antisocial acts in persons with developmental difficulties is further confounded by the effects of co-morbid mental illness, effects of low IQ and the effects of institutionalisation (Baker *et al.* 1970). The lack of a single unitary behaviour which exemplifies violent and non-violent crime, crimes against property, sexual crimes and arson poses considerable difficulties in characterising criminal behaviour as a behavioural phenotype. The heterogeneity within populations and the varied definitions have resulted in outcomes which may not be easily generalizable.

CURRENT RESEARCH EVIDENCE

The challenge of behaviour genetics is to connect the proximal genetic cause to identifiable molecular changes which may be associated with structural changes. These molecular and structural changes will form the basis for cognitive and emotional dysfunctions which will heighten the risk of acquisition of antisocial tendencies in suboptimal environments (Blair *et al.* 2006).

Behavioural genetics has sought to meet the challenge of investigating proximal genetic influences through the use of two genetic paradigms, namely qualitative genetics and molecular genetics. Both these genetic paradigms have their specific strengths and challenges as discussed later (see Steyaert and Fryns 2002 for a review). Current evidence suggests that most behavioural disorders including those presenting with antisocial behaviours are, for most part, not determined by single gene effects. It is likely that antisocial disorders are inherited through polygenic mechanisms where a number of genes or qualitative trait loci (QTL) act in concert with each other and with environmental influences to produce the resultant behaviours. The QTL singly are not necessary or sufficient to produce the disorder.

Even in genetic syndromes where single gene effects are prominent, it is likely that not every individual shows the expected outcome in relation to complex behaviours (Hodapp and Dykens 2009). Single gene disorders may lead instead to a spectrum of qualitative and quantitative impairments through various genetic mechanisms such as anticipation, chance, gender effects and effects of other genes (Steyaert and Fryns 2002).

Qualitative behaviour genetics

Qualitative genetics looks at the extent to which a particular disorder or trait is genetically determined. It seeks to clarify 'how much' genetics affects the disorder in question. It provides models of genetic causation which can then be used to study the promising genes. It is also said to provide the best available evidence for environmental influences as most disorders have heritability of less that 100 per cent. Insights from qualitative research have elucidated on the various forms these environmental mechanisms my take. It has been particularly important in highlighting that even salient environmental influences do not have uniform effects on children growing up in the same families (Plomin and Davis 2009). Children, subject to their unique genetic endowments, also create specific experiences within environments. This has been called genotype environment co-relation (GEC) which may exert its effects through active, passive and evocative effects (Plomin *et al.* 1997).

These effects have been seen to affect the expression of antisocial traits in several ways. Passive GEC effects are perpetuated by parents with antisocial behaviours in providing genetic loading and environmental risk factors such as marital discord. In addition, an evocative correlation occurs when genetically influenced behaviours such as aggression in offspring may evoke negative reactions from carers.

Active GEC occurs when the genetic conditions predispose the individual to seek particular experiences, including partners with similar profiles (assortative mating), which also increases the trans-generational transmission of risk behaviours (Holmes and Thapar 2004; Plomin and Davis 2009; Rutter *et al.* 1999a). In distinction to this, reciprocal effects between nature and nurture have been designated as 'gene environment interaction' (Plomin and Davis 2009). Quantitative genetics has used several paradigms to elucidate genetic influences.

Familial studies

Studies of antisocial behaviours in both childhood and adulthood have highlighted that these problems cluster within families. Farrington, Gundry and West (1975) found that convicted teenagers were likely to have parents with previous convictions. Kandel *et al.* (1988) compared the occurrence of criminal behaviours in children and found that the offspring of fathers with criminal histories had five times the risk than those without.

Rutter *et al.* (1999b) confirmed that criminality in parents was associated with a fourfold increase in delinquency in their offspring. However, it has been acknowledged that familial clustering may reflect not only shared genetic endowments but also common environment and parenting influences. Twin studies and adoption studies have been used to clarify these issues.

Twin studies

Twin studies are based on the premise that identical or monozygotic (MZ) twins share 100 per cent of their genetic complement. Hence any concordance in the rates of any traits or disorders is likely to reflect genetic influences in distinction to fraternal or dizygotic (DZ) twins who share only 50 per cent of their genes.

Data from recent studies (Goldsmith and Gottesman 1996) have shown high concordance rates for delinquency of 95 per cent for monozygotic twins and 73 per cent for dizygotic twins suggesting that delinquency may indeed run within families. However, the slender differences between MZ and DZ concordance rates favour shared environment as being critical.

Twin studies depend on accurate assessment of zygosity. They are significantly affected by attrition bias where the non-participating families are likely to have higher risks of psychopathology. Twins also share prenatal environmental influences which may minimise solely genetic effects. Twin pregnancies are also complicated by higher risk of perinatal complications including premature births and low birth weight. This would be of particular import in twin studies of intellectual disabilities (Rutter *et al.* 1999a).

Adoption studies

Adoption studies have been used as natural experiments to clarify the distinction between genetic and environmental influences. The premise is that high rates of disorder in biological but not adoptive parents would suggest genetic influences.

Adoption studies use different paradigms to look at rates of disorders among adopted offspring of affected parents. They compare the rates of disorder in biological and adoptive parents. They also compare the rates of the disorder in adoptees with affected biological parents/unaffected adoptive parents with those where both set of parents are affected.

Mednick *et al.* (1986) showed that rates of criminal behaviours were higher in adoptive parents but the rates were higher still if both biological and adoptive parents were affected. Adoption studies by Cloninger and Gottesman (1987) and Cadoret *et al.* (1995) substantiate that though genetic influences are important there remains a significant environmental contribution. Adoption studies may be confounded by effects of significant perinatal influences, biases in adoptive parents being carefully selected and biological parents having higher rates of psychopathology. Assortative mating between two biological parents will significantly influence adoption data.

Some authorities have questioned familial, twin and adoption studies on conceptual and methodological grounds (Joseph 2001). They argue that though twin studies are based on the fact that both MZ and DZ twins share the same environment, this may be a false assumption as MZ twins may be treated more similarly than DZ twins, creating a unique 'microenvironment' that would substantially influence results. Adoption studies similarly are subject to selective placement factors. Joseph argues that despite various methodological problems, in the main the bulk of adoption and twin studies do not support a genetic basis for antisocial behaviours.

Studies have also separated data from twin and adoption studies based on age, where it has been suggested that shared genetic factors are particularly important in the persistence of antisocial behaviours into adulthood (Holmes and Thapar 2004). It would seem important to know whether this remains true in young persons with developmental disability (Hodapp and Dykens 2009). Genetic influences also seem to be more prominent for non-violent delinquency as compared to violent criminality (Rhee and Waldman 2007).

Gender differences have been postulated in juveniles in that there is greater support for a genetically mediated trajectory of aggressive behaviours in girls whereas an environmentally mediated trajectory to non-aggressive behaviours is better supported in boys (Tuvblad, Eley and Lichtenstein 2005). Heritability is also significantly influenced by the presence of co-morbid disorders, especially hyperactivity (Silberg, Meyer and Pickles 1996).

In the study of a particular risk factor in the form of callous unemotional traits it was found that genetic factors accounted for two-thirds of the difference between children with this trait and the population, particularly in children with significant group heritability and lack of shared environmental influences (Viding *et al.* 2005).

Molecular genetics

Molecular genetics seek to discover the genetic mechanisms of individual disorders or conditions. It elucidates *how* genes exert their genetic effects.

Traditional techniques have included association studies, linkage studies and animal models. There have been more recent developments in the form of genome-wide associations (GWA) and the mapping of non-coding RNA (Plomin and Davis 2009).

Linkage studies follow the backward approach from behaviour to genes in tracing the co-inheritance of a DNA marker and trait within families to detect genes with large effect size. This has proved to be a particularly fruitful approach in single gene disorders with a clear phenotype but has not been as successful in neuropsychiatric disorders with complex traits (Plomin and Davies 2009). Linkage studies may have a useful interface with the study of specific behaviour phenotypes linked to known genetic referents within family pedigrees.

A landmark linkage study by Brunner *et al.* (1993) described an association between abnormally aggressive and criminal behaviours and monoamine oxidase A (MAO-A) deficiency in several males with mild mental retardation from single large Dutch kindred. Using linkage analysis the locus was assigned to the p11–21 region on the X chromosome and the causative mutation was found to be a single missense mutation of a single nucleotide of the gene.

Further studies delineated that functional polymorphisms in the MAO-A gene can also mediate the impact of traumatic early life events in the propensity for antisocial behaviours in later life.

In a study by Caspi, McClay and Moffit (2002) involving major longitudinal study of a birth cohort of 1,037 children in Dunedin, New Zealand the researchers examined 442 males in the group for differences in the promoter region of the gene which determines how much MAO-A is produced. The investigators explored the interactions of the participants' genetic endowments with their environmental circumstances in relation to how experiences of maltreatment between the ages of 3 and 11 years affected the later antisocial propensities of participants with either a high or low MAO-A activity. They found that antisocial behaviours were significantly increased in the group that had both low MAO-A activity and a history of severe maltreatment.

It has been acknowledged that children with intellectual disabilities are four to ten times more likely to be abused. It seems particularly pertinent to investigate if similar mediators exist in the population with intellectual disabilities (Hodapp and Dykens 2009).

It is by no means certain that finding the loci will ensure that the multiple genes are found or that their pathogenic mechanisms can be definitively ascertained. Association studies use the forward approach from genes to behaviours in focusing on the presence of candidate genes using DNA markers in coding regions. This allows the study of effects of both individual genes and several candidate genes. However, these studies may only be able to detect large effects and the molecular basis for their effects may be difficult to discern (Steyaert and Fryns 2002).

Molecular genetics has looked at variations in the expression of genes coding for various putative neurotransmitters that may be involved in aggression, particularly monoamines.

Serotonin has been consistently implicated in the neurobiology of aggression (Lesch and Merschdorf 2000). The regulation of 5-HT release from serotonergic neurons via 5-HT1a and b autoreceptors has emerged as candidate mechanisms in animal models. Knockout models looking at targeted disruption of 5-HT1B receptors have been associated with aggression. MAO-A gene codes for the enzyme monoamine oxidase A that plays a vital role in the catabolism of monoamine neurotransmitters including serotonin, norepinephrine and dopamine. There have been experimental studies concluding that MAO-A is less frequently associated with occurrence of aggression in situations of low provocation but significantly predicts behaviour in a high provocation situation (McDermott et al. 2009).

Candidate gene approaches have been used to characterise ADHD which has probable shared genetic etiology with and is a risk factor for conduct disorder (Holmes and Thapar 2004). Dopamine transporter gene DAT1 and dopamine receptor gene DRD4 have been put forward as susceptibility loci for ADHD (Thapar et al. 1999).

Animal models have been used to delineate the molecular basis of the gene environment interaction in producing aggressive behaviours. Mice have been particularly useful in having homologous gene regions to humans. Methods have included study of natural mutations and selective breeding to identify genes with smaller effects.

The transgenic approach is based on the introduction of transgenic mutant genes into the genome. These have been deemed akin to human dysmorphy syndromes in producing behaviour phenotypes that can be studied.

The knockout approach involves inactivation of specific genes with subsequent loss of functions. The impact of this loss of function on behaviours is then used to study the mechanism of action of the gene. These have included targeted disruption of 5-HT1B receptor gene which has been associated with increased aggression in mice (Saudou et al. 1994). Accessible invertebrate and rodent models have been used to delineate experience dependent and sexually dimorphic gene expression in aggression (Miczek et al. 2007).

Recent advances in molecular genetics have included the shift towards genome-wide association studies that aim to sequence the entire genome of each individual with the goal of identifying sets of genes, each of small effect, that can be used to predict and prevent problems in childhood. There has also been particular interest in non-coding RNAs which are deemed to have a regulatory function over the protein coding regions of DNA, which have been the focus of more traditional molecular genetics methods. This method may be particularly fruitful in the study of disorders with polygenic inheritance (Plomin and Davis 2009).

Neural basis for genetic influences

Blair *et al.* (2006), in their study of the construct of psychopathy in particular, have put forward possible specific emotional dysfunctions (reduced empathy and guilt) which are substantially genetically mediated. The genetic influences are said to mediate their effects through the disruption of the functional integrity of the neural systems including the amygdala and orbital and ventrolateral frontal cortex. This manifests in the form of cognitive deficits where a child is unable to form normative negative associations between the distress of others and his or her own actions. This prevents normal socialisation and renders a child at greater risk of learning antisocial behaviours contingent on environmental influences.

Contribution of behaviour phenotype to behaviour genetics

The term 'behaviour phenotype' was introduced by Nyhan in 1972 to describe particular behaviours which are integrally associated with specific genetic syndromes. Flint and Yule (1994) elaborated this definition to include 'characteristic patterns of motor, cognitive, linguistic and social abnormalities which are consistently associated with a biological disorder'. Implicit in this definition is the assumption that biogenetic disorders are causally linked to the behaviours so much so that 'a behaviour phenotype should consist of distinctive behaviours that almost occurs in every case of a genetic or chromosomal disorder and rarely if at all in any other condition' (Flint and Yule 1994). Some authors have merely stipulated a 'heightened probability that people with a given syndrome will exhibit behavioural and developmental sequelae relative to those without the syndrome'(Dykens 1995). In line with this, some behaviours are very unique to the genetic syndrome, such as the type of self-mutilation seen in Lesch-Nyhan syndrome. Other behaviours may be more generic and in some cases may present as an increased frequency of disorder occurring in the general population.

Behaviour phenotypes are of particular interest when it is possible to use the phenotypic features to locate a gene of interest by deletion mapping (Skuse 2000). There have been very few studies looking at behaviours with a polygenic inheritance (Hodapp and Dykens 2009). There has not been any identified syndrome with aggression as sole or primary phenotype. The possibility of a gene directly encoding the entirety of aggressive behaviours seems unrealistic (Brunner 1996). However, several disorders have aggression as a prominent part of their behaviour phenotype.

Within the tradition of behaviour phenotypes, the focus of behaviour genetic research has been the study of dysmorphy syndromes with known genetic causes and established behaviour phenotype (O'Brien and Yule 1995). This may prove valuable in elucidating the mechanisms by which known genetic changes produce their effects on behaviours without the reliance on allelic variants. This has led Harris (2002) to designate behaviour phenotypes as 'portals into the developing brain' (p.625). However, there are several challenges in defining the pathway from the genotype to the phenotype.

The study of behaviour phenotypes is based on several assumptions. The first assumption is that the behaviours are causally linked to genetic mechanism and not merely secondary sequelae to developmental insults. The second assumption is that the relationship is sufficiently direct to enable the elucidation of causal mechanisms (Flint and Yule 1994). Moreover the genotype may be variously expressed in each individual and may be modified by developmental stage and environmental influences (Dykens, Hodapp and Finucane 2000). The occurrence and phenomenology may also be significantly affected by the severity of the associated intellectual disabilities (O'Brien 2006).

There have been difficulties in defining particular behaviour as a behaviour phenotype especially within rare syndromes with variable expression. The small numbers of cases and also methodological difficulties in evolving validated instruments for uncommon behaviours (Flint 1998) are some of the difficulties encountered.

PRACTICE ISSUES

Ethical implications of genetic research

Despite the science of behaviour genetics being in its nascence there has been considerable speculation about the impact it may have on the practice of forensic psychiatry (Appelbaum 2005). These concerns seem in line with the established tradition of science and theory influencing legal practice.

It has been argued of late that with increasing sophistication within science there is a very real possibility of a fundamental paradigm shift with forensic psychiatry morphing to forensic neuropsychiatry. It has been postulated that better brain behaviour relationship will lead to traditional 'psychosocially determined mental processes being complemented by biopsychosocially determined neural processes' particularly in determining criminal responsibility and guiding more efficient risk assessments (Witzel *et al.* 2008, p.113). It has also been proposed that biological approaches open up further avenues for treatment.

Other authorities have not been quite as sanguine. Eastman and Campbell (2006) have argued that there continues to be a fundamental mismatch between the questions that the legal system asks and the questions that science can answer. This is particularly true of behavioural genetics which looks at predisposition to crime within populations rather than specific intent on the part of the individual. Eastman and Campbell opine that we have not achieved a congruence between biology and behaviour as yet to explain away free will and personhood.

This is particularly true in relation to genetic endowment being used to exculpate criminal responsibility. The defence of 'genetic determinism' has been advanced (Johnson 1998) particularly in the light of the findings of Brunner *et al.* (1993) and Caspi *et al.* (2002) regarding low levels of MAO-A enhancing the risks for antisocial behaviours. This has raised fundamental questions of whether these genetically determined conditions could be deemed to significantly reduce the individual's capacity to choose adaptive behaviours. To date this defence has not been accepted because of the tenuous causal links between enzyme defects and individual acts (Appelbaum 2005).

It has been argued that biogenetic factors may well be introduced as mitigators during sentencing. However, it has been conversely proposed that lack of current treatment options for these factors when present actually heightens the risk of the individual re-offending.

A reasoned stance has looked at how information from biologic influences can guide civil laws modifying exposure to environmental influences (Witzel *et al.* 2008). It may well form the basis for more evidence-based early interventions to modify the trajectory into future criminal behaviours.

Case example

Max was the eldest of three children. His parents separated during his early infancy and he continued to live with his mother and older siblings until the age of six when all the children were taken into care on grounds of neglect, exposure to domestic abuse and physical abuse. There was concern at the time that all children appeared to have poor language development and socialisation. Max had been reviewed by child mental health services in early childhood for aggression and behaviour problems and he moved between several care placements in his teenage years on account of his aggression to carers and property. At the age of 16 Max was 190 cm tall and he was becoming increasingly difficult to control when he became upset or angry. He was charged with intimidating behaviour in public following an altercation at a local shop, when he accidentally knocked over some items with his backpack. During this time his father attempted to re-establish contact. This led to Max attempting to abscond from care; during this time he was charged with arson after attempting to set fire to a wastepaper basket at his care home in an attempt to be moved back with his father. He was found unfit to plead and admitted as a patient to a secure unit. On examination of his karyotype he was found to have XYY syndrome. Max also had significant receptive language and executive function that were much lower than expected, given his IQ which was in the borderline range.

He responded to secure containment and offence-related work, and responded to psycho-education about the behaviour phenotype associated with his condition. He also received specific speech and language and educational input to improve his understanding of language and he was taught problem solving strategies (including aggression replacement training) to help manage his anger. He was able to gain a degree of insight into the impact his tall stature had on his social interactions. He has been able to access a voluntary self-help organisation for persons with his condition.

CONCLUSIONS

Behaviour genetics has elucidated that antisocial behaviours have a high heritability but also exemplifies the complex interplay between genetic endowment and environmental influences. Challenges remain in evolving meaningful and homogenous phenotypes to optimise the innovations arising from the recent advances in molecular genetics.

There is much to hope that continuing progress will enable early identification of risk factors which would lead the way for targeted interventions within high risk groups to limit developmental liabilities. The recent developments in this field also raise important ethical and legal dilemmas if genetic diagnosis and intervention become a reality.

REFERENCES

Appelbaum, P. (2005) 'Behavioral genetics and the punishment of crime.' *Psychiatric services 56*, 1.

Baker, D., Telfer, M.A., Richardson, C.E. and Clark, E.R. (1970) 'Chromosome errors in men with antisocial behaviours.' *Journal of the American Medical Association 214*, 5, 869–878.

Blair, R.J.R., Peschardt, K.S., Budhani, S., Mitchell, D.G.V. and Pine, D.S. (2006) 'The development of psychopathy.' *Journal of Child Psychology and Psychiatry and Allied Disciplines 47*, 3, 262–275.

Brunner, H.G. (1996) 'MAOA deficiency and abnormal behaviour: Perspectives on an association.' *Ciba Foundation Symposium 194*, 155–164.

Brunner, H.G., Nelen, M., Breakefield, X.O., Ropers, H.H. and van Oost, B.A. (1993) 'Abnormal behavior associated with a point mutation in the structural gene for monoamine oxidase A.' *Science 262*, 578–580.

Cadoret, R.J., Yates, W.R., Troughton, E., Woodworth, G. and Stewart, M.A. (1995) 'Genetic and environmental interactions in the genesis of aggression and conduct disorders.' *Archives of General Psychiatry 52*, 916–924.

Caspi, A., McClay, J. and Moffit, T.E. (2002) 'The role of the genotype in the cycle of maltreatment by children.' *Science 297*, 851–854.

Cloninger, C.R. and Gottesman, I.I. (1987) 'Genetic and Environmental Factors in Antisocial Behaviour Disorders.' In S.A. Mednick, T.E. Moffit and S.A. Stack (eds) *Causes of Crime: New Biological Approaches*. Cambridge: Cambridge University Press.

Court Brown, W.M. (1962) 'Sex chromosomes and the law.' *Lancet 2*, 503–509.

Dykens, E.M. (1995) 'Measuring behaviour phenotypes: Provocations from the new genetics.' *American Journal on Mental Retardation 99*, 522–532.

Dykens, E.M., Hodapp, R.M. and Finucane, B.M. (2000) 'Towards Etiology-based Work.' In *Genetics and Mental Retardation Syndromes: A New Look at Behaviours and Interventions*. Baltimore, MD: Paul H Brookes.

Eastman, N. and Campbell, C. (2006) 'Neuroscience and legal determinism of criminal responsibility.' *Nature Neuroscience 7*, 311–318.

Farrington, D.P., Gundry, G. and West, D.J. (1975) 'The familial transmission of criminality.' *Medicine, Science and the Law 15*, 177–186.

Flint, J. (1998) 'Behaviour phenotypes: Conceptual and methodological issues.' *American Journal of Medical Genetics 81*, 235–240.

Flint, J. and Yule, W. (1994) 'Behaviour Phenotype.' In M. Rutter, E. Taylor and L. Hesrov (eds) *Child and Adolescent Psychiatry: Modern Approaches*. Third edition. London: Blackwell Scientific.

Fontaine, N., Carbonneau, R., Vitaro, F., Barker, E.D. and Tremblay, R.E. (2009) 'A critical review of studies on the developmental trajectories of antisocial behaviours in females.' *Journal of Child Psychology and Psychiatry 50*, 4, 363–385.

Geerts, M., Steyaert, J. and Fryns, J.P. (2003) 'The XYY syndrome: A follow-up study on 38 boys.' *Genetic Counselling 14*, 3, 267–279.

Gibson, M. (2002) *Born to Crime: Cesare Lombroso and the Origins of Biological Criminology*. Westport, CT: Praeger.

Goldsmith, H.H. and Gottesman, I.I. (1996) 'Heritable Variability and Variable Heritability in Developmental Psychopathology.' In M.F. Lenzenwegger and J.J. Haugaard (eds) in *Frontiers of Developmental Psychopathology*. New York, NY: Oxford University Press.

Hahn Rafter, N. (1997) *Creating Born Criminals*. Champaign, IL: University of Illinois Press.

Harris, J. (2002) 'Behavioral Phenotypes of Neurodevelopmental Disorders.' In K.L. Davis, D. Charney, J.T. Coyle and C. Nemeroff (eds) *Neuropsychopharmacology: The Fifth Generation of Progress*. Brentwood, TN: American College of Neuropsychopharmacology.

Hodapp, R.M. and Dykens, E.M. (2009) 'Intellectual disabilities and child psychiatry: Looking to the future.' *Journal of Child Psychology and Psychiatry 50*, 1–2, 99–107.

Hofvander, B., Ossowski, D., Lundstorm, S., Anckarsater, H. (2009) 'Continuity of aggressive antisocial behaviour from childhood to adulthood: The question of phenotype definition.' *International Journal of Law and Psychiatry 32*, 4, 224–234.

Holmes, J. and Thapar, A. (2004) 'Genetics in Juvenile Antisocial Behaviours.' In S. Bailey and M. Dolan (eds) *Adolescent Forensic Psychiatry*. London: Arnold.

Johnson, M. (1998) 'Genetic technology and its impact on culpability for criminal actions.' *Cleveland State Law Review 46*, 443–470.

Joseph, J. (2001) 'Is crime in the genes? A critical review of twin and adoption studies of criminality and antisocial behavior.' *Journal of Mind and Behavior 22*, 179–218.

Kandel, E., Mednick, S.A., Kirkegaard-Sorenson, L., Hutchings, B. *et al.* (1988) 'IQ as a protective factor for subjects at a high risk for antisocial behaviours.' *Journal of Consulting and Clinical Psychology 54*, 224–226.

Lesch, K.P. and Merschdorf, U. (2000) 'Impulsivity, aggression, and serotonin: A molecular psychobiological perspective.' *Behavioral Sciences and the Law 18*, 5, 581–604.

Loeber, R. and Hay, D. (1997) 'Key issues in the development of aggression and violence from childhood to early adulthood.' *Annual Review of Psychology 48*, 371–410.

McDermott, R., Tingley, D., Cowden, J., Frazetto, G. and Johnson, D.P.D. (2009) 'Monoamine oxidase: A gene (MADA) predicts behavioural aggression following provocation.' *Proceedings of the National Academy of Sciences 106*, 7, 2118–2123.

Mednick, S.A., Moffitt, T., Gabrielli, W. and Hutchings, B. (1986) 'Genetic Factors in Criminal Behaviours: A Review.' In D. Olwens, J. Block and M. Radke-Yarrow (eds) *Development of Antisocial and Prosocial Behaviours*. London: Academic Press.

Miczek, K.A., de Almeida, R.M.M., Kravitz, E.A., Rissman, E.F., de Boer, S.F. and Raine, A. (2007) 'Neurobiology of escalated aggression and violence.' *Journal of Neuroscience 27*, 44, 11803–11806.

Moffit, T.E. (1993) 'Adolescence limited and life course persistent antisocial behaviour: A developmental taxonomy.' *Psychological Review 100*, 674–701.

Nyhan, W.L. (1972) 'Behaviour phenotype in organic disease: Presidential address to the Society of Pediatric Research (May 1st, 1971).' *Pediatric Research 6*, 1–9.

O'Brien, G. (2006) 'Behaviour phenotypes: Causes and clinical implications.' *Advances in Psychiatric Treatment 12*, 338–348.

O'Brien, G. and Yule, W. (1995) 'Why Behavioural Phenotypes?' In G. O'Brien and W. Yule (eds) *Behavioural Phenotypes*. London: McKeith Press.

Plomin, R. and Davis, O.S.P. (2009) 'The future of genetics in psychology and psychiatry: Microarrays, genome-wide associations, and non-coding RNA.' *Journal of Child Psychology and Psychiatry 50*, 1–2, 63–71.

Plomin, R., Defries, J.C., McClearn, G.E. and Rutter, M. (1997) *Behavioral Genetics*. Third edition. New York, NY: WH Freeman.

Rhee, S.H. and Waldman, I.D. (2007) 'Behavior Genetics of Criminality and Aggression.' In Y.-K. Kim (ed.) *The Cambridge Handbook of Violent Behavior and Aggression*. New York, NY: Springer.

Ross, J.L., Zeger, M.P., Kushner, H., Zinn, A.R. and Roeltgen, D.P. (2009) 'An extra X or Y chromosome: Contrasting the cognitive and motor phenotypes in childhood in boys with 47XYY syndrome or 47XXY Klinefelter syndrome.' *Developmental Disabilities Research Reviews 15*, 4, 309–317.

Rutter, M., Silberg, J., O'Connor, T. and Simonoff, E. (1999a) 'Genetics and child psychiatry: I Advances in quantitative and molecular genetics.' *Journal of Child Psychology and Psychiatry 40*, 1, 3–18.

Rutter, M., Silberg, J., O'Connor, T. and Simonoff, E. (1999b) 'Genetics and child psychiatry: II Empirical research findings.' *Journal of Child Psychology and Psychiatry 40*, 1, 19–55.

Saudou, F., Amara, D.A., Dierich, A., LeMeur, M. *et al.* (1994) 'Enhanced aggressive behaviour in mice lacking 5HT-1β receptor.' *Science 265*, 1875–1878.

Scrivner, C.R., Kaufman, S., Eisensmith, R.C. and Woo, S.L.C. (1995) 'The Hyperphenylalani-naemias.' In C.R. Scrivner, A.L Beaudet, D.Valle and W.S. Sly (eds) *The Metabolic and Molecular Basis of Inherited Disease*. Seventh edition. New York, NY: McGraw Hill Professional

Silberg, J.L., Meyer, J. and Pickles, A. (1996) 'Heterogeneity among juvenile antisocial behaviours: Findings from the Virginia Twin Study of Adolescent Behavioural Development.' In G.R. Bock and J.A. Goode (eds) *Genetics of Criminal and Antisocial Behaviours*. Chichester: John Wiley.

Skuse, D.H. (2000) 'Behaviour phenotypes: what do they teach us?' *Archives of Disease in Childhood 82*, 222–225.

Steyaert, J. and Fryns, J.-P. (2002) 'Psychiatric genetics: The case of single gene disorders.' *European Child and Adolescent Psychiatry 11*, 201–209.

Thapar, A., Holmes, J., Poulton, K. and Harrington, R. (1999) 'Genetic basis of attention deficit and hyperactivity.' *British Journal of Psychiatry 174*, 105–111.

Tuvblad, C., Eley, T.C. and Lichtenstein, P. (2005) 'The development of antisocial behaviour from childhood to adolescence: A longitudinal twin study.' *European Child and Adolescent Psychiatry 14*, 4, 216–225.

Viding, E., Blair, R.J.R., Moffit,T.E. and Plomin, R. (2005) 'Evidence for substantial genetic risk for psychopathology in 7-year-olds.' *Journal of Child Psychology and Psychiatry 46*, 592–597.

Witzel, J., Walter, M., Bogerts, B., Northoff, G. (2008) 'Neurophilosophical perspectives of neuroimaging in forensic psychiatry: Giving way to a paradigm shift?' *Behaviour Sciences and the Law 26*, 113–130.

Chapter 13

ACQUIRED BRAIN INJURY IN ADOLESCENTS WITH FORENSIC NEEDS

Ekkehart Staufenberg and Ernest Gralton

INTRODUCTION

Acquired brain injury (ABI) is an important and sometimes unrecognised cause of disability in a proportion of adolescents presenting to secure services and has serious long-term health, economic and social consequences.

This chapter seeks to achieve the following:

- Raise the readers' awareness of the emerging neurofunctional as well as biopsychosocial complexities and sequelae of traumatic acquired brain injury in children and young people. The goal is to prompt the reader to pursue more specialised studies in areas of particular clinical interest.

- Provide an overview of some of the current knowledge and evidence based in the emerging field of clinical brain injury work in children and young people.

- Emphasise the importance and relevance of traumatic acquired brain injury in the developing brain for all stages of the affected individual's subsequent chronological age trajectory.

RESEARCH EVIDENCE

ABI is one of the most frequent causes of death and long-term disability in childhood (Bruns and Hauser 2003). Long-term follow up of these children indicates that recovery is far from assured and their problems can persist and even worsen (Taylor and Alden 1997). The general public understanding of the problems of individuals with ABI is still relatively poor (Chapman and Hudson 2010).

The second International Conference on Concussion in Sport in Prague (McCrory *et al.* 2005) reached consensus expert agreements on definitional and outcome focused clinical evidence specific to sport-related traumatic concussive injuries to the brain. Standards were set for acute clinical care and future research strategies. The consensus statement posits shared clinical, pathological and biomechanical injury characteristics which help delineate the concussive head injury:

- Concussion is caused by direct trauma to the head, face, neck or elsewhere on the body prompting an 'impulsive' force being transmitted to the head.

- Concussion typically results in prompt onset of short-lived impairment of neurological function that resolves spontaneously.

- Concussion may result in neuropathological changes, but the acute clinical symptoms largely reflect a functional disturbance rather than structural injury.

- Concussion results in a graded set of clinical syndromes that may or may not involve loss of consciousness. Resolution of the clinical and cognitive symptoms typically follows a sequential course.

- Concussion is typically associated with grossly normal structural neuroimaging studies.

- Post-concussive symptoms may be prolonged or persistent.

The UK Paediatric Traumatic Brain Injury Study Steering Group (Parslow *et al.* 2005) sets out clinical epidemiological population data (age range <18 years) for traumatic acquired brain injury and incorporates risk ratios and outcomes set against social deprivation status as ascertained by Townsend scores.

The US-based Sara Jane Brain Project (SJBP) published a 'National Paediatric Acquired Brain Injury Plan' (Voogt, Savage and Jacobs 2009) which formulates a hitherto uniquely systemic model of prevention and care for children and young people with traumatic acquired brain injury; it has yet to be matched by comparable initiatives across other national or across EU countries.

The UK National Institute for Clinical Excellence (NICE 2007) has published guidance for early management of brain injury in document CG056, *Triage, Assessment, Investigation and Early Management of Head Injury in Infants, Children and Adults*, which is due for review in 2011.

The new guidance will address the following clinical domains:

- What should happen before someone with a head injury reaches hospital?

- Who should go to hospital?

- The checks and tests that should be carried out and the action that should be taken once the test results are known

- The care people should receive if they have been discharged from hospital within 48 hours

- The symptoms that healthcare professionals should watch out for after a head injury

- How information should be exchanged between different healthcare professionals

- The information and advice that should be made available to people with head injuries and their carers.

Whilst severe brain injury and moderately severe brain injury are acknowledged aetiologies for change to the lives of both the children and young people as well as their families, it is only gradually more widely accepted that milder traumatic brain injury can also cause medium to long-term adversity. Such sequelae are increasingly recognised to be associated with neurogenetic and developmental predisposing, and precipitating. Hence they potentially maintain individual vulnerability and/or protective variables characteristic not only for a population cohort as a whole, but also for young individual victims of acquired traumatic brain injury.

Neurocognitive, social, emotional and psychological sequelae, including high risk or offending conducts, may some day benefit from emerging neuroprotective strategies – neurorehabilitative approaches which, together with improved preventative framework, including legislation, hope to reduce both incidence and sequelae of traumatic brain injury in children and young people.

The epidemiological studies of traumatic brain injury in children receiving intensive care in the UK report a prevalence rate for admission to intensive care units for children and young people (up to 14 years) of 5.6 per 100,000 (Parslow *et al.* 2005).

The UK Paediatric Traumatic Brain Injury Study Steering Group (Parslow *et al.* 2005) reports a significantly elevated mean Townsend score of psychosocial deprivation for these admissions; ABI resulting from pedestrian accidents remain the most prevalent cause in children over ten years (36%), with a summer holiday peak. The mortality rate in western countries for children and young people with traumatic brain injury is higher than the combined mortality rate from all childhood diseases (National Centre for Injury Prevention and Control 2000).

Both the National Centre for Injury Prevention and Control study (2000) and Read *et al.* (2001) remark that the relatively highest rate of traumatic brain injury sustained by children and adolescents coincides with chronological age strata when physical ability would appear to be exceeding the corresponding developmental maturational milestone and age of the ABI victim concerned (Berney, Favier and Rilliet 1995). The authors reported predominantly low impact injuries in infants and young children. Higher impact injuries resulted from accidents involving motor cars, and more serious falls were more prevalent in children over nine years of age. These reported findings are broadly consistent across the UK and the US National Epidemiological Studies (Parslow *et al.* 2005; Voogt, Savage and Jacobs 2009).

The highest incidence of ABI is children aged up to four years and adolescents aged 15–19. Some studies suggest that the most common sources of ABI for children below 14 are falls and for the 15–25 year age group it is more likely to be motor vehicle accidents (particularly motorbikes) and sporting injuries (Browne and Lam 2006; McKinlay *et al.* 2008; Weiss, Agimi and Steiner 2010). Overall ABI is more common in males (Langlois, Rutland-Brown and Wald 2006).

Infants and young children who are claimed to have suffered 'shaken baby syndrome' are in fact more likely to have suffered blunt trauma, often by throwing against a hard surface (Duhaime *et al.* 1987). In adolescents there is increasing concern about the occurrence of ABI that is a result of inter-juvenile assault (Lundy *et al.* 2010).

Traumatic acquired brain injury in childhood and young people

Traumatic brain injuries are customarily characterised as those injuries to the brain tissue which result from an external impact on the skull. Alternatively, and more rarely, traumatic brain injury may arise from circumstances in which no direct impact on the skull takes place. Acceleration/deceleration mechanisms of brain matter precipitates the pathophysiological processes and mechanisms underlying acute, but also medium term and longer term traumatic brain injury and related outcomes.

In the acute phase after ABI the severity of injury is usually categorised as mild, moderate or severe according to the Glasgow Coma Scale (GCS) (Teasdale and Murray 2000). The Paediatric Glasgow Coma Scale for Children's validity and reliability as compared with its adult parent version has recently been reported. Holmes *et al.* (2005), to date the largest epidemiological study, divided 2043 children and young people into two cohorts (cohort 1 (N=327): < 2 years, and cohort 2 (N=1716): > 2 years). Comparing the two patient groups with findings on CT scans, the Paediatric Glasgow Coma Scale outperformed the standard GCS for children under two years of age in the evaluation of the severity of the blunt traumatic brain injury. The Paediatric Glasgow Coma Scale was found to be particularly accurate in its evaluation of pre-verbal children with regards to the need for acute intervention as indicated and correlated with CT findings (Holmes *et al.* 2005).

A range of common, core symptoms of ABI has been described (Matouk and Kulkarni 2007; Miller 1993; Parslow *et al.* 2005). The categorisation of severity of a traumatic brain injury (with or without an associated skull fracture) employs composite strands of information including clinical observations, and neuroradiological as well as psychometric and neuropsychiatric signs and symptoms.

Signs and symptoms associated with mild head injury:

- raised, swollen and/or bruised area over site of impact

- laceration of scalp – differing degrees

- reports of headache

- irritability

- disorientation regarding time, place, passage of time

- light headedness and/or dizziness

- motor imbalance

- nausea

- potential sensitivity to noise and light

- tinnitus

- fatigue/lethargy

- hypervigilance/agitation, e.g. anxiousness with raised motor activity levels.

Moderate-to-severe head injury may include a range of the above symptoms and signs but, in addition, will show clinical signs and symptoms indicative of:

- fluctuations of awareness, alertness and consciousness levels including coma

- persisting headache

- repeated nausea and vomiting

- dysarthria

- post-traumatic amnesia

- ataxia

- hemiplegia or hemiparesis

- temperature dysregulation – sweating/chill

- pallor of skin

- seizures

- perplexion (sensitive/persecutory ideations together with psychomotor agitation)

- irritability

- deep laceration of the scalp

- skull fracture (open and/or penetrating)

- orbital haematoma (*brillenhaematom*, e.g. spectacles haematoma)

- fluid or blood loss from the ear

- rhinorrhoea

- vegetative state

- locked-in syndrome.

There are a range of interacting complex mechanisms that are likely to underlie neuronal cells loss after ABI, some of which may form the basis of a range of future treatments (Stoica and Faden 2010). There is evidence that migrating neuroblasts can replace damaged neurones: there are other hormones such as nerve growth factor that can influence neuronal repair (Chiaretti *et al.* 2008). There are still just a couple of pharmacological agents with any significant evidence to assist recovery after acute ABI in adults (Wheaton, Mathias and Vink 2009). New forms of neuroimaging, particularly diffusion tensor imaging or DTI, are likely to be helpful in monitoring the progress of brain recovery, particularly in adolescents (Wilde *et al.* 2008).

For a comprehensive guide to the assessment of ABI in adolescents see Begali (1992) or Ylvisaker (1998). The most appropriate text for families and social or educational professionals is Semrud-Clikeman (2001).

PRACTICE ISSUES

All adolescents, but particularly those with developmental disabilities, presenting with behavioural problems to secure services should routinely have enquiries about earlier head injury. A history of a head injury with loss of consciousness, sometimes recurrent (but often without medical attention), is quite common in this population. A young person's significant problems following an ABI are frequently misattributed to other factors (Laatsch *et al.* 2007).

ABI is associated with a number of serious impairments including sleep disorders, sexual dysfunction, bladder and bowel incontinence, dysphagia and systemic metabolic dysregulation which may arise and/or persist for months to years post-injury (Masel and DeWitt 2010; Pillar *et al.* 2003). ABI also leads to a significant longer-term risk of epilepsy (Annegers and Pasternak Coan 2000; Christiansen *et al.* 2009) including complex partial seizures that may be difficult to recognise.

There remains a high frequency of hypothalamic-pituitary hormone deficiency patients with ABI, with approximately 25 per cent patients showing one or more pituitary hormone deficiencies. These can include growth hormone (GH) and adrenocorticotropic hormone (ACTH) and pan-hypopituitism (Behan *et al.* 2008). Screening for hypothalamic pituitary deficiency should be a routine in the management of adolescents with a history of ABI (Acerini *et al.* 2006; Niederland *et al.* 2007). Hypopituitarism can remain undiagnosed and untreated in many cases, with serious consequences for adolescent development, recovery and rehabilitation. Not only is GH replacement important in maintaining normal growth in GH deficient adolescents, but it has also been shown to improve cognitive rehabilitation (Reimunde *et al.* 2011).

ABI is associated with a variety of longer-term cognitive deficits including problems with arousal, attention, concentration, language, memory (verbal and nonverbal) and executive function, that is, problems with planning, organising, set shifting, sequencing, judgement and impulse control (Rao and Lyketsos 2000). Slowing of information processing speed seems to be a general consequence of ABI in childhood (Konrad *et al.* 2000). Children with severe ABI have long-term deficits in social problem solving skills (Janusz *et al.* 2002), and these may be a target for specific treatment interventions (Chertkoff Walz *et al.* 2009).

Classifications for personality change due to traumatic brain injury exist in both major diagnostic systems, namely ICD-10 (WHO 1992) and DSM-IV (APA 1994). In children, however, brain injury occurs in the context of brain development, and the long-term impact of the trauma depends not only on the site and extent of neuronal damage but also the stage of brain development. Deviation from development may be a more suitable paradigm than personality change in children and adolescents suffering from ABI (Max, Robertson and Lansing 2001).

Middleton (2001) has identified the constellation of impulsive behaviour – poor attention, increased irritability and anger, disinhibition, lethargy and inertia – as common sequelae of ABI.

In children who suffered significant developmental changes (frequently called personality change by parents and carers) following ABI the most common problems were affective instability followed by aggression, disinhibition or markedly impaired social judgement, and more occasionally, apathy or paranoia (Max *et al.* 2001).

However, many of these symptoms overlap with other childhood developmental disorders including oppositional defiant disorder and attention deficit hyperactivity disorder (ADHD) that may be pre-existing. ADHD, in particular, is a risk factor for developing ABI, and post-ABI children with high levels of psychosocial adversity are more likely to go on to meet criteria for secondary ADHD (Geering *et al.* 1998).

More severe instances of ABI during the preschool years are associated with a marked increase in the prevalence during mid-adolescence of psychiatric symptoms consistent with a diagnosis of ADHD, conduct disorder/oppositional defiant disorder, substance abuse and mood disorder (McKinlay *et al.* 2009).

Children with ABI are more likely to leave school early, experience social isolation and psychologic disturbance, and have difficulty finding paid employment. Their problems may not be evident initially post-injury and they may develop secondary problems of adjustment. Alternatively, they may emerge as the child fails to meet expected developmental milestones (Anderson and Catroppa 2006). There is a strong association between injury severity and outcomes including educational attainment and adaptive behaviour (Catroppa *et al.* 2008). There are high levels of disability incurred by patients even with mild ABI and with more than five years post-injury (Whitnall *et al.* 2006). Young people post-ABI can have relatively subtle balance and gait-related problems (Katz-Leurer *et al.* 2008) that can impact adversely on functional and social performance. Overall, in adulthood, a large proportion of the children who sustained severe preschool ABI are unemployed and socially isolated (Chevignard, Brooks and Truelle 2010).

Criminal behaviour does appear to increase in populations of adults and adolescents after ABI (Farrer and Hedges 2011; Morrell *et al.* 1998). This is likely to be due to the impairments brought about by ABI, particularly impairments in emotional regulation, increased irritability, executive function deficits and impaired socio-emotional communicative skills (Tonks *et al.* 2009). There is also evidence of an elevated rate of some harmful behaviours like increased alcohol consumption following ABI (Horner *et al.* 2005).

Erroneous ideas that a young person has 'recovered' from an earlier ABI can mean that information is not passed on when children make key transitions such as entering secondary education, where developmental demands inevitably increase. Frontal lobe injury in preadolescence may be relatively invisible as the frontal lobe is still 'developmentally silent' – it can manifest several years later when the expected social competence and executive function of later adolescence fails to emerge (Forsyth 2010; Tonks *et al.* 2009).

A treatment programme must be multidisciplinary and include pharmacotherapy, psychological therapy, physiotherapy, speech and language therapy, occupational therapy, remedial education, recreation and vocational training.

The usual approach to rehabilitation is to train individuals to perform various activities using alternative strategies, enabling them to compensate for their cognitive deficits and thus lessening the functional impact of the impairment (Anderson and Catroppa 2006). The Pediatric Evaluation of Disability Inventory (PEDI) is one of the most appropriate instruments to document functional skill acquisition in young people (Haley *et al.* 2010). Computer-based problem solving training for adolescents with ABI has shown early promise (Wade *et al.* 2010). Both applied behaviour analysis and positive behaviour supports have been used, but the best evidence is probably for occupational therapy-based context-sensitive approaches highlighting interventions embedded in functional routines of everyday life. These need to be integrated flexibly together to take into account the individual needs of each young person (Ylvisaker *et al.* 2005).

There are a variety of very well documented neuropsychiatric complications of ABI, particularly depression and post-traumatic stress disorder (PTSD), with more uncertainty about the direct links with psychosis and mania (Kim *et al.* 2007). However, when they do occur they will require appropriate psychopharmacological treatement. Anxiety disorders, mania, dysthymia, depressive symptoms and PTSD are all potential consequences of ABI. Severe obsessional syndromes may develop in up to one-third of children following ABI; this is not associated with the severity of injury (Grados *et al.* 2008). Unfortunately there is relatively little research evidence for psychopharmacological treatment of adolescents with ABI, and the vast majority of the research is from the adult population. Identified seizures need to be treated using agents that do not significantly impair cognition like carbamazepine, valproic acid, clobazam and topiramate (Ylvisaker *et al.* 2005).

Methylphenidate has been shown to be helpful in improving information processing speed in patients with attentional problems post-ABI (Willmott and Ponsford 2009) and on other cognitive domains like memory, executive function, sensory-perceptual-motor skills and global cognition (Writer and Schillerstrom 2009). The best evidence for the management of agitation or aggression after ABI appears to be for for propanolol (Fleminger, Greenwood and Oliver 2006).

Drugs with anticholinergic effects should be avoided at all costs as basal forebrain cholinergic systems are thought to play an important role in brain recovery after ABI (Conner, Chiba and Tuszynski 2005). When antipsychotic medication is required to treat bipolar disorder, psychotic symptoms or behavioural dyscontrol, atypicals are recommended as anti-dopaminergic effects of some medication may impair cognitive recovery (Hoffman *et al.* 2008; Writer and Schillerstrom 2009).

A healthy functioning family unit is critical for a good outcome for survivors of childhood ABI (Perrott, Taylor and Montes 1991). There is evidence for a few specific intensive family supported interventions improving outcomes for young people with chronic impairment after ABI (Braga, Da Paz and Ylvisaker 2005). Children with significant impairments will require long-term management and rehabilitation with particular emphasis on developmental transitions like school and adolescence (Anderson and Catroppa 2006). Sexual development is a particularly problematic issue for adolescents with ABI and requires significant support and intervention (Simpson and Simons 2010).

Considering the significant long-term morbidity of ABI there are still very few treatments based on verifiable outcomes (Laatsch *et al.* 2007). This may be because young people with ABI are a very heterogenous population (Slomine and Locascio 2009). Many young people with ABI do not have access to good long-term rehabilitation options (Di Scala, Osberg and Savage 1997) with the vast majority returning to the family home, regardless of whether this is the right setting to meet their complex needs. Some families encounter very significant stress coping with these young people (Armstrong and Kerns 2003; DeMatteo *et al.* 2006). Children from socially disadvantaged families where access to resources is limited are probably in need of the most ongoing rehabilitation support (Anderson and Catroppa 2006). Community integration is a complex outcome, with many contributing variables. It includes aspects such as independent living, social relationships, schooling and, later in life, employment (Chevignard, Brooks and Truelle 2010).

Follow up for children and adolescents with ABI should be long term and extended into early adulthood, in order to both prevent and treat problems that are likely to emerge with the increasing developmental demands of adult life (Chevignard *et al.* 2010).

Case study

William, a prepubescent 14-year-old boy, was detained in a secure training centre on remand following his arrest on a number of charges including robbery and assault causing actual bodily harm. He had to be isolated from his peers because he was aggressive and unstable. William had a number of previous convictions for violent and non-violent offences with community sentences, but his compliance with the youth offending team had been poor. According to his mother, William had been a very active toddler with impaired concentration but overall he had met his developmental milestones. He had started school at the age of four years and was coping reasonably well.

At the age of six, while riding his bike alone, he suffered a serious head injury as he was not wearing a helmet. He was knocked unconscious (possibly for several minutes). A neighbour alerted the ambulance and he was taken to the local hospital where he was kept in for several days under observation. He appeared to make a reasonable recovery and was discharged without follow up.

His mother reported that following his return to school teachers commented that he found it difficult to integrate back into the class. His ability in literacy in particular appeared to have gone backwards. He was irritable at school and at home and more prone to outbursts of anger and temper tantrums. William's sleep was chronically disturbed at night and he was often awake in the early hours of the morning. His stepfather reacted with increasingly severe physical punishment to William's more frequent outbursts of defiance at home. William was more frequently in violent conflict with peers at primary school and subject to a number of fixed exclusions. He coped particularly poorly with the transition to secondary school, was frequently truant and associated with older more able antisocial youth. On at least one occasion he was quite badly beaten around the head with a stick.

After admission to the psychiatric unit, his overall IQ was 74 but he had more significant executive function and social deficits than predicted by his IQ. Mental state examination revealed recurrent odd gastrointestinal somatic symptoms associated with feelings of intense anxiety without obvious precipitant. William's EEG was found to be abnormal with generalised spike and wave activity in his right temporal area although he had never had any documented motor seizures. His pituitary function was normal but he had significant gross motor dyspraxia. His mood and anxiety improved significantly with a trial of antiepileptic medication and melatonin for his sleep disturbance, and he integrated into a multidisciplinary rehabilitative programme.

CONCLUSIONS

ABI is an important but underrecognised issue in young people with developmental disabilities presenting to secure services. Young people with developmental disability, particularly those with ADHD, are most likely more prone to suffering from ABI. Even relatively mild injury can have serious long-term sequelae for some young people and contributes to worsening of pre-existing developmental problems. Some of the manifestations of ABI can be delayed into adolescence with the failure of key areas of neurological function particularly in the frontal lobes. Obtaining a full developmental history, including ABI, is important to understanding the developmental trajectory of adolescents with complex developmental disabilities who require secure care.

REFERENCES

Acerini, C.L., Tasker, R.C., Bellone, S., Bona, G., Thompson, C.J. and Savage, M.O. (2006). 'Hypopituitarism in childhood and adolescence following traumatic brain injury: The case for prospective endocrine investigation.' *European Journal of Endocrinology 155*, 5, 663–669.

American Psychiatric Association (APA) (1994) *Diagnostic and Statistical Manual of Mental Disorders*. Fourth edition. Washington, DC: APA.

Anderson, V. and Catroppa, C. (2006) 'Advances in postacute rehabilitation after childhood-acquired brain injury: A focus on cognitive, behavioral, and social domains.' *American Journal of Physical Medicine and Rehabilitation 85*, 9, 767–778.

Annegers, J.F. and Pasternak Coan, S. (2000) 'The risks of epilepsy after traumatic brain injury.' *Seizure 9*, 7, 453–457.

Armstrong, K. and Kerns, K.A. (2003) 'The assessment of parent needs following paediatric traumatic brain injury.' *Pediatric Rehabilitation 5*, 149–160.

Begali, V. (1992) *Head Injury in Children and Adolescents*. Second edition. Brandon, VT: Clinical Psychology Publishing Company.

Behan, L.A., Phillips, J., Thompson, C.J. and Agha, A. (2008) 'Neuroendocrine disorders after traumatic brain injury.' *Journal of Neurology, Neurosurgery and Psychiatry 79*, 753–759.

Berney, J., Favier, J. and Rilliet, B. (1995) 'Head injuries in children: A chronicle of a quarter of a century.' *Children's Nervous System 11*, 256–264.

Braga, L.W., Da Paz, A.C.J. and Ylvisaker, M. (2005) 'Direct clinician-delivered versus indirect family-supported rehabilitation of children with traumatic brain injury: A randomized controlled trial.' *Brain Injury 19*, 10, 819–831.

Browne, G.J. and Lam, L.T. (2006) 'Concussive head injury in children and adolescents related to sports and other leisure physical activities.' *British Journal of Sports Medicine 40*,163–168.

Bruns, J. and Hauser, W. (2003) 'The epidemiology of traumatic brain injury: A review.' *Epilepsia 44*, 10, 2–10.

Catroppa, C., Anderson,V.A., Morse, S.A., Haritou, F. and Rosenfeld, J.V. (2008) 'Outcome and predictors of functional recovery 5 years following pediatric traumatic brain injury (TBI).' *Journal of Pediatric Psychology 33*, 7, 707–718.

Chapman, R.C.G. and Hudson, J.M. (2010) 'Beliefs about brain injury in Britain.' *Brain Injury 24*, 6, 797–801.

Chertkoff Walz, N., Owen Yeates, K., Wade, S.L. and Mark, E. (2009) 'Social information processing skills in adolescents with traumatic brain injury: Relationship with social competence and behavior problems.' *Journal of Pediatric Rehabilitation Medicine 2*, 4, 285–295.

Chevignard, M.P., Brooks, N. and Truelle, J.L. (2010) 'Community integration following severe childhood traumatic brain injury.' *Current Opinion in Neurology 23*, 6, 695–700.

Chiaretti, A., Antonelli, A., Genovese, O., Pezzotti, P.D. *et al.* (2008). 'Nerve growth factor and doublecortin expression correlates with improved outcome in children with severe traumatic brain injury.' *Journal of Trauma-Injury Infection and Critical Care 65*, 1, 80–85.

Christiansen, J., Pedersen, M.G., Pedersen, C.B., Sidenius, P., Olsen, J. and Vestergaard, M. (2009) 'Long-term risk of epilepsy after traumatic brain injury in children and young adults: A population-based cohort study.' *Lancet 373*, 1105–1110.

Conner, J.M., Chiba, A.A. and Tuszynski, M.H. (2005) 'The basal forebrain cholinergic system is essential for cortical plasticity and functional recovery following brain injury.' *Neuron 46*, 2, 173–179.

DeMatteo, C.A., Cousins, M.A., Lin, C.-Y.A., Law, M.C., Colantonio, A. and Macarthur, C. (2006) 'Exploring postinjury living environments for children and youth with acquired brain injury.' *Archives of Physical Medicine and Rehabilitation 89*, 9, 1803–1810.

Di Scala, C., Osberg, J. and Savage, R. (1997) 'Children hospitalised for traumatic brain injury: Transition to post-acute care.' *Journal of Head Trauma Rehabilitation 12*, 1–10.

Duhaime, A.C., Gennarelli, T.A., Thibault, L.E., Bruce, D.A., Margulies, S.S. and Wiser, R. (1987) 'The shaken baby syndrome: A clinical, pathological, and biomechanical study.' *Journal of Neurosurgery 66*, 3, 409–415.

Farrer, T.J. and Hedges, D.W. (2011) 'Prevalence of traumatic brain injury in incarcerated groups compared to the general population: A meta-analysis.' *Progress in Neuropsychopharmacology and Biological Psychiatry 35*, 2, 390–394.

Fleminger, S., Greenwood, R.J. and Oliver, D.L. (2006) 'Pharmacological management for agitation and aggression in people with acquired brain injury.' *Cochrane Database of Systematic Reviews 4*, CD003299.

Forsyth, R.J. (2010) 'Back to the future: Rehabilitation of children after brain injury.' *Archives of Disease in Childhood 95*, 7, 554–559.

Geering, J.P., Brady, K.D., Chen, A., Vasa, R. *et al.* (1998) 'Premorbid prevalence of ADHD and development of secondary ADHD after closed head injury.' *Journal of the American Academy of Child and Adolescent Psychiatry 37*, 6, 647–654.

Grados, M.A., Vasa, R.A., Riddle, R.A., Slomine, B.S. *et al.* (2008) 'New onset obsessive-compulsive symptoms in children and adolescents with severe traumatic brain injury.' *Depression and Anxiety 25*, 5, 398–407.

Haley, S.M., Coster, W.I., Kao, Y.C., Dumas, H.M. *et al.* (2010) 'Lessons from use of the pediatric evaluation of disability inventory: Where do we go from here?' *Pediatric Physical Therapy 22*, 1, 69–75.

Hoffman, A.N., Cheng, J.P., Zafonte, R.D. and Kline, A.E. (2008) 'Administration of haloperidol and risperidone after neurobehavioral testing hinders the recovery of traumatic brain injury-induced deficits.' *Life Sciences 83*, 17–18, 602–607.

Holmes, J.F., Palchak, M.J., McFarlane, T. and Kuppermann, N. (2005) 'Performance of the paediatric Glasgow coma scale in children with blunt head trauma.' *Academic Emergency Medicine* 12, 9, 814–181.

Horner, M.D., Ferguson, P.L., Selassie, A.W., Labbate, L.A., Kniele, K. and Corrigan, J.D. (2005) 'Patterns of alcohol use 1 year after traumatic brain injury: A population-based, epidemiological study.' *Journal of the International Neuropsychological Society 11*, 3, 322–330.

Janusz, J., Kirkwood, M., Yeates, K. and Taylor, H. (2002) 'Social problem-solving skills in children with traumatic brain injury: Long-term outcomes and prediction of social competence.' *Child Neuropsychology 8*, 3, 179–194.

Katz-Leurer, M., Rotem, H., Lewitus, H., Keren, O. and Meyer, S. (2008) 'Relationship between balance abilities and gait characteristics in children with post-traumatic brain injury.' *Brain Injury 22*, 2, 153–159.

Kim, E., Lauterbach, E.C., Reeve, A., Arciniegas, D.B. *et al.* (2007) 'Neuropsychiatric complications of traumatic brain injury.' *Journal of Neuropsychiatry and Clinical Neurosciences 19*, 106–127.

Konrad, K., Gauggel, S., Manz, A. and Schöll, M. (2000) 'Inhibitory control in children with traumatic brain injury (TBI) and children with attention deficit/hyperactivity disorder (ADHD).' *Brain Injury 14*, 10, 859–875.

Laatsch, L., Harrington, D., Hotz, G., Marcantuono, J. *et al.* (2007) 'An evidence-based review of cognitive and behavioral rehabilitation treatment studies in children with acquired brain injury.' *Journal of Head Trauma Rehabilitation 22*, 4, 248–256.

Langlois, J.A., Rutland-Brown, W. and Wald, M.M. (2006) 'The epidemiology and impact of traumatic brain injury: A brief overview.' *Journal of Head Trauma Rehabilitation 21*, 5, 375–378.

Lundy, C.T., Woodthorpe, C., Hedderly, T.J., Chandler, C., Lasoye, T. and McCormick, D. (2010) 'Outcome and cost of childhood brain injury following assault by young people.' *Emergency Medicine Journal 27*, 9, 659–662.

Masel, B. and DeWitt, D. (2010) 'Traumatic brain injury: A disease process, not an event.' *Journal of Neurotrauma 27*, 8, 1529–1540.

Matouk, C.H. and Kulkarni, A.V. (2007) 'Acute brain injury.' In D. MacGregor, A. Kulkarni, P. Dirks and P. Rumney (eds) *Head Injury in Children and Adolescence*. London: McKeith Press.

Max, J.E., Robertson, B.A.M. and Lansing, A.E. (2001) 'The phenomenology of personality change due to traumatic brain injury in children and adolescents.' *Journal of Neuropsychiatry and Clinical Neurosciences 13*, 161–170.

McCrory, P., Johnston, K., Meeuwisse, W., Aubry, M. *et al.* (2005) 'Summary and agreement statement of the 2nd international conference on concussion in sport, Prague 2004.' *British Journal of Sports Medicine 39*, i78–i86.

McKinlay, A., Grace, R., Horwood, J., Fergusson, D. and MacFarlane, M. (2009) 'Adolescent psychiatric symptoms following preschool childhood mild traumatic brain injury: Evidence from a birth cohort.' *Journal of Head Trauma Rehabilitation 24*, 3, 221–227.

McKinlay, A., Grace, R.C., Horwood, L.J., Fergusson, D.M., Ridder, E.M. and MacFarlane, M.R. (2008) 'Prevalence of traumatic brain injury among children, adolescents and young adults: Prospective evidence from a birth cohort.' *Brain Injury 22*, 2, 175–181.

Middleton, J.A. (2001) 'Brain injury in children and adolescents.' *Advances in Psychiatric Treatment 7*, 257–265.

Miller, J.D. (1993) 'Head injury.' *Journal of Neurology, Neurosurgery and Psychiatry 65*, 5, 440–447.

Morrell, R.F., Merbitz, C.T., Jain, S. and Jain, S. (1998) 'Traumatic brain injury in prisoners.' *Journal of Offender Rehabilitation 27*, 3–4, 1–8.

National Centre for Injury Prevention and Control (2000) *Traumatic Brain Injury in the United States: Assessing Outcomes in Children – Summary and recommendations from the Expert Working Group, Atlanta, GA, October 26–27, 2000.* Atlanta, GA: National Center for Injury Prevention and Control. Available at www.cdc.gov/traumaticbraininjury/assessing_outcomes_in_children.html, accessed on 25 December 2010.

National Institute for Health and Clinical Excellence (NICE) (2007) *Triage, Assessment, Investigation and Early Management of Head Injury in Infants, Children and Adults.* London: NHS NICE. Available at www.nice.org.uk/CG056, accessed on 25 December 2010.

Niederland, T., Helga, M., Gal, V., Bertelan, A., Abraham, C.S. and Kovaks, J. (2007) 'Abnormalities of pituitary function after traumatic brain injury in children.' *Journal of Neurotrauma 24*, 1, 119–127.

Parslow, R.C., Morris, K.P., Tasker, R.C., Forsyth, R.J. and Hawley, C.A. (2005) 'Epidemiology of traumatic brain injury in children receiving intensive care in the UK.' *Archives of Disease in Childhood 90*, 1182–1187.

Perrott, S., Taylor, H. and Montes, J. (1991) 'Neuropsychological sequelae, familial stress, and environmental adaptation following pediatric head injury.' *Developmental Neuropsychology 7*, 1, 69–86.

Pillar, G., Averbooch, E., Katz, N., Peled, N., Kaufman, Y. and Shahar, E. (2003) 'Prevalence and risk of sleep disturbances in adolescents after minor head injury.' *Pediatric Neurology 29*, 2, 131–135.

Rao, V. and Lyketsos, C. (2000) 'Neuropsychiatric sequelae of traumatic brain injury.' *Psychosomatics 41*, 2, 95–103.

Read, S.R., Roesler, J.S., Gaichas, A.M. and Tsai, A.K. (2001) 'The epidemiology of traumatic brain injury in Minnesota.' *Archives of Paediatric Adolescent Medicine 155*, 784–789.

Reimunde, P., Quintana, A., Castañón, B., Casteleiro, N. *et al.* (2011) 'Effects of growth hormone (GH) replacement and cognitive rehabilitation in patients with cognitive disorders after traumatic brain injury.' *Brain Injury 25*, 1, 65–73.

Semrud-Clikeman, M. (2001) *Traumatic Brain Injury in Children and Adolescents: Assessment and Intervention.* New York: The Guilford Press.

Simpson, G. and Simons, M. (2010) 'Promoting positive sexual development among children and adolescents after acquired brain injury.' *Social Care and Neurodisability 1*, 1, 19–30.

Slomine, B. and Locascio, G. (2009) 'Cognitive rehabilitation for children with acquired brain injury.' *Developmental Disabilities Research Reviews 15*, 2, 133–143.

Stoica, B. and Faden, A. (2010) 'Cell death mechanisms and modulation in traumatic brain injury.' *Neurotherapeutics 7*, 1, 3–12.

Taylor, H.G. and Alden, J. (1997) 'Age related differences in outcomes following childhood brain insults: An introduction and overview.' *Journal of the International Neuropsychological Society 3*, 555–567.

Teasdale, G.M. and Murray, L. (2000) 'Revising the Glasgow coma scale and coma score.' *Intensive Care Medicine 26*, 2, 153–154.

Tonks, J., Slater, A., Frampton, I., Wall, S.E., Yates, P. and Williams, W.H. (2009) 'The development of emotion and empathy skills after childhood brain injury.' *Developmental Medicine and Child Neurology 51*, 1, 8–16.

Voogt, R.D., Savage, R.C. and Jacobs, H.E. (2009) 'North American Brain Injury Society's seventh annual conference on brain injury.' *Journal of Head Trauma Rehabilitation 5*, 392–412.

Wade, S.L., Walz, N.C., Carey, J., Williams, K.M. *et al.* (2010) 'A randomized trial of teen online problem solving for improving executive function deficits following pediatric traumatic brain injury.' *Journal of Head Trauma Rehabilitation 25*, 6, 409–415.

Weiss, H., Agimi, Y. and Steiner, C. (2010) 'Youth motorcycle-related hospitalizations and traumatic brain injuries in the United States in 2006.' *Pediatrics 126*, 6, 1141–1148.

Wheaton, P., Mathias, J.L. and Vink, R. (2009) 'Impact of early pharmacological treatment on cognitive and behavioral outcome after traumatic brain injury in adults: A meta-analysis.' *Journal of Clinical Psychopharmacology 29*, 5, 468–477.

Whitnall, L., McMillan, T.M., Murray, G.D. and Teasdale, G.M. (2006) 'Disability in young people and adults after head injury: 5–7 year follow up of a prospective cohort study.' *Journal of Neurology, Neurosurgery and Psychiatry 77*, 5, 640–645.

Wilde, E., McCauley, S., Hunter, J., Bigler, E. *et al.* (2008) 'Diffusion tensor imaging of acute mild traumatic brain injury in adolescents.' *Neurology 70*, 12, 948–955.

Willmott, C. and Ponsford, J. (2009) 'Efficacy of methylphenidate in the rehabilitation of attention following traumatic brain injury: A randomised, crossover, double blind, placebo controlled inpatient trial.' *Journal of Neurology, Neurosurgery and Psychiatry 80*, 5, 552–557.

World Health Organization (WHO) (1992) *International Classification of Diseases 10 Classification of Mental and Behavioural Disorders: Clinical Descriptions and Diagnostic Guidelines.* Geneva: WHO.

Writer, B.W. and Schillerstrom, J.E. (2009) 'Psychopharmacological treatment for cognitive impairment in survivors of traumatic brain injury: A critical review.' *Journal of Neuropsychiatry and Clinical Neurosciences 21*, 4, 362–370.

Ylvisaker, M. (1998) *Traumatic Brain Injury Rehabilitation: Children and Adolescents.* Second edition. Oxford: Butterworth-Heinemann.

Ylvisaker, M., Adelson, P.D., Braga, L.W., Burnett, S.M. *et al.* (2005) 'Rehabilitation and ongoing support after pediatric TBI: Twenty years of progress.' *Journal of Head Trauma Rehabilitation 20*, 1, 95–109.

Chapter 14

THE LEGAL CONTEXT FOR ADOLESCENTS WITH DEVELOPMENTAL DISABILITIES
An International Perspective

Teresa Flower and Ernest Gralton

INTRODUCTION

Adolescents are often viewed as disadvantaged when faced with problems that bring them into contact with the law. Individuals with an intellectual disability are more likely than others to experience vulnerability in interacting with persons in authority, to confess, to be found incompetent to testify or stand trial, be led by the interviewer, be denied trial and be sentenced to incarceration (Marinos *et al.* 2008). Young offenders with a developmental disability are over-represented in youth justice settings worldwide (Shelton 2006). Young offenders with conduct disorder are likely to have lower verbal abilities than their peers which may place them at a specific disadvantage in a legal setting (Chitsabesan *et al.* 2007). Young offenders also show high rates of psychiatric morbidity both in community and custodial settings, with a diagnosis of attention deficit hyperactivity disorder (ADHD) being a common co-morbid diagnosis. The developmentally disabled youth is particularly vulnerable in a custodial setting where bullying and coercion may be commonplace.

There are two main legal issues that will be covered in this chapter: the issue of legal responsibility for committing a crime and the capacity to stand trial.

The age of criminal responsibility varies according to jurisdiction. In most countries where the legal system is derived from Anglo Saxon common law, the age of criminal responsibility is usually at age ten, with doli incapax (literally 'incapable of crime') allowing some flexibility until age 14. There is some variation in the age of criminal responsibility in some jurisdictions depending on the seriousness of the crime. In some European countries, the age of criminal responsibility is higher, with diminished responsibility being used for those under the age of 18. Some of the variation is shown below in Table 14.1 (Australian Law Reform Commission 2010; Juvenile Justice Panel 2010); however, the most up to date and comprehensive review of this issue is by Cipriani (2009).

Table 14.1 Age of criminal responsibility	
Age	**Country**
7	Cyprus, Liechtenstein, Malawi, Papua New Guinea, Switzerland, India, Tasmania (Australia)
8	Scotland, Northern Ireland, Australian Capital Territory
9	Malta
10	England, Wales, Remaining Australian States and Territories (New South Wales, Queensland, Northern Territory, Victoria, Western Australia)
12	Greece, Canada, Netherlands, San Marino, Turkey, France, Scotland, Ireland
13	Niger
14	Austria, Bulgaria, Germany, Hungary, Italy, Latvia, Lithuania, Romania, Slovenia, Uganda, China, New Zealand
15	Czech Republic, Denmark, Estonia, Finland, Iceland, Norway, Slovakia, Sweden
16	Andorra, Poland, Portugal, Spain
18	Belgium, Luxembourg

In the US, the age of criminal responsibility varies from age 7 to 10 from state to state but the important question involves the issue of legislative transfer from juvenile to adult court; this is clearly of great importance in countries which have the death penalty. Ireland raised its age from 7 to 12 in 2006 (Criminal Justice Act Ireland 2006). The Law Society in the UK has also called for an increase in the age of criminal responsibility (Baski 2010) but there is no indication that this is likely to occur. There has also been significant debate about the age of criminal responsibility in Australia, including giving the law flexibility depending on a young person's individual level of understanding of their crime (Urbas 2000).

The question of the capacity of intellectually disabled adolescents to stand trial is rarely formally addressed in legislation applying to children and adolescents. Legislation which tackles the associated concepts of fitness to stand trial and mental impairment is usually drafted with adults in mind and may not consider the particular issues associated with the developmentally disabled adolescent. The question of capacity may be avoided by lawyers as this can lead to delays in the trial process and more complicated sentencing. It has been argued that where there is specific legislation drafted for young people who offend this takes into account their developmental needs and is usually orientated to the welfare of the young person rather than having an explicitly punitive role as in adult sentence (Children, Youth and Families Act 2005, Victoria, Australia). The vast majority of offending committed by adolescents is minor and thus will not usually involve lengthy sentences. Legislation concerning fitness to stand trial, if designed for the adult offender, may impose a longer sentence for the young person than the usual tariff for that particular offence under the relevant child and youth act. For example, an intellectually disabled adolescent who is found guilty of assault under youth legislation may have a penalty of a few months supervision imposed by the court. However, if found not guilty as a result of mental impairment under legislation designed for adults, he or she might, in some jurisdictions, potentially face a supervision order of up to 25 years.

RESEARCH EVIDENCE

Evaluation of the issues surrounding children's and adolescents' capacity to be held responsible for their actions and stand trial has not been well researched. There are a number of reasons for this, including a lack of consistency throughout the world regarding the rights and responsibilities of young offenders. Different jurisdictions rely on differing historical contexts regarding the legal status of children's competency; thus common law jurisdictions rely on historical precedent whereas in the US case law is determined by reference to the constitution. This has resulted in quite different approaches to the legal rights of children between common law jurisdictions, European jurisdictions and the US.

In the US, the question of capital punishment has led to the development of instruments to evaluate competency (Grisso and Appelbaum 1998). Whilst there has been some research into developing instruments appropriate for use in children, there is little research which has evaluated such tools in the developmentally disabled adolescent offender population.

Woolard, Repucci and Redding (1996) consider that research regarding children and their legal responsibility should concentrate on first, identifying children's capacities relevant to law and second, identifying circumstances under which their performance varies. Clearly, therefore, the specific legal context in which children are adjudicated requires further discussion. As an adjunct to this, specific research concerning their capacity and performance will be considered later in the chapter.

The MacArthur Competence Assessment Tool – Criminal Adjudication (MACCAT-CA) (Poythress *et al.* 1999) is an assessment instrument that has been designed to look at competence to stand trial. It is a structured interview that uses questions about a hypothetical legal situation that assesses knowledge in three areas: 1) understanding, which focuses on the roles of courtroom personnel; 2) reasoning, which involves recognising information relevant to a defence case and legal decision making, and 3) appreciation, which assesses whether thinking is impaired by other factors (e.g. delusional thinking). It differs from most other competency assessment instruments by having a teaching component. Although the instrument was originally designed for use in adults it has been the subject of a modest number of studies in adolescent offender populations, including those with developmental disabilities (Grisso *et al.* 2003; Warren *et al.* 2003). The authors comment that adolescents tended to make judgements which reflected greater compliance with adults (e.g. plea bargaining) and choices which reflected lower psychosocial maturity. There was an association between lower age, lower IQ and competency to stand trial; adolescents aged 11–13 with an IQ between 60 and 74 were found to have significantly impaired competency in the area of understanding and appreciation. Out of the group of 11–13 year olds, 50 per cent of those with an IQ in the range of 60–74 and 30 per cent of those with an IQ in the 75–89 range lacked the necessary capacity to stand trial. In the 14–15 age group 40 per cent of those with an IQ in the 60–74 range and 25 per cent of those with an IQ in the range 75–89 lacked capacity. Whilst capacity improved with age and cognitive ability, two-thirds of the sample of juvenile defendants had an IQ associated with the risk of being found incompetent to stand trial as a result of impaired understanding or reasoning.

Doli incapax

In some jurisdictions the principle of doli incapax (incapable of crime) applies. Doli incapax is a rebuttable presumption found in common law jurisdictions. It arises from the belief that children are less responsible for their actions than adults (Crofts 2003). It refers to a young person (usually between the ages of 10 and 14) who lacks the capacity to distinguish between an act which is 'seriously wrong' and one which is merely 'mischievous' as described in R v. Gorrie 1918 (Johnston 2006). The onus is on the prosecution to prove that the young person knew that what s/he was doing was seriously wrong at the time of the alleged offence. Doli Incapax was abolished in England and Wales following the trial of Thompson and Venables in 1996 for the murder of James Bulger in the Crime and Disorder Act (1998) while the presumption had been abolished in Canada a decade earlier. In the second reading of the bill on 8 April 1998 (House of Commons 1998), Jack Straw, the then Home Secretary, stated:

> The concept of doli incapax was developed when the major sanction against children who offended was the death penalty. In the days when children were hanged for stealing sheep, it was probably wise for the courts to establish clearly that offenders knew that they had committed a flagrant offence, rather than being guilty of mere naughtiness. Now the sanctions have changed entirely. Lawyers acting for offenders between the ages of 10 and 13 use the presumption of doli incapax incapacity to commit evil – to run rings around the court system, and to avoid proper sanctions for young offenders.
>
> Something else has changed since the reign of Edward III. I think that children now understand the difference between right and wrong at an earlier age…[they] know that when they take someone else's property or assault someone, they are committing an offence for which they ought to be punished.

There continues to be technical legal debate as to whether the bill abolished only the rebuttable presumption of doli incapax rather than the defence of doli incapax. Doli incapax still applies in some states of Australia and in New Zealand (Klinger 2007) and other former commonwealth countries, most often being applied in trials concerning offending committed by developmentally disabled offenders (Bartholomew 1998).

Fitness to stand trial

One of the main legacies of the Magna Carta for the Anglo Saxon legal world is that accused people should be able to participate in their trial which is of course a separate issue from whether they can be held responsible for a crime. In order to participate the accused needs to be able to understand the process that is happening. In common law jurisdictions, criteria for fitness to plead are based upon two nineteenth century cases involving deaf mutes, R v. Dyson 1831 and R v. Pritchard 1836 (Exworthy 2006; Gibbons *et al.* 1999), where it was established that the defendant should 'be of sufficient intellect to comprehend the proceedings, to know that he might challenge any one of you to whom he might object and to comprehend the details of the evidence'. The 'test' for fitness has evolved to fall into four main areas: an appreciation of the charges and the potential consequences for the defendant; an ability to understand the trial process; the potential for the defendant to participate in the process; and the ability to work collaboratively with a lawyer on the proposed defence. In England and Wales, fitness to plead was rarely raised in the nineteenth and early twentieth century as the consequences of doing so were serious. Under the Criminal Procedure (Insanity) Act (1964), there was provision for indefinite detention for those found unfit to plead, thus it was only in the best interests of those charged with committing the most serious crimes to be found unfit. The Criminal Procedure (Insanity and Unfitness to Plead) Act (1991) introduced a 'trial of the facts' before a jury, following a declaration of unfitness and allowed for four dispositions: a hospital order; a supervision and treatment order; a guardianship order; and an absolute discharge. The Domestic Violence, Crime and Victims Act (2004) moved the determination of fitness by a jury in favour of a judge, which is then followed by a 'trial of the facts', determined by a jury. The court then must decide 1) whether to make a hospital order under s.37 of the Mental Health Act (1983) accompanied by a restriction order under s.41; 2) to make a supervision order; or 3) discharge the defendant absolutely (De Souza 2007).

The relevant case law for young people is from R(P) v Barking Youth Court (2002), where a 16-year-old youth with an intellectual disability (full scale IQ of 52) was found fit to plead on the basis of observations of the youth made by justices during the course of the trial. P was granted judicial review in which the procedure of the justices was termed 'wholly inappropriate' and in his judgment, Wright J stated that the matter could be heard in the magistrates court through a combination of s37(3) of the Mental Health Act read in conjunction with the Powers of Criminal Courts (Sentencing) Act (2000).

Procedure for dealing with young intellectually disabled offenders in England and Wales is currently laid down in the Crown Prosecution Service document on legal guidance, *Young Offenders* (CPS 2010). Consideration is to be given to the seriousness of the offence, the circumstances of any previous offending, the nature of the youth's mental disability or disorder, the likelihood of repetition and the availability of any suitable alternatives to prosecution. Prosecutors are advised to consult widely and be aware of the opinions of relevant welfare agencies, 'particularly about the offender's stage of development or understanding of the offence and the perceived likelihood of repetition, the likely effect of proceedings on his or her mental state and the relevant welfare options'. Prosecutors are instructed not to bring cases to court until they have gathered all relevant information and a plea should not be accepted until the prosecutor has reviewed the file. A fair trial involves the following:

- The youth has to understand what he is said to have done wrong.

- The court must be satisfied that the youth had the means of knowing an act or omission was wrong at the time of the act or omission.

- The youth had to understand what, if any, defences were available to him.

- The youth must have a reasonable opportunity to make relevant representations if he wished to do so.

- The youth must have the opportunity to consider what representations he wished to make once he had understood the issues involved (R (TP) v. West London Youth Court 2005).

However, it is not clear that these are principles that can be challenged in court, other than through a formal application to be declared unfit to plead. To an extent, the role of the presumption of doli incapax has been taken up by fitness hearings, articulated by Smith J in her judgment in CPS v. P (2007).

> One of the listed requirements of a fair trial is that the defendant should know that what he is alleged to have done is wrong, which is in effect the test for doli incapax. Thus it appears to me that there is a large measure of overlap between the issues of 'sufficient understanding of right from wrong', fitness to plead, 'ability to stand trial' and 'the fairness of the trial'… A child who, due to immaturity or lack of understanding, does not know that what is alleged against him is seriously wrong may well also…be unable to participate effectively in a trial.

In an examination of fitness to plead in English and Welsh Home Office records between 1976 and 1988, Grubin (1991) found that those electing to be found unfit to plead were predominantly males in their 20s and 30s with a diagnosis of schizophrenia. However, 25 per cent suffered from a significant intellectual disability and, for those under continuing detention, intellectual disability was the prominent diagnosis. A more recent review by James et al. (2001) looked at 479 court referrals to a psychiatrist and found that the most frequent reason for being found unfit was an inability to follow the course of a trial, followed by not being able to give instructions to a legal representative. However, the authors did not survey the mentally impaired population and this research may not, therefore, reflect the situation of the developmentally disabled adolescent.

There is concern from the Law Commission (2010) that the development of the law in England and Wales has been piecemeal and a more coherent approach is now required. A number of parties have suggested that each trial will need to have a different threshold for fitness to plead depending on the complexity of the evidence, an approach not favoured by the Law Commission.

In Australia, whilst following common law, most states and territories base legislation on the 'Presser criteria' (R v Presser 1958). These were summarised by Smith J, of the Victorian Supreme Court (Law Reform Commission 1994) as:

- to understand what he or she is charged with

- to plead to the charge and to exercise his or her right to challenge jurors

- to understand generally the nature of the proceedings

- to follow what is going on in court and to understand the substantial effect of any evidence given against him or her

- to decide what defence he or she will rely upon and make this and his or her version of the facts known to the court.

In the jurisdiction of Victoria, Australia, within the Crimes (Mental Impairment and Unfitness to be Tried) Act (1997) a person may be found unfit to plead on just one of the above criteria.

In North America, the term competency to stand trial is preferred. The ruling in Dusky v. the United States (1960) provides the basis for all US states' statutes concerning competence to stand trial. Grisso *et al.* (2003) have divided competency into the specific functional abilities of understanding, reasoning and appreciation. Understanding refers to the basic comprehension of the purpose and the nature of the trial, reasoning refers to the capacity to supply relevant information to the defendant's lawyer and appreciation refers to the ability to apply information to the defendant's own situation. In the face of an increasing trend for adolescents to be tried as adults (legislative transfer) assessment of competency has become more formalised and a range of instruments for testing competency have been developed.

More recent developments in US law have reviewed the status of the death penalty (Steinberg and Scott 2003). In Atkins v. Virginia (2002) the US Supreme Court ruled against the death penalty for persons with mental retardation as this would constitute 'cruel and unusual punishment', outlawed by the eighth amendment of the constitution. In the decision, Justice Paul Stevens wrote 'Because of their disabilities in areas of reasoning, judgment, and control of their impulses, [they] do not act with the level of moral culpability that characterizes the most serious adult criminal conduct.' In Roper v. Simmons (2005) the Supreme Court voted to overturn the death penalty for adolescents on the grounds that this, too, constituted cruel and unusual punishment. The ruling overturned a previous ruling which allowed the death penalty for ages 16 and above. In their submission to the court, the American Psychiatric Association presented evidence that the adolescent brain continues to mature into the twenties thus suggesting that an adolescent's ability to make appropriate decisions may still be developing (American Psychiatric Association 2004).

Current advances in neuroscience have demonstrated continuing myelination and pruning of the prefrontal cortex throughout adolescence which may in turn suggest that executive functioning may not be fully developed even in late adolescence (Blakemore and Choudhury 2006). Other studies have examined the role of dopamine in the adolescent brain and posited that increases in dopaminergic activity in adolescence are linked to adolescent 'thrill seeking' behaviour (Steinberg 2009). These advances in neuroscience have been received enthusiastically by lawyers in the US, although the significance of the findings appears to have been overstated; it may be premature to draw conclusions about more abstract concepts such as the maturity of judgement and reasoning based on neuroimaging. It is also difficult to predict how useful advances in neuroscience will be for the intellectually disabled offender as brain development in this group has been impacted by a wide variety of different agents such as birth trauma, genetics, head injury, infection and substance use. However, this is clearly an area which will be of increasing importance in the future (Popma and Raine 2006).

Case description

> Sam, aged 15, has an intellectual disability which falls into the moderate range, with a full scale IQ of 55. He lives at home with his mother. His parents divorced when he was five. His intellectual disability was first noticed in kindergarten and he received early assistance prior to attending a special school. Sam's mother works as a hairdresser close to home. Sam is well known in the local community and has a Saturday job in the butcher shop. He enjoys playing electronic games and will spend time at the local internet cafe where he likes to help the owner.
>
> On one occasion the cafe owner asked Sam to help a nine-year-old girl with one of the computers. As Sam leant over to help the girl, it is alleged that he touched her inappropriately in the groin area. The girl became distressed and left the cafe. Her mother informed the police who subsequently interviewed Sam. Sam was later charged with one count of indecent assault.

Sam's mother sought legal advice and their solicitor requested an adjournment from the court in order to obtain a psychiatric assessment investigating Sam's capacity to stand trial and his ability to form criminal intent. The solicitor provided the psychiatrist with background information including a transcript of the police interview with Sam, a copy of the charge sheet and victim's statement, a copy of a recent cognitive assessment and a school report.

The police record of interview commenced with Sam being informed of his rights. However, when the police attempted to get Sam to explain what they had said in his own words in order to gauge his understanding of the caution, he struggled to do so and needed considerable assistance and prompting. Many of Sam's responses to questions were limited to one word answers which did not necessarily indicate that he had understood the question. Sam's mother was present during the interview as the 'appropriate adult', but did not intervene in the interview process.

The following is an excerpt from the transcription of the interview between Sam and the police. Sam is in the process of being informed of his rights:

Q: You may communicate with, or attempt to communicate with, a legal practitioner. Do you understand that?

A: Yes.

Q: Can you tell me what a legal practitioner is?

A: I don't know.

Q: You don't know? Okay. Do you know a solicitor?

A: Yes.

Q: What is a solicitor?

A: When they have a question to you.

Q: Is it like a lawyer?

A: Yes.

Q: Is it lawyers that deal with stuff at court?

A: Yes.

Q: And can help you with advice?

A: Yeah.

Q: Do you understand all that?

A: Yeah.

On reading this transcript, Sam's lawyer had concerns about Sam's capacity to stand trial and requested a psychiatric report. Sam's lawyer forwarded copies of previous psychological assessments including a Wechsler Intelligence Scale for Children (WISC) IQ assessment (Wechsler 2003).

Sam's mother attended the psychiatric assessment with Sam. Sam presented as a tall youth who looked older than his chronological age. His speech was characterised by poor articulation which made him difficult to understand. His fluency and grammar were impaired. He made and maintained eye contact and a good rapport was established. There was no evidence that Sam suffered from a psychiatric disorder. Sam gave no history of substance use and there was no generalised pattern of antisocial behaviour. Sam had a history of ADHD and had been prescribed stimulants in the past.

Sam was aware of the nature of the charges as these had been explained to him. He stated that he had only meant to help the girl. It was difficult to establish any premeditated element to the alleged offence; there was no evidence that he had planned the assault.

When asked about the role of his lawyer, Sam could not remember who this might be. On being prompted he replied 'She's nice. She helps me.' He was not able to distinguish the role she played as distinct from the other 'workers' in his life.

Sam described the court as a 'big building'. He did not understand the implications of entering a guilty plea. He had not heard of a jury. He did not know how he might challenge evidence in court and looked down when the police were mentioned, remaining silent. At this point Sam's mother explained that he was afraid of being 'locked up' by the police.

Examination of Sam's school record indicated that in the year prior to the alleged offence he had also touched a girl at his school in a sexual manner. The school had arranged a course of counselling with a psychologist who specialised in treating sexual offending in developmentally disabled adolescents, and this was still in progress.

Fitness

The report by the psychiatrist indicated that Sam was not fit to plead. In particular, concern was raised about his ability to follow the course of a trial. This was based on likely concentration difficulties given Sam's history of ADHD and his relatively low performance on the language items of the WISC (Wechsler 2003).

The report was forwarded to the Department of Public Prosecutions who did not drop the charges but requested an independent psychological assessment of Sam's fitness to stand trial.

Trial

Sam appeared before the magistrate in the Children's Court. The matter was adjourned and transferred to the County Court as fitness to plead could not be heard in a Children's Court. After many delays, Sam's case was heard as a fitness to plead contest which involved the empanelling of a jury before Sam. Psychiatric evidence involved cross examination of the psychiatric report obtained by Sam's solicitor. In addition to psychiatric evidence, evidence was heard from an independent psychologist appointed by the Department of Public Prosecutions, who estimated that Sam's intellectual functioning was at the level of an eight-year-old. A WISC IQ assessment (Wechsler 2003) had been repeated which demonstrated that Sam achieved higher scores on performance than verbal domains. The jury found that Sam was unfit to plead on all of the 'Presser criteria' (R v. Presser 1958). Sam was then placed on a non-custodial supervision order for a period of five years.

PRACTICE ISSUES

Discussion

Sam's case illustrates many of the difficulties encountered by developmentally delayed young offenders. Sam's was a minor offence but an offence likely to arouse public concern. In many cases, when faced with a young offender who falls into the moderately intellectually disabled range, police may drop the charges or limit their involvement to a caution. Having been charged, Sam presents a dilemma for the legal system as in order for justice to be fair, Sam must be able to participate in his trial. However, Sam's capacity to participate is hindered by his limited understanding of the legal process. As a result of his lawyer seeking a psychiatric assessment regarding his ability to stand trial, Sam's case is adjourned and subject to a series of delays which prolong the adjudication process. Sam is eventually placed on a supervision order for five years thus continuing his involvement with the legal system until he reaches the age of 22. In contrast, had Sam pleaded guilty to the charge, because it is a low tariff offence, Sam might have been placed on probation for 12 months, possibly with no conviction recorded. Arguably, the systems designed to protect the developmentally disabled offender have led to a more serious sentencing outcome for Sam.

The dilemma appears to be between acknowledging the concerns of the community with regard to offences committed by developmentally disabled offenders whilst balancing the need for sentencing and a disposition which acknowledges the disadvantage that these offenders face within the youth justice system.

Psychiatrists are not uncommonly asked to give an expert opinion on the issue of unfitness to plead. There will be some variation between jurisdictions on the number of issues that need to be considered. Evidence of intellectual ability based on historical psychometric testing and records of educational attainment (particularly where educational provision has had to be substantially altered to meet the developmental needs of the young person) can be very helpful. Many of the young people in this category have complex co-morbid disabilities in addition to intellectual impairment and the court may need assistance to understand how these co-morbid problems interact, in particular to adversely affect the ability to advise counsel and to follow the evidence in court. Functioning in a court setting is highly dependent on an individual's language ability, particularly receptive language. Co-morbid conditions like attention deficit hyperactivity disorder can adversely affect concentration and the ability to sit appropriately in the courtroom. High trait anxiety and a variety of sensory sensitivities can adversely affect the ability of an individual with autism to tolerate an unfamiliar setting. Each person will have a unique combination of strengths and impairments that a clinician will need to take into account in advising the court on fitness to plead.

Most legislation does not consider the question of criminal intent in relation to the developmentally disabled youth. In Sam's case it was argued that his offence was not planned or premeditated but impulsive and that Sam lacked a mature understanding of appropriate social behaviour. It is not unusual for developmentally disabled offenders to be charged with sexual offences; often these may be as a result of inappropriate touching of staff or other residents whilst in the residential care system. There is an increased emphasis on accountability and responsibility in the out of home care system and staff may be encouraged to press charges in order that the young offender can learn that such actions are wrong and take responsibility (Crown Prosecution Service 2010). However, it is doubtful that the courts are the right place to reinforce notions of responsibility as the timeliness of the outcome limits this, in addition to the young person's inability to participate in the process.

It has been argued that autistic youth find it more difficult to form criminal intent as they lack the ability to empathise with others and form theory of mind (Barry-Walsh and Mullen 2004). The defence would be that if they cannot understand how another person might feel or react then they cannot comprehend the impact of the offence upon the victim. For example, Joe, an autistic boy, forms a romantic attachment to Clare, one of his classmates. Resulting from social skills deficits he does not know how best to act on his interest. In order to be close to Clare he begins to follow her and even sits behind her on the bus to school. Clare does not appreciate his attentions and becomes alarmed, complaining to the police and describing the behaviour as stalking. However, Joe has no concept of the distress his behaviour has caused, having merely wanted to be in close proximity to the object of his affection. In this case, Joe is guilty of the actus reus but arguably lacks the capacity to form mens rea.

A defence of mental impairment is rarely pursued by young people in the criminal justice system; this is in part due to the more severe penalties they face (lengthy supervision orders in some jurisdictions). It may also be due to the lower incidence of psychotic illness in this population compared with adult offenders (McGaha *et al.* 2001), as most mental impairment defences involve a psychotic illness. Whilst there is little provision made for adolescents in legislation referring to issues of impairment and fitness to plead, there is also a dearth of research, outside of the US, which considers these issues in this population. Whilst sentences are lower and less punitive in the youth courts and procedure is less formal (no wigs and gowns), in many jurisdictions (South Australia is one example) more serious offences are dealt with in the higher courts where children are treated as adults. However, there appears to be little accommodation made by the higher courts to develop a practice which is more youth friendly and easier to comprehend. It was argued that the two young boys who were tried for the murder of James Bolger did not have a fair trial; representations to the European Court of Human Rights focused on the protocol associated with a higher court as a significant factor inhibiting their participation. The inevitable march of the mantra of 'adult time for adult crime' should be reason for examining current legislation and introducing some further safeguards to protect the very young and developmentally disabled offender.

On some occasions the court can make adjustments that may allow a vulnerable defendant to participate and be fit to plead. This can include the judge or magistrate reducing the formality of the process, playing a more active role in advising the various parties and controlling the process, particularly its complexity and pace.

The UK CPS guidelines (Crown Prosecution Service 2010) for assisting intellectually disabled youths at court suggest a number of strategies, including taking frequent breaks, using concise and simple language, taking additional time to explain court proceedings, being proactive in ensuring the youth has access to support, explaining the charge, explaining possible outcomes and sentences and ensuring that cross examination is carefully controlled so that questions are kept short. Other provisions include providing the young person with an intermediary during the preparation phase prior to court (C v. Sevenoaks Youth Court 2009) and allowing the youth to give evidence via a live video link. There is a need for research to examine the success of these measures and the frequency with which they are implemented.

CONCLUSIONS

There is a paucity of information regarding legislation designed to protect the rights of developmentally disabled young offenders. Matters may be dealt with on an ad hoc basis, for example by not pressing charges, or more formally, as has been illustrated by Sam's case. There appears to be a paucity of legislation designed specifically for the needs of young intellectually disabled offenders. For adult intellectually disabled offenders, legislation regarding mens rea is usually designed as a variant of M'Naughten rules. However, the majority of adults who are found not guilty through mental impairment or insanity have been diagnosed with a psychotic illness (McGaha *et al.* 2001). Custodial facilities and placement options are more often designed for the mentally ill population rather than the developmentally disabled. The Law Commission in the UK is proposing a single test for decision making capacity to determine whether someone is fit to plead at the outset of proceedings which would rely on a unitary construct, rather than individually assessing a range of capacities specific to every trial. This may make assessment more straightforward but whether it will meet the needs of young people with complex developmental disabilities remains to be seen.

Further suggestions for change might include separate legislation aimed at impaired and developmentally disabled youth, with more flexible sentencing options. Diversionary programmes have shown to be successful with identified offender groups committing minor offences. For example, in a scheme for indigenous juvenile offenders in the Northern Territory, Australia using precourt diversion, 76 per cent of those diverted did not reoffend within a year (Cunningham 2007). Group conferencing has an established track record for offending Maori youth in New Zealand. Similar schemes are in place for adult mentally impaired offenders. Finally, specialised mental health courts exist in some jurisdictions like Queensland (Queensland Courts 2008) and it may be that a youth mental health court could offer the most consistency and best practice.

REFERENCES

American Psychiatric Association (2004) *Amicus Brief*. Available at www.scribd.com/doc/2071334/American-Psychological-Association-amicus-brief-in-Roper-v-Simmons-Applicable-to-Juvenile-Life-Without-Parole-Campaign, accessed on 25 December 2010.

Atkins v. Virginia (2002) 536 U.S. 304. Available at www.law.cornell.edu/supct/html/00-8452.ZS.html, accessed on 25 December 2010.

Australian Law Reform Commission (2010) *Children's Involvement in Criminal Justice Processes*. Available at www.alrc.gov.au/publications/18-childrens-involvement-criminal-justice-processes/age-thresholds-criminal-justice-pro, accessed on 25 December 2010.

Barry-Walsh, J. and Mullen, P. (2004) 'Forensic aspects of Asperger's syndrome.' *Journal of Forensic Psychology and Psychiatry 15*, 96–107.

Bartholomew, T. (1998) 'Legal and criminal enactment of the Doli Incapax defence in the Supreme Court of Victoria, Australia.' *Psychiatry, Psychology and Law 5*, 1, 95–105.

Baski, C. (2010) 'The age of criminal responsibility is much too low.' *The Law Gazette,* 20 August. Available at www.lawgazette.co.uk/blogs/news-blog/the-age-criminal-responsibility-much-too-low, accessed on 25 December 2010.

Blakemore, S.J. and Choudhury, S. (2006) 'Development of the adolescent brain: Implications for executive function and social cognition.' *Journal of Child Psychology and Psychiatry 47*, 3–4, 296–312.

C v. Sevenoaks Youth Court (2009) EWHC 3088. Available at www.mentalhealthlaw.co.uk/C_v_Sevenoaks_Youth_Court_(2009)_EWHC_3088_(Admin), accessed on 25 December 2010.

Children, Youth and Families Act (2005) Available at www.austlii.edu.au/au/legis/vic/consol_act/cyafa2005252, accessed on 26 May 2011.

Chitsabesan, P., Bailey, S., Williams, R., Kroll, L., Kenning, C. and Talbot, L. (2007) 'Learning Disabilities and the educational needs of young offenders.' *Journal of Children's Services 2*, 4, 4–17.

Cipriani, D. (2009) *Children's Rights and the Minimum Age of Criminal Responsibility: A Global Perspective.* Farnham: Ashgate.

Crime and Disorder Act (1998) Available at www.legislation.gov.uk/ukpga/1998/37/contents, accessed on 5 July 2011.

Crimes (Mental Impairment and Unfitness to be Tried) Act (1997) Available at www.austlii.edu.au/au/legis/vic/consol_act/ciautbta1997472, accessed on 25 December 2010.

Criminal Justice Act Ireland (2006) Available at www.citizensinformation.ie/en/justice/children_and_young_offenders/children_and_the_criminal_justice_system_in_ireland.html, accessed on 25 December 2010.

Criminal Procedure (Insanity) Act (1964) Available at www.mentalhealthlaw.co.uk/Criminal_Procedure_(Insanity)_Act_1964, accessed on 25 December 2010.

Criminal Procedure (Insanity and Unfitness to Plead) Act (1991) London: HMSO. Available at www.legislation.gov.uk/ukpga/1991/25/contents, accessed on 25 December 2010.

Crofts, T. (2003) 'Doli Incapax: Why children deserve its protection.' *Murdoch University Electronic Journal of Law 10*, 3, 1–15.

Crown Prosecution Service (CPS) (2010) *Youth Offenders* (Legal guidance). London: CPS. Available at www.cps.gov.uk/legal/v_to_z/youth_offenders/#a17, accessed on 3 June 2010.

Crown Prosecution Service (CPS) v. P (2007) EWHC 946. Available at www.mentalhealthlaw.co.uk/CPS_v_P_(2007)_EWHC_946_(Admin), accessed on 25 December 2010.

Cunningham, T. (2007) 'Pre-court diversion in the Northern Territory: Impact on juvenile reoffending.' *Trends and Issues in Crime and Criminal Justice 339*, June.

De Souza, D. (2007) 'The concept of unfitness to plead.' *British Journal of Forensic Practice 9*, 3, 7–15.

Domestic Violence, Crime and Victims Act (2004) Available at www.legislation.gov.uk/ukpga/2004/28/contents, accessed on 5 July 2011.

Dusky v. United States (1960) 362 U.S. 402. Available at http://supreme.justia.com/us/362/402/case.html, accessed on 25 December 2010.

Exworthy, T. (2006) 'Commentary: UK perspectives on competency to stand trial.' *Journal of the American Academy of Psychiatry and the Law 234*, 466–471.

Gibbons, P., Mulyran, N., Mcleev, A. and O'Connor, A. (1999) 'Criminal responsibility and mental illness in Ireland 1850–1995: Fitness to plead.' *Irish Journal of Psychological Medicine 16*, 2, 51–56.

Grisso, T. and Appelbaum, P.S. (1998) *MacArthur Competence Assessment Tool for Treatment (MAC-CAT-T)*. Sarasota, FL: Professional Resource Press.

Grisso, T., Steinberg, L., Woolard, J., Cauffman, E. *et al.* (2003) 'Juveniles' competence to stand trial: A comparison of adolescents' and adults' capacities as trial defendants.' *Law and Human Behavior 27*, 333–363.

Grubin, D (1991) 'Unfit to plead in England and Wales, 1976–1988: A survey.' *British Journal of Psychiatry 158*, 540–548.

House of Commons (1998) *Crime and Disorder Bill: Second Reading*, 8 April. Available at http:// yourdemocracy.newstatesman.com/parliament/orders-of-the-day/HAN14654273, accessed on 25 December 2010.

James, D.V., Duffield, G., Blizard, R. and Hamilton, L.W. (2001) 'Fitness to plead: A prospective study of the interrelationships between expert opinion, legal criteria and specific symptomatology.' *Psychological Medicine 31*, 139–150.

Johnston, M. (2006) *Doli Incapax: The Criminal Responsibility of Children*. Paper presented at the Children's Magistrates' Conference. Sydney: Children Law News.

Juvenile Justice Panel (2010) *General Comment Number 10: Children's Rights in Juvenile Justice. Fact Sheet #4: Ensuring Appropriate Age Limits of Criminal Responsibility*. Available at www. juvenilejusticepanel.org/resource/items/D/C/DCI_GC10FactSheet4_EnsureAppropriateA-geofCR08_EN.pdf, accessed on 25 December 2010.

Klinger, S. (2007) 'Youth competence on trial.' *New Zealand Law Review 2*, 235–270.

Law Commission (2010) *Unfitness to Plead: A Consultation Paper*. Consultation paper no.197. Available at www.justice.gov.uk/lawcommission/docs/cp197_Unfitness_to_Plead_consultation. pdf, accessed on 8 July 2011.

Law Reform Commission (1994) *Discussion Paper 35 – People with an Intellectual Disability and the Criminal Justice System: Courts and Sentencing Issues*. Sydney: Law Reform Commission, New South Wales. Available at www.lawlink.nsw.gov.au/lrc.nsf/pages/DP35CHP4, accessed on 25 December 2010.

Marinos, V., Griffiths, D., Gosse, L., Robinson, J. and Olley, G.J. (2008) 'Legal Rights and Persons with Intellectual Disabilities.' In F.A. Owen and D. Griffiths (eds) *Challenges to the Human Rights of People with Intellectual Disabilities*. London: Jessica Kingsley Publishers.

McGaha, A., Otto, R.K., McClaren, M.D. and Petrila, J. (2001) 'Juveniles adjudicated incompetent to proceed: A descriptive study of Florida's competence restoration program.' *Journal of the American Academy of Psychiatry and the Law 29*, 4, 427–437.

Mental Health Act (1983) London: HMSO. Available at www.dh.gov.uk/en/Publicationsandstatistics/ Legislation/Actsandbills/DH_4002034, accessed on 25 December 2010.

Popma, A. and Raine, A. (2006) 'Will future forensic assessment be neurobiologic?' *Child and Adolescent Psychiatric Clinics of North America 15*, 2, 429–445.

Powers of Criminal Courts (Sentencing) Act (2000) London: HMSO. Available at www.legislation. gov.uk/ukpga/2000/6/contents, accessed on 25 December 2010.

Poythress, N.G., Nicholson, R., Otto, R.K., Edens, J.F., Bonnie, R.J., Monahan, J. and Hoge, S. (1999) *Professional Manual for the MacArthur Competence Assessment Tool – Criminal Adjudication (MacCATCA)*. Odessa, FL: Psychological Assessment Resources.

Queensland Courts (2008) *Mental Health Court*. Available at www.courts.qld.gov.au/4428.htm, accessed on 25 December 2010.

R v. Presser (1958) VR 45. Available at www.qcjc.com.au/practice/econtent/1/2/22/the-test-for-fitness-for-trial, accessed on 25 December 2010.

Roper v. Simmons (2005) 543 U.S. 551. Available at www.law.cornell.edu/supct/html/03-633.ZS.html, accessed on 25 December 2010.

R(P) v. Barking Youth Court (2002) EWHA admin 734. Available at www.mentalhealthlaw.co.uk/R_(P)_v_Barking_Youth_Court_(2002)_EWHC_734_(Admin), accessed on 25 December 2010.

R(TP) v. West London Youth Court (2005) EWHC 2583. Available at www.mentalhealthlaw.co.uk/R_(TP)_v_West_London_Youth_Court_(2005)_EWHC_2583_(Admin), accessed on 25 December 2010.

Shelton, D. (2006) 'A study of young offenders with learning disability.' *Journal of Correctional Health Care 12*, 1, 36–44.

Steinberg, L. (2009) 'Adolescent development and juvenile justice.' *Annual Review of Clinical Psychology 5*, 459–485.

Steinberg, L. and Scott, E. (2003) 'Less guilty by reason of adolescence.' *American Psychologist 58*, 12, 1009–1018.

UN Convention on the Rights of the Child (1989) Available at www.unicef.org/crc, accessed on 25 December 2010.

Urbas, G. (2000) 'The age of criminal responsibility.' *Trends and Issues in Criminal Justice 181*. Canberra: Australian Institute of Criminology.

Warren, J.I., Aaron, J., Ryan, E., Chauhan, P. and DuVal, J. (2003) 'Correlates of adjudicative competence among psychiatrically impaired juveniles.' *Journal of the American Academy of Psychiatry and Law 31*, 299–309.

Wechsler, D. (2003) *Wechsler Intelligence Scale for Children – Fourth UK Edition (WISC-IV UK)*. London: The Psychological Corporation.

Woolard, J.L., Repucci, N.D., Redding, R. (1996) 'Theoretical and methodological issues studying children's capacities in legal contexts.' *Law and Human Behaviour 20*, 3, 219–228.

Chapter 15

ART PSYCHOTHERAPY FOR ADOLESCENTS WITH DEVELOPMENTAL DISABILITIES
An Inner World Examined Through Images

Mary Barnes

INTRODUCTION

This chapter will describe the provision of art psychotherapy and the particular advantages of this process when working with adolescents with developmental disabilities and a forensic background. The first section will describe research into working with this client group, and other relevant literature. The next part will explore issues such as referral, assessment, treatment and endings, followed by a case study illustrating the art psychotherapy process.

The basis of art psychotherapy lies within the two strands of art and psychoanalysis; as with other psychotherapies, art psychotherapy depends on building a dependable therapeutic relationship in which feelings and thoughts can be explored as they arise in the session. As the relationship between client and therapist becomes more trusting, links can be made between present behaviour and the patient's past. When these links can be recognised, the young person is afforded the beginning of control over his or her anxieties and impulses, and a feeling of containment.

Art making is central to the process, alongside the building of a therapeutic relationship, so materials are provided for the patients to use as they wish. The content of sessions is not usually planned or directed but within firm boundaries of time and space. The young person is free to bring to the sessions what he or she chooses. Art is able to replace the function of speech by allowing expression of what cannot (as yet) be put into words. In other cases, where the client is very talkative or articulate, words can become a defensive screen for things which are being avoided, and working with art materials can be a way of bypassing this. In this way art can be an expression and a communication, on both a conscious and unconscious level. The art work presented in the case study will be seen to be vitally important to understanding the inner world of a troubled young woman, both for herself and the therapist. In addition to this, the making of the art itself enhanced her feelings of mastery and self-esteem as she grew in skill and confidence.

With this particular client group, attachment issues are paramount as many have suffered abuse and neglect. We know from both observation and from neurological evidence that these issues affect the development of the brain and the ability to make relationships. The case study describes a patient whose life had been characterised by neglect and violence from her carers. The difficult beginnings of relating to this traumatised young woman in art psychotherapy sessions illustrate the damaged nature of her way of functioning and the value for her of long-term therapy.

RESEARCH EVIDENCE

Much has been written by art psychotherapists working with various forms of developmental disability. For example, contributors to Rees (1998) cover a wide range of topics including group work and supervision with this client group. Evans and Dubowski (2001) describe working developmentally, for example, by helping children to advance their skills beyond the scribbling stage towards representation, which parallels a growth in communication and ultimately in the self. In an extensive case study, Case (2005) describes the different approaches she used as different phases of therapy progressed with a child with autistic features and severe confusional presentation. Damarell and Paisley (2008) write of art psychotherapy as useful in times of transition for learning disabled children.

This literature follows the debate about art psychotherapy and learning disability held at a conference at the Hertfordshire College of Art and Design in 1984, where several key papers were presented. Apart from art psychotherapy giving validation to the inner world, the debate asked some important questions: How does therapy work with those for whom communication is impaired? Is it to do with communication or is the art standing by itself as an important link with reality? Is the making of art therapeutic in itself? Is it the relationship with the therapist, sustained over a long period of time which is beneficial? How do the developmental stages fit into the therapy process? The view was expressed that psychotherapy works within a relationship where the clients choose what they will do with the allotted time and materials; that this is particularly significant for a clientele who are often restricted in choice. The participants strongly disputed the prevailing view that developmentally disabled people have no need of attention to their inner life. A purely behaviourist approach, common with this client group, can be focused on only reducing unacceptable behaviour and reinforcing the 'good', which may lead to patients feeling that their anger and frustration are not validated. Sinason (1992) writes of a parallel process in the psychoanalytic psychotherapy profession, where analytic work and research with learning disabled children began in 1989 at the Tavistock Clinic in London. She has explored the trauma frequently suffered by the developmentally disabled, and the tendency of those who work with this clientele to defend themselves against this painful knowledge. Although the literature covers a range of age and disability, the issues explored are all relevant to the specialised work which is the subject of this book.

PRACTICE ISSUES

Art psychotherapy provision in Malcolm Arnold House at St Andrew's Healthcare formerly comprised a full-time post, but at present consists of one part-time therapist working across the four wards of the unit. A designated therapy room with water supply and storage for art work is not available due to shortage of space, which can make consistent work difficult.

Referral for art psychotherapy can be made by any staff member who feels that this treatment will be helpful for a particular young person, with the backing of the multi-disciplinary team. Referrers are asked to complete a form which summarises the patient's difficulties and life experiences. Most importantly, the referrers are asked to comment on whether they feel the patient has an awareness of his or her problems and a desire to work on them. Here we are trying to see if the young person has the beginnings of insight and the capacity to reflect on and explore his or her feelings and relationships with a view to change. In other words can the young person be helped to think, rather than to react and act out?

Once a referral has been made, and a discussion has taken place between the therapist, the referrer and other relevant professionals, the therapist and patient meet to talk about what art psychotherapy entails and its potential benefits. If the patient wants to proceed, he or she will be offered four to six assessment sessions. This is a mutual assessment for both therapist and patient. Can they work together in a productive way? Can the patient persist when times get tough? Can the patient see the point in continuing; can he or she believe there is something worth having?

It is often hard to predict who will engage, and the process of engagement with this client group can take time and perseverance on the part of the therapist. A major contributing factor is that most of the young people have experienced trauma and insecure attachments. Their capacity to trust another person, particularly an adult who is perceived to be in authority, has often been severely tested, if it exists at all. The work of the ward staff, who contain and deal with extremes of behaviour on a day-to-day basis, is a fundamental part of treatment for these young people. For many it is their first experience of feeling safe, contained and cared for, and it is on this foundation that therapy and psychological work can be built.

Engaging patients can be thought about as finding a way of bringing them into what Winnicott (1971) calls a state of being able to play. He says:

> Psychotherapy has to do with two people playing together. The corollary of this is that where playing is not possible then the work done by the therapist is directed towards bringing the patient from a state of not being able to play into a state of being able to play. (p.38)

Winnicott would describe the inability to play as a symptom of mental ill health, and playing as being therapeutic in its own right.

After referral and assessment, weekly sessions are offered. The engagement phase is primarily concerned with building trust and the foundation of a therapeutic relationship. This will be described in the case study, where persistence was needed with a hostile and unpredictable patient who through the art process gradually grew to trust the therapist. As far as possible, the boundaries of the sessions are held consistently, with sessions held at the same time in the same place each week, and notice given of the therapist's absences. This enables a feeling of reliability to grow. Although art psychotherapy is usually non-directive, in this phase it might be necessary to be prescriptive with the patient. As in the case study, sharing the art-making process and playing drawing games can be a helpful way of initiating a relationship.

In the middle phase of treatment, trust has been established and the patient is committed to the sessions, bringing his or her own material to work on. Patients with a learning difficulty can find verbalisation difficult and the therapist needs to help the patients think about what their work is about. Transference issues can arise, where the therapist becomes in the patient's unconscious a figure from the past, usually a parent. When this happens, the therapist will be used as a projection for powerful feelings which might be hostile and rejecting. The therapist can explore this with the patient and make links with the patient's inner world.

The therapist and patient regularly review progress by putting out all the art work and looking at it together. This can be a chance for both to make connections between different pieces of work, or to find new meanings in it. It is also an opportunity to be amazed at what they have produced.

This client group have often suffered abrupt and traumatic separations, so the ending of therapy is important and ideally something that is worked towards in order that earlier endings are not replicated. However, in this setting the practicalities of moving on mean it is not always possible to know a leaving date much in advance, leaving little time for the severing of what has often become an important relationship.

Case description

Anna arrived at the unit at the age of 17 after being placed under a section of the Mental Health Act and detained in hospital for a series of violent assaults. She had previously been held in prison but, because of her moderate developmental disability and features which indicated her having an autistic spectrum disorder, she was accepted for inpatient treatment.

Anna is the oldest child of a large family from a northern English coastal town. Her birth and early milestones were apparently normal but at the age of three, symptoms of disturbance became evident – incontinence, rocking, and failure to thrive. She was placed on the 'At Risk Register' for neglect, but it seems that further intervention from social services was not forthcoming. Anna's mother was reported to be 'emotionally detached' and her father to have a tendency to quickly become aroused to intense anger and violence.

Neglect is defined as a carer deliberately or by inattentiveness causing suffering, or failing to provide the essential elements for a child's development (Children Act 1989). It is highly probable that in Anna's case her mother's inability to provide her with emotional warmth and regulation was a factor in the impairment of Anna's development in intelligence, social skills and ability to regulate her feelings. Early privation would lead not only to impaired development, but to overwhelming anxiety and the building of extreme defences against dependence, factors which became evident in therapy.

When Anna was four, her father left and was replaced by a man whose behaviour towards the children was reported to be abusive and punitive. Anna told me that she had no memories of being played with or of being a carefree child. At the age of 14 Anna ran away to live with her father, who was apparently controlling and violent. It seemed he allowed her large quantities of alcohol, which began to play a big part in her life, along with inappropriate sexual behaviour with himself, his friends and strangers. It sounds as if Anna began to use sex as a way of seeking love and affection, and that alcohol was a way of deadening dreadful feelings of deprivation and emptiness. Anna's behaviour became increasingly aggressive, which can be thought of as violence in response to failed attachment needs (de Zulueta 1993). It is against this background, and at the point when her father said he could no longer cope with her and she had to go, that she committed a series of extremely violent offences and was arrested.

It can be seen from this brief summary that Anna's attachment figures were both neglectful and abusive. This would have prevented the formation of secure attachment, and instead lead to a disorganised attachment, characterised by avoidance, anxiety about closeness, and disassociation. Holmes writes that disorganised attachments are

> associated with traumatic care-giving. Trauma overwhelms and disrupts the psychological immune system altogether. Disorganised responses and narratives lack any clear coherent strategy for self-protection. They are likely to arise when a care-giver is...the source of threat, an extreme example of which is seen in child abuse. (Holmes 2001, p.3)

The effect of this attachment style would be seen in our therapeutic encounter.

Anna can also be considered as typical of what has been called 'complex trauma', a term used to describe the experience of 'multiple, chronic, and prolonged, developmentally adverse traumatic events, most often of an interpersonal nature...and early-life onset' (van der Kolk 2008, p.46). Van der Kolk distinguishes between isolated traumatic incidents which can lead to a diagnosis of post traumatic stress disorder (PTSD), and chronic early maltreatment, which has 'pervasive effects on the development of mind and brain' (p.47) and might lead to complex or developmental trauma in which the victim cannot respond appropriately to minor stresses but instead will react with 'hyperactivity, aggression, defeat or freeze responses' (p.55). There is an ensuing dissociation and disorientation, misinterpreting of events, and the need to be always on guard (van der Kolk 2008).

Referral and presentation

Anna was referred for art psychotherapy soon after her arrival on the unit. However, she was not able to engage in any work at this time because of her overwhelming anxiety and defensiveness. It was decided to postpone therapy until offence-related work with the forensic psychologist had been established. Around 12 months later, by which time Anna had formed a relationship with the psychologist, she was re-referred before the psychologist was due to go on maternity leave. The reasons for referral were given as the need to work with attachment and affect regulation.

Anna presented as an attractive teenager who on first meeting appeared flat and affectless, hardly making eye contact. She was characterised by low self-esteem, extreme anxiety, and anger, all of which lay hidden under a controlled exterior, but which because of her difficulty with regulating her feelings would emerge in sudden angry outbursts or in uncontrollable elation. She expressed despair at having any future and at the indifference of her family, who made no contact with her. She coped with her feelings by withdrawing, often appearing indifferent or cut off from the life of the ward, gleaning sustenance from sitting alone reading. In therapy sessions she often initially gave no sign of recognition or contact with me and I found that she needed to be gently coaxed out of herself at these times. It was only after six months of weekly therapy that Anna began to say goodbye at the end of each session, and to use the therapist's name.

She had difficulty sustaining peer relationships. She was extremely sensitive to anything which she perceived as a slight, which would cause her to retreat. Conversely she was fearful if she felt she might have hurt or offended staff that she liked, was not able to 'read' faces and reactions well, and would be apologetic on these occasions as if she feared she had done irreparable damage.

Engagement in therapy

As previously mentioned, the first few sessions with Anna were difficult. She seemed to feel unsafe and overwhelmed, although less so than at the initial meeting. Her hostility and anxiety were palpable to the therapist. Anna was angry with her psychologist for leaving, and denigrated art psychotherapy, saying she didn't need help and that she couldn't draw or paint, so what was the use?

To allow Anna a sense of control and safety, the therapist made it clear that they would meet for only six sessions and after this she could decide whether or not to continue with therapy. Because of her anxiety about using the art materials, the therapist suggested that she and Anna work together. For example, they might draw on the same sheet of paper, or play variations of the squiggle game where a quick 'squiggle' by the therapist is turned into something else by the patient, and vice versa (see Winnicott 1971). This game allows a 'to and fro' relationship to develop (important when the 'to and fro' of early parent/infant interaction has been missing) and for the possibility of imaginative free association and creativity. Anna also introduced guessing word games, they drew each other, and copied pictures by famous artists. Anna gradually became more trusting within the relationship, but it was noticeable that whenever there was a space between activities she was overcome with panic and would rush around the room shouting and giggling, opening cupboards, 'looking for something to do'. It seemed she had no capacity for inner containment. At other times she was strongly resistant, asking if the therapist would just go for a walk with her, testing the boundaries of the sessions.

In the fourth session the therapist suggested using torn paper to make a collage, because she felt that Anna's denigration of her own abilities was paralysing her. Anna immediately took to this. The tearing seemed to afford her an outlet for anxiety, and the sticking together of the fragments an experience of 'gathering up the pieces'. The first picture was of a little girl holding up her arms as if to be picked up (Figure 15.1). It is important to say that this was a joint activity with Anna working herself and simultaneously directing the therapist in what she should do. She had found a way of having ownership of the work without doing it on her own, for which at that time she had no confidence.

Figure 15.1

She became more committed to the sessions, but was noticeably sensitive to anything which could be seen as criticism, or simply if the demeanour of the therapist was such that she couldn't 'read' it on a particular day. She would furiously accuse her of being angry with her, or thinking she was stupid. The process of tearing and sticking was obviously significant to her and in a later session the therapist reflected that it perhaps mirrored her mental process when she felt to be 'in pieces' and needed to be put back together. Anna appeared to think about this metaphor and be able to understand it. It was the beginning of Anna's thinking about herself and how her work related to what was going on inside her; in other words that the images she made might have some meaning for her.

The collage work continued for several months. Anna's final collage was a self-portrait (Figure 15.2). This piece of work was of great significance for her, allowing herself to be seen, depicted against a grey wall which she said was the wall of the therapy room but also the walls of the prison in which she felt herself to be, metaphorically and literally. She added an image of an angel behind her head, which she said represented a guardian angel who watched over her. In future sessions, Anna often took this picture out and looked at it quietly, saying, 'This is me.'

Figure 15.2

In these early sessions can be seen the establishing of a therapeutic relationship through the art making, in a non-threatening way. This illustrates the concept of the triangular relationship of therapist, patient and art work – the response of each person to the art work, and their response to each other. Making images can be a safe way of relating because the focus is on the image, not the patient. For many of the young people in our service, especially those with autistic traits, a sustained face-to-face encounter might be too intense and confusing. With Anna, 'working with' was paramount, allowing her support but also facilitating her growing sense of mastery and control over the materials. She was established in the therapy, feeling safe with the therapist. Realising the therapy was of help to her, she asked for an extra weekly session.

Middle phase: the drawings

Anna's work now moved to a new phase. Feeling very low after a bereavement, Anna initiated some messy finger painting, in which she revelled. For several weeks she regressed to playing with the paint like a toddler, perhaps acting out an important developmental stage she had missed out on. In addition, O'Brien (2004) suggests, mess-making in therapy can be a way of 'keeping thought at bay', a form of dissociation when feelings become unbearable. The sessions took place in a conference room with no access to water, so the mess had to be contained. However, Anna was largely able to restrict it to the limits of the table, indicating she was still able to access her more adult self.

She then discovered charcoal, a medium of rich possibilities which she was able to use to embody her feelings of loss (Figure 15.3). A series of striking images were made over the following few months. The pictures were still made together, with Anna always asking the therapist to start ('Make the first mark, Mary') and after this intervention being able to continue. The powerful images, full of affect and atmosphere, continued with a series of seascapes, in which tiny boats were buffeted by storms, lightening flashed and jagged black rocks jutted out of the sea. Over time, the drawings gradually became more serene, with beaches added in which two people would sit together or play in the rock pools. The scenes consequently became crowded and intensely colourful, packed with activity and life.

However, unsafe and threatening elements always entered the drawing in the form of red crabs, black rocks, or a figure in difficulty in the water. Anna began to include lifeguards and life-belts in the pictures. As they worked, the therapist would 'wonder aloud' to herself about what the people were doing, why the boats were crashing, what the lightning meant. In response to this, Anna gradually began to think for herself, commenting more on what she had drawn and what it meant to her, bringing up memories and feelings from childhood, as well as relating her pictures to present-day feelings. The therapist encouraged Anna to think about her images rather than just make them, to help her to make conscious the unconscious fantasies and feelings that pervaded them, and thus for her to move on.

It was clear that not only did Anna now trust the therapist, but also that her confidence in herself had grown so that she was able to persist if something didn't work, or could ask for help. Her envy of the therapist's ability, which in the first sessions had come out as furious self-denigration, no longer seemed an issue as she was now creating objects of which she was intensely proud.

Figure 15.3

Finding a face

A year into therapy, despite steady overall progress, Anna suffered a setback when her medication was changed. She had flashbacks and felt so uncontained that she self-harmed and threatened suicide. She felt unable to do much in the next session except to draw a tiny gravestone and female figure, covered in red. It was as if all her confidence and accomplishments had been obliterated. In disgust she poured black paint over her drawing, until there was a pool of black, then screwed up the sodden sheet and put it in the bin. The therapist said she felt this was a very important piece of work; the black mess was showing how Anna had been feeling inside. Anna retrieved it from the bin and began to mould it into a face. She asked the therapist to make a face too and they both struggled with forming faces out of paper so wet it didn't hold together (Figure 15.4, left).

Figure 15.4

Significantly, Anna said, 'Tomorrow, when they're dry, we'll put some colour on them' (Figure 15.4, right). She had retrieved some hope, a connection with the healthy creativity she had fostered over the past year. This was to be the start of an important phase of work, a series of life-sized plaster heads: men, women, children and a baby. It seemed that in some way Anna was making a family, while simultaneously searching for a way of reproducing inner states of mind. The heads went through constant transformation and alteration using paint and plaster. For example, at one point, Anna painted them all white, obliterating the personalities of the different figures, and negating weeks of hard work. She could not account for this but the therapist wondered if she was re-enacting some sense of feeling obliterated herself as a child. Sometimes faces were rejected because their expressions were too harsh or frightening, and the therapist suggested they were evoking punitive authority figures from Anna's past.

This body of work was extremely important, because in a profound way the figures were embodied images of her inner world. It was impossible for her to put into words, but she was able to say they were part of a story that had to be told. It was noticeable that over this period of time she was becoming more separate from the therapist, instead of merged with her, having developed trust in herself through allowing herself to be dependent. For example, she would ask the therapist to work on her 'own' work, as well as working with Anna on hers.

Ending phase

After over two years on the unit, Anna was felt to have matured sufficiently to move to a less secure, adult environment. This was both longed for and feared by Anna. Over the closing weeks the therapist and Anna talked about the changes that she had made within herself over her two years of art psychotherapy and the sadness they would both feel in ending their work together. Anna had clearly gained in self-confidence, and had been able to make a trusting relationship in which she felt accepted for herself. She had also moved from a position of hostility and unpredictability at the start of therapy to make a stable relationship which had the seeds of reciprocity. For example, she would sometimes enquire how the therapist was, or whether she was finding a bit of work difficult; this would have been unthinkable two years prior.

Although Anna recognised there would always be situations which would make her feel angry, she had learned largely to interpose thought between stimulus and action, a process her traumatic early years had failed to provide her with. Struggling with the art materials to make more and more complex pieces of work had provided Anna with a situation where her frustration was tried to its limits, and she learned the capacity to persevere with the difficult processes inherent in making art work. Moreover the therapist was able to act as a model for her in both thinking carefully about the work and its execution, and persisting with the difficulties that arose.

Anna's final images were a consolidation of all her work, a series of delicate plaster models which featured the sea, caves, boats with anchors, and figures. She felt that her images were about safety and hopefulness and it was clear that they were deeply important to her. The therapist was reminded of Louis Bourgeois' statement 'All art comes from terrific failures and needs that we have. It is about the difficulties of being a self because one is neglected... Art is a way of recognising oneself' (Storr and Herkenhoff 2003, pp.124–125).

Before she left, the therapist and Anna reviewed the two years' work, which when laid out covered the floor of a large room. They discussed each piece of work and how it had originated, how it linked together and how it showed a development in Anna's thinking. For example, Anna had forgotten how the black, messy face had been the start of her making heads, and the therapist reminded her of how this had been transformed into a bright multi-coloured 'Picasso' face (Figure 15.4, right). Anna tried to lift the face to see the black beneath. Then she said, 'Look, see how sad the eyes are!'

Looking at the final models, the therapist suggested that they symbolised the point that Anna had now reached, of being able to contain her thoughts and feelings to a large extent, something she had been incapable of when she arrived at the unit. This self-containment could have been the basis for deeper therapeutic work and it was unfortunate that Anna had to move away at this point in time. However, it could be said that her ending was good in that she was able to show normal feelings of ambivalence and sadness, knowing that many people had cared for her and were sad too, and appreciate what she was leaving behind.

CONCLUSIONS

The case study shows how art images made in therapy can be helpful in that they are connected with the self and are symbols that can be thought about. The ability to think about something in an abstract way (mentalisation, or symbolic functioning) is crucial, since for the client group which is the subject of this book, trauma and neglect have often prevented the development of this capacity. The individual will go from stimulus to reaction with no thought in between, resulting in aggression and violence, unless this ability can be developed. O'Brien (2004) writes of how neural pathways which are atrophied through traumatic experience can be developed by the experience of thinking about something with another person, and that the therapeutic situation can provides a consistent container for this work. Holmes (2001) writes that

> The very act of artistic production creates the container for feelings that may have been lacking in childhood and puts the patient into a state of relatedness to himself and the world that may have been stunted in the traumatic environment in which he grew up. (p.11)

Both Holmes (2001) and de Zulueta (2008) see art as an integrating technique which influences the right brain hemisphere where memories and traumatic experiences are stored. For a verbally disadvantaged person, using art materials can be a way to express and communicate difficult thoughts and feelings. Moreover, the opportunity to make a sustained therapeutic relationship can give a reparative experience of attachment, leading to a growth in trust and self-esteem.

Art psychotherapy can thus provide a unique service for patients who are at the beginning of developing a capacity to think, to reflect on their experiences and to make sense of their lives. It is hoped that in some small way what has been outlined in this chapter is the value and contribution that art psychotherapy can bring to the organisation and how it can directly contribute towards the creative and emotional development of developmentally disabled adolescents. In order for this process to be fully effective, art psychotherapy has to be practised in an appropriate and reliable environment so that provision for this kind of intervention is to be fully established and continued into the future.

The contributor would like to thank Angela Foster, Heidi Friis and Tessa Dalley for their valuable contributions, which helped my thinking at various stages in the writing of this chapter.

REFERENCES

Case, C. (2005) *Imagining Animals: Art, Psychotherapy and Primitive States of Mind.* London: Routledge.

Children Act (1989) London: HMSO.

Damarell, B. and Paisley, D. (2008) 'Growing up can be so hard to do: The Role of Art Therapy During Crucial Life Transitions and Change in the Lives of Children with Learning Disabilities.' In C. Case and T. Dalley (eds) *Art Therapy with Children: From Infancy to Adolescence.* London: Routledge

De Zulueta, F. (1993) *From Pain to Violence: The Traumatic Roots of Destructiveness.* London: Whurr Publishers.

De Zulueta, F. (2008) 'Developmental Trauma in Adults: A response to Bessell van der Kolk.' In S. Benema and K. White (eds) *Trauma and Attachment: The John Bowlby Memorial Conference Monograph 2006.* London: Karnac.

Evans, K. and Dubowski, J. (2001) *Art Therapy with Children on the Autistic Spectrum: Beyond Words.* London: Jessica Kingsley Publishers.

Holmes, J. (2001) *The Search for the Secure Base: Attachment Theory and Psychotherapy.* London: Brunner-Routledge.

O'Brien, F. (2004) 'The making of mess in art therapy: Attachment, trauma and the brain.' *Inscape* 9, 1, 2–13.

Rees, M. (ed.) (1998) *Drawing on Difference: Art Therapy with People who have Learning Difficulties.* London: Routledge.

Sinason, V. (1992) *Mental Handicap and the Human Condition: New Approaches from the Tavistock.* London: Free Association Books.

Storr, R. and Herkenhoff, P. (2003) *Louise Bourgeois.* London: Phaidon Press.

Van der Kolk, B. (2008) 'The John Bowlby memorial lecture 2006. Developmental Trauma Disorder: A New, Rational Diagnosis for Children with Complex Trauma Histories.' In S. Benamer and K. White (eds) *Trauma and Attachment: The John Bowlby Memorial Conference Monograph 2006.* London: Karnac.

Winnicott, D.W. (1971) *Playing and Reality.* London: Tavistock Publications.

Chapter 16

FORENSIC ISSUES IN ADOLESCENTS WITH DEVELOPMENTAL DISABILITIES IN COMMUNITY SETTINGS

Sarah H. Bernard

INTRODUCTION

The mental health needs of children and adolescents with learning disability and forensic issues can prove a challenge to community services. The complexities of the assessment include an understanding of risk, the nature of the mental health difficulties, and how the young person's intellectual level impacts on these factors.

Whilst community services for adolescents with offending behaviours are a focus for service development, this is not the case for the group of young people with significant developmental disabilities who offend. Such services remain under-developed and under-resourced, compounded by the lack of an evidence base on which to develop these much needed and often highly specialised services (Hodapp and Dykens 2008). This, combined with the inevitable anxieties these young people create, results in a challenge for the frequently numerous agencies working with the child and his/her family (Bernard and Turk 2009).

This chapter will consider the current evidence which supports the development of community forensic services for children and adolescents with learning disability. The assessment and management of these young people will be considered.

RESEARCH EVIDENCE

The lack of mental health provision for children and adolescents with learning disability is widely recognised and well documented (Allington-Smith 2006;

Simonoff 2005). Community services are expected to provide wide ranging expertise, both in assessment and management (Bernard and Turk 2009; Royal College of Psychiatrists 2004). A multidisciplinary and/or multiagency approach is generally recommended (Bernard 2009).

Adolescent forensic services frequently see young people with mild learning disability. There is evidence that those with a mild learning disability demonstrate a higher rate of offending behaviour when compared to their non-learning disabled peers (Dickson, Emerson and Hatton 2005; Hodgins 1992). Many studies of young offenders with learning disability have concentrated on residential populations including those in specialist education provision and secure units (Gunn, Maden and Swinton 1991; Hall 2000; Richardson 1969).The incidence in a community population is less certain. Studies have indicated that, for those young people with learning disabilities, offenders are more likely to have a mild learning disability, are more likely to have social and communication deficits and psychiatric co-morbidities and lack stability during childhood (Hall 2000). As the intellectual level falls there is an expectation that specialist learning disability services will become involved with young people who present with high-risk or offending behaviour (Royal College of Psychiatrists 2004).

The advantages of community-based interventions as opposed to hospital or institutional treatments have been studied in adolescents without learning disability. The outcomes have been found to be variable (McCord 1978; O'Donnell, Lydgate and Fo 1979). The evidence base for adolescents with learning disability is lacking although interventions for the adult learning disabled population have been more successful (Dinani et al. 2010). Studies of adults have demonstrated successful community-based interventions for the management of anger, sexualised behaviours and fire setting (Allan et al. 2001; Lindsay et al. 2004).

The presentation of the offending behaviours is wide ranging and, in part, dependent on the young person's level of intellectual disability. Those with a mild learning disability, with no additional disabling conditions, present similarly to those without learning disability. Those with more significant learning disabilities and/or co-morbid physical or sensory disabilities or autistic spectrum disorder demand an understand of how their level of intellectual functions and/or their co-morbidities impact on their presentation; this is the underlying aetiology of the offence and their management.

People with autism are recognised as being at a particular risk of offending. Lack of understanding of acceptable social norms and boundaries and a liking for routine predispose those on the autistic spectrum to behaviours such as stealing, sexually inappropriate behaviours, aggression and trespassing (Gabriels and Hill 2007). Obsessions and compulsions can also result in offending behaviours.

In the adult population those with a learning disability and offending behaviour are likely to suffer from a range of disorders, including autistic spectrum disorders and other social and communication disorders, personality disorders, mood disorders and psychosis in addition to the more non-specific label of challenging behaviour. In adolescence the situation is similar although a label of personality disorder is less frequently applied.

Presentations will include aggression to people, property and animals, sexually inappropriate behaviours, fire setting and persistent stealing. This is not dissimilar to adolescents without a learning disability who offend but the offences are less well planned and are more likely to come to the prompt attention of others.

In the past segregation and custodial care was the preferred option when managing the risk posed by people with learning disability who offended (Alaszewski, Parker and Alaszewski 1999). More recently the need for an individualised approach, if possible within the community, has been recognised (Reed 1992). Many of these people can be safely managed in the community albeit with the need for well developed and well resourced services (Cambridge 2007).

PRACTICE ISSUES

The development of specialist mental health services for children and adolescents with learning disability and mental health or behavioural problems lags behind the development of Child and Adolescent Mental Health Services (CAMHS) for their non-learning disabled peers. It also lags behind the development of community services for adults with learning disabilities (Bernard and Turk 2009). This is also the case when considering services for young people with learning disability who offend.

Community services for young people with learning disability have been developed on a tiered model of service. The primary tier is the front-line of clinical service provision and includes general practitioners and health visitors (Lawrenson *et al.* 1997). Secondary levels of service are, in general, unidisciplinary and community based and include school-based services, early intervention services and parenting support. Young people with learning disability who offend frequently bypass these two tiers of service. Once the young person has come to the attention of other agencies it is important to ensure that tiers one and two are aware, and involved with, the young person's assessment and management.

Tertiary level services are multidisciplinary and include local, borough-based CAMHS provision with a range of professional expertise. This might include, in addition to psychiatry and clinical psychology, speech and language therapy, occupational therapy, specialist social work and psychotherapy amongst others. There is not always specialist learning disability provision at this level and service provision will be dependent on local arrangements and resources.

Quaternary services are supra-regional and/or highly specialised services including outpatient facilities, day patient provision and hospital inpatient care. These highly specialised services vary in the expertise they offer depending on the nature of the service. Some will offer management of young people who offend within a learning disability service whilst others will offer this within the forensic adolescent provision.

There is an expectation that the mental health provision for young people with learning disability should be based within the existing local CAMHS provision. This is on the understanding of the need for ring-fenced time and a sufficient level of expertise and commitment from the service. In certain situations, including young people with moderate/severe learning disability and offending or high-risk behaviour, there will be a requirement for quaternary services to become involved in conjunction with the local service provision.

Decisions concerning the assessment and management of young people, whether or not they have a learning disability, should be the least restrictive in order to respect the rights and freedom of the individual concerned. This adds support to the need to develop comprehensive community-based services for adolescents with learning disability who offend rather than considering custodial or residential care as the first or only option.

Routes and nature of referrals

The route into services varies and referrals are likely to come from a wide range of sources. Some young people will already be involved with or known to the criminal justice system including Youth Offending Teams (YOTs), the police, prison, and young offenders units. Others will not be known to the criminal system and are likely to be referred from social care, education or CAMHS.

There is, at times, a perhaps understandable reluctance to involve the police with people who are disabled as there is a fear of labelling an already stigmatised young person as having a criminal behaviour (McBrien and Murphy 2006; McNulty, Kissi-Deborah and Newsom-Davies 1995). Prison, for those who have been charged with and/or have been found guilty of an offence, is not generally regarded as the optimum route of disposal. Instead the psychiatry and behavioural needs of the young person will demand a comprehensive and appropriate multidisciplinary mental health assessment followed by recommendation and implementation of treatment and management strategies. The aim should be to keep the young person in the community whilst ensuring the risks can be safely managed.

ASSESSMENT

As with any assessment, identification of the presenting complaint is the starting point. This, when considering problems of a forensic nature, will be clarification of the index offence or the risk behaviour which has raised concerns.

The boundaries between mental health and social care can be particularly blurred when addressing the assessment needs of young people with learning disabilities. This boundary is, at times, artificial and driven by financial constraints resulting from separate health and social care budgets. Many of these cases will require expensive and prolonged periods of multidisciplinary and multiagency care assessment, management and care.

There will often be multiple agencies involved and identification of these agencies at the start of the assessment process will aid communication and coordination. Access to reports and assessments previously carried out allows for lack of repetition during the assessment and ensures that all information is considered as part of the assessment process. A case manager approach aids coordination of the case as does the identification of keys workers from the, not infrequent, multiple agencies which are involved with the young person.

Identification of the immediate risk likely to be encountered during the assessment process is a crucial part of planning the assessment. This includes an awareness of any specific behaviour that the young person presents with which presents a risk, and adaptation of the environment to ensure safety.

Assessment would, in general, take place over a number of sessions and involve work in the outpatient department and in the community. The child, his or her family, school staff, social workers and any other agencies are all likely to contribute to the assessment. Planning a meeting well in advance optimises attendance.

Consideration of the young person's capacity and ability to consent must be taken into account when assessing the young person. For children under 16 years of age, the child's parents, or those who have parental responsibility, consent on behalf of the child. The Mental Capacity Act applies to children aged 16–17 years but there is an overlap with the Children Act 1989. Depending on circumstances, if the young person lacks capacity, then one, other or both Acts will apply. In addition, again depending on the situation, the Mental Health Act 1983 or the High Court's inherent powers to deal with cases involving young people may also apply. It should be assumed, for young people aged

16 years and over, that they have capacity unless proved otherwise. Even if the young person is assessed as not having capacity he or she must be helped to make decisions. Decisions must be in the best interest of the young person whilst addressing the safety and well-being of others.

The following areas of enquiry should be considered as part of the assessment:

- developmental history including the prenatal period, perinatal events, birth, neonatal period, infancy and early childhood to the current time

- schooling

- separations

- trauma and abuse

- forensic history

- family history

- medical history

- psychiatric history

- network of social support.

Assessment of the young person's psychometric and cognitive profile enables interpretation of the offence or high-risk behaviour in light of the level of the child's functioning. Tools that assist in the clarification of diagnoses might also be helpful, such as the Autism Diagnostic Interview (ADI) (Lord, Rutter and Le Couteur 1994) or the Autism Diagnostic Observation Schedule (ADOS) (Lord *et al.* 2000).

When assessing young people with moderate or severe learning disability, deficiencies and abnormalities of verbal communication can complicate the assessment process. Suggestibility can lead to inaccuracies and, in certain cases, the use of objective measures of suggestibility assist the assessment process (Singh and Gudjonsson 1992).

An understanding of the details of the events surrounding the offence/risk behaviour is obviously a key part of the assessment process. Circumstances leading to the incident, what actually occurred at the time of the incident and the consequences of the incident must be detailed using information from a range of sources. Information obtained should include the details of the investigation of the initial allegation.

An understanding of the child/young person will include discussion of:

- his or her areas of interest

- how the child believes the offence has impacted on him- or herself, the victim and others

- remorse

- future plans for further actions

- placement – home, family, school or other settings such as respite care.

An assessment of the risk which the child or young person poses to him- or herself or other is another key area of the assessment. There are many manualised risk assessment tools such as the Structured Assessment of Violence Risk in Youth (SAVRY) (Borum, Bartel and Forth 2006). Whilst they are of value for those with mild learning disabilities, they become less useful for those with moderate/severe levels of intellectual disability.

At the completion of the assessment, the multidisciplinary team should be able to reach a formulation of the case that includes a multiaxial diagnosis (WHO 1992). The axes of the classification system permit consideration of most aspects of the child or young person's presentation. They cover the following areas:

- Axis I – Psychiatric disorder, for example autism, attention deficit hyperactivity disorder (ADHD), psychosis

- Axis II – Specific developmental disabilities, for example specific reading retardation

- Axis III – Global level of disability (mental retardation): mild, moderate, severe or profound as defined by IQ

- Axis IV – Medical conditions/syndromes including epilepsy

- Axis V – Psychosocial stressors

- Axis VI – Overall level of social disability.

Interventions

The immediate consideration when planning interventions/treatment following assessment is the level of risk posed by the young person and whether he or she can be safely managed in the community. This will depend on several factors including:

- the nature of the offence

- the risk to self and others

- the current placement and the level of supervision that can be provided.

In many situations it will be clear that the young person cannot be managed in the community. This will be the situation for those charged with very serious offences such as murder, attempted murder, serious arson attacks, serious sexual assault and persistent highly aggressive incidents. In other instances the situation will not be as clear. Examples include persistent and escalating levels of aggression, sexually inappropriate behaviours, repeated minor episodes of arson and serious threats of harm to others that have not yet been acted upon. When the situation is unclear it is important that expert services are involved with the assessment of immediate risk.

The child's placement will also dictate whether interventions can be offered in the community. If the child is living at home with younger siblings and the offence is one of sexually inappropriate behaviour then there are clearly risks involved with allowing the child to remain in the home environment. Alternative community provision will demand consideration rather than automatic removal to a more secure environment.

The option and range of community treatment and management will depend on the nature of the offence or the risk behaviour. It will also depend on psychiatric co-morbidities, the child's level of learning disability and other disabilities. Interventions can, and should, be preventative. Therefore, children and adolescents at risk of offending will demand a service in addition to those who have already offended or been in contact with the police.

Interventions to be considered are:

- preventative work
- psycho-education
- parenting work
- behavioural: individual and/or group
- medication
- environmental changes.

The range of behavioural work includes individual and group-based sessions. Issues such as anger management (Rose, O'Brien and Rose 2009), sexualised behaviours and fire setting can be addressed.

There is also a role for medication. This will be either in order to treat a specific disorder such as ADHD, obsessive-compulsive disorder (OCD), psychosis or a mood disorder or to consider the non-specific reduction of aggression and arousal.

The family, school and respite care services will be required to work jointly. This can be a challenge as input might be intensive and is likely to include the management of risk. Assessment of risk has to be ongoing with a clear plan should community work fail or the risk become too great to manage safely.

Transitional planning to adult services must be commenced in a timely manner. The pathway to adult services is frequently unclear. The contractual arrangements for the provision of care for these young people are frequently complex, involving negotiation between many different agencies.

PREVENTION

CAMHS services also have a responsibility to consider prevention of mental health and behavioural problems. Young people with learning disabilities are at an increased risk of offending behaviour if they experience socioeconomic deprivation and instability within the family, and have impaired social or communication skills (McCarthy 2000). Links between early behavioural problems and later antisocial behaviours have been demonstrated (Lindsay *et al.* 2009; Robins 1978). It is thus important that behavioural strategies and interventions target this group.

Case description

Allen is a 15-year-old male with severe learning disability and autistic spectrum disorder. He presented with a longstanding history of inappropriate touching of women's buttocks and thighs. At the time of referral he had been taken into police custody but released without charge into the care of his elderly, single mother.

Allen was born six weeks prematurely following an induced labour because of concerns about severe intrauterine growth restriction. His weight, at birth, was on the 4th percentile for his gestational age. Investigation of his growth restriction revealed no abnormalities. He required oxygen by mask for the first six hours of his life and spent three weeks on the neonatal unit. He was bottle-fed and his early neonatal period was uneventful.

Early milestones were delayed. His mother did not recall him smiling. He sat at ten months, crawled at 14 months and walked at two years. He did not babble or use gestures to communicate. He developed some words but lost these at 18 months. By five years of age he was using single words to communicate.

At play group he showed little interest in the other children apart from stroking their arms and legs in a gentle and non-threatening manner.

From infancy he accessed the child development service and at four years of age he was diagnosed with autism and learning disability. He attended a special needs nursery and moved to a school for children with severe learning disability at 4.5 years of age.

At school he persisted in stroking children's legs. He also started to stroke the legs of strangers in the community. This did not cause significant concerns until he was ten years of age when he became pubertal. It was evident, at this stage, that the stroking behaviour was associated with some sexual arousal. On some occasions the stroking would be followed by masturbation. Allen was referred to the local CAMHS. His case was discussed then immediately referred to the neurodevelopment stream of the CAMHS service.

Allen was fully assessed. The diagnosis of autism was not disputed. Psychometric assessment confirmed an uneven profile, with his verbal IQ being in the severe learning disability range (30) but his performance IQ being in the moderate learning disability range (48). This verbal/performance discrepancy supported the diagnosis of autism.

Allen could not expand on his interest in stroking, simply saying 'I like it.' He did not recognise that the behaviour might be inappropriate. In discussion with Allen's mother and the staff at his school it was evident that the behaviours were presenting a difficulty in all environments and a behaviour programme was instituted. This programme included psychosexual education, distraction techniques, rewards for appropriate behaviours and environmental adaptations allowing Allen private time for masturbation. The strategies were not successful and Allen's behaviour escalated. He would pull people over in an attempt to stroke their thighs whilst exposing himself and masturbating.

Allen was referred to a tier 4 specialist, outpatient service for adolescents with learning disability and offending or high-risk behaviour. As part of this assessment the following were reviewed:

- diagnosis
- psychometry
- functional analysis of behavioural disturbance
- risk
- possible interventions – behavioural and psychopharmacological
- placement.

The diagnosis of autism was supported. Psychometric assessment confirmed the results of previous testing. Functional analysis supported the functions of the behaviour as being sensory and sexual with an obsessive-compulsive element. Some of the strategies that had been implemented by the school were found to be reinforcing the behaviours rather than diminishing them. The risk to others was moderate but likely to continue to escalate.

The multidisciplinary team and the other agencies involved with Allen supported a trial of community intervention that included:

- behavioural management aimed at the introduction of alternative sensory stimulation
- structured private time for masturbation with clear visual cues
- distraction strategies
- trial of medication aimed at reduction of compulsive elements of behaviour (SSRI)
- consistency across all environments with psychiatric and psychological support to school and respite.

Initially, the interventions resulted in a reduction in the frequency of the touching behaviour. This improvement was maintained for several months. The behaviours subsequently became more persistent with prolonged attempts to stroke others whilst being sexually aroused. Reassessment concluded with recommendations for a greater level of consistent behavioural intervention. The behaviours were found to be presenting a high risk to others and Allen's family could no longer manage him safely at home.

Allen was moved to an autism specific residential educational placement with access to a waking hour curriculum, behavioural psychology and psychiatry input. Currently the frequency and intensity of the behaviours have diminished and Allen is accessing educational and leisure activities.

CONCLUSIONS

- There is a role for specialist community services for adolescents with learning disabilities who offend or present with high-risk behaviours.
- Services should be multidisciplinary and be able to work with a wide range of agencies.
- Comprehensive assessment is important in understanding the reasons for the offending behaviour and identifying co-morbidities.
- Risk assessment is a crucial part of community service provision.
- Interventions and management often require a significant allocation of resources as they are likely to be intensive and prolonged.

REFERENCES

Alaszewski, H., Parker, A. and Alaszewski, A. (1999) *Empowerment and Protection: The Development of Policies and Practices in Risk Assessment and Risk Management in Services for Adults with Learning Disabilities.* London: Mental Health Foundation.

Allan, R., Lindsay, W.R., Macleod, F. and Smith, A.H.W. (2001) 'Treatment of women with intellectual disabilities who have been involved with the criminal justice system for reasons of aggression.' *Journal of Applied Research in Intellectual Disabilities 14,* 4, 340–347.

Allington-Smith, P. (2006) 'Mental health of children with learning disabilities.' *Advances in Psychiatric Treatment 12,* 130–138.

Bernard, S.H. (2009) 'Mental health and behavioural problems in children and adolescents with learning disabilities.' *Psychiatry 8,* 10, 387–390.

Bernard, S.H. and Turk, J. (2009) *Developing Mental Health Services for Children and Adolescents with Learning Disabilities: A Toolkit for Clinicians.* London: RCPsych Publications.

Borum, R., Bartel, P. and Forth, A. (2006) T*he Structured Assessment of Violence Risk in Youth (SAVRY).* Lutz, FL: Psychological Assessment Resources.

Cambridge, P. (2007) 'Taking Risks in Assessing and Managing Risks.' In S. Carnaby (ed.) *Learning Disability Today.* Brighton: Pavilion Publishing.

Dickson, K., Emerson, E. and Hatton, C. (2005) 'Self-reported antisocial behaviour: Prevalence and risk factors amongst adolescents with and without intellectual disability.' *Journal of Intellectual Disability Research 49,* 820–826.

Dinani, S., Goodman, W., Swift, C. and Treasure, T. (2010) 'Providing forensic community services for people with learning disabilities.' *Journal of Learning Disabilities and Offending Behaviour 1,* 1, 58–63.

Gabriels, R.L. and Hills, D.E. (2007) *Growing Up With Autism.* London: The Guilford Press.

Gunn, J., Maden, T. and Swinton, M. (1991) *Mentally Disordered Prisoners.* London: Institute of Psychiatry.

Hall, I. (2000) 'Young offenders with a learning disability.' *Advances in Psychiatric Treatment 6,* 278–286.

Hodapp, R.M. and Dykens, E.M. (2008) 'Intellectual disabilities and child psychiatry: Looking to the future.' *Journal of Child Psychology and Psychiatry 50,* 1–2, 99–107.

Hodgins, S. (1992) 'Mental disorder, intellectual deficiency and crime: Evidence from a birth cohort.' *Archives of General Psychiatry 49,* 476–483.

Lawrenson, R., Rohde, J., Bott, C., Hambleton, I. and Farmer, R. (1997) 'Trends in the need for services for people with learning disabilities: Implications for primary care.' *Health Trends 29,* 2, 37–41.

Lindsay, W.R., Allan, R., Parry, C., Macleod, F. *et al.* (2004) 'Anger and aggression in people with intellectual disabilities: Treatment and follow-up of consecutive referrals and a waiting list comparison.' *Clinical Psychology and Psychotherapy 11,* 4, 225–264.

Lindsay, W.R., Holland, A.J., Taylor, J.L., Michie, A. *et al.* (2009) 'Diagnostic information and adversity in childhood for offenders with learning disabilities referred to and accepted into forensic services.' *Advances in Mental Health and Learning Disabilities 3,* 4, 19–24.

Lord, C., Risi, S., Lambrecht, L., Cook, E.H. *et al.* (2000) 'The autism Diagnostic Observation Schedule – Generic: A standard measure of social and communication deficits associated with the spectrum of autism.' *Journal of Autism and Developmental Disorders 30,* 3, 205–233.

Lord, C., Rutter, M. and Le Couteur, A. (1994) 'Autism Diagnostic Interview – Revised.' *Journal of Autism and Developmental Disorders 24*, 659–686.

McBrien, J. and Murphy, G. (2006) 'Police and carers' views of reporting of alleged offences by people with intellectual disabilities in one local authority.' *Journal of Forensic Psychiatry 127*, 1181–1184.

McCarthy, J. (2000) 'Commentary.' *Advances in Psychiatric Treatment 6*, 285–286.

McCord, J.A. (1978) 'A thirty year follow-up of treatment effects.' *American Psychology 33*, 284–289.

McNulty, C., Kissi-Deborah, R. and Newsom-Davies, I. (1995) 'Police involvement with clients having intellectual disabilities: A pilot in South London.' *Mental Handicap Research 8*, 129–136.

O'Donnell, C.R., Lydgate, T. and Fo, W.S.O. (1979) 'The buddy system: Review and follow-up.' *Child Behaviour Therapy 1*, 161–169.

Reed, J. (1992) *Review of Health and Social Services for Mentally Disordered Offenders and Others Requiring Similar Services: Final Summary Report (Reed Report)*. London: HMSO.

Richardson, H.J. (1969) *Adolescent Girls in Approved Schools*. London: Routledge and Kegan Paul.

Robins, L. (1978) 'Sturdy childhood predictors of adults' antisocial behaviour. Replications from longitudinal studies.' *Psychological Medicine 8*, 611–622.

Rose, J., O'Brien, A. and Rose, D. (2009) 'Group and individual cognitive behavioural interventions for anger.' *Advances in Mental Health and Learning Disabilities 3*, 4, 45–50.

Royal College of Psychiatrists (2004) Council Report CR123. London: Royal College of Psychiatrists.

Simonoff, E. (2005) 'Children with psychiatric disorders and learning disabilities.' *British Medical Journal 330*, 742–743.

Singh, K.K. and Gudjonsson, G.H. (1992) 'Interrogative suggestibility among adolescent boys and its relationship with intelligence, memory and cognitive set.' *Journal of Adolescence 15*, 155–161.

World Health Organization (WHO) (1992) *International Classification of Diseases 10 Classification of Mental and Behavioural Disorders: Clinical Descriptions and Diagnostic Guidelines*. Geneva: WHO.

Chapter 17

MODELS OF SECURE INPATIENT CARE FOR ADOLESCENTS WITH DEVELOPMENTAL DISABILITIES

Ernest Gralton, Charlotte Staniforth and Yve Griffin

INTRODUCTION

What is a model of care or a treatment philosophy and why would it be important to have one? Many health services say they have a model or philosophy that underpins the delivery of care. However, there does not appear to be a clear distinction between a treatment philosophy and a model in psychiatric healthcare provision and the terms are often used interchangeably. A philosophy can be defined as a system of theories on the nature of things or conduct whereas a model often describes a repeated pattern or a standard of excellence. For the purpose of this chapter we have defined both the philosophy and model in mental healthcare as the set of principles that underlie the consistent delivery of treatment and guide the wider therapeutic interactions between staff and patients.

It is probably important to have an underlying model or treatment philosophy in order to ensure a consistency of approach. Philosophical ideas are useful in guiding the formation of appropriate relationships between patients and staff in healthcare settings (Halpern 2003). There is concern about the lack of evidence base of models for inpatient secure services (Crowhurst and Bowers 2002). A multidisciplinary team will come from a variety of backgrounds often with contrasting models of care and differing views on how they are best implemented (Mason, Williams and Vivian-Byrne 2002).

It is important for any model for the care of young people to be grounded in developmental principles. A developmental perspective includes an understanding of three core elements: brain maturation, the environmental interface and the mastery of key developmental tasks (Harris 2000). Because neurodevelopmental disorders are by their very nature complex and interrelated, single treatments in isolation are very unlikely in themselves to produce significant and sustained effects. Multiple modalities of treatment must be combined through multidisciplinary working with a variety of professionals. This produces a complex treatment system with varying professional perspectives, relationships, priorities and goals. It can sometimes produce inappropriate rivalries or members of a team who feel marginalised or that their work is undervalued or misunderstood. The model has to encompass the perspectives of a variety of staff in a way that ensures that everyone (including the young person) appreciates that the input of every individual is interrelated and vital in the ongoing progress of the young person.

Basic training for most staff working in mainstream adolescent forensic services is recognised as inadequate (Boles 2004). Adolescents are still undergoing significant brain development with more neuro-plasticity than adults. The demands made by adolescent populations on staff teams are significantly higher than the adult population and they require a high level of structured activity and routine (Rose 2004). It is not unreasonable to assume that for even more specialised secure services there is a very significant training requirement for staff to allow them to work effectively with developmentally disabled adolescents requiring secure care.

RESEARCH EVIDENCE

There are treatment models that have been recently used to underpin the philosophy of adult secure inpatient care. The most notable has been dialectical behaviour therapy (DBT), which was originally devised for borderline personality disorder but has also been applied as a treatment modality for patients in forensic mental health services (McCann, Ball and Ivanoff 2000). This model is promising but the training is expensive and prolonged and it requires strong leadership to maintain (Wix 2003).

The Tidal Model based partly on the ideas of Hildegard Peplau has been developed and implemented into some secure inpatient psychiatric services in Newcastle upon Tyne in the UK. This is a multidimensional humanist model with a particular emphasis on empathic understanding (Barker 2001). The approach is seen as a nursing rather than a multidisciplinary model and is critical of medical models of psychiatric care. Concern has been expressed that the model does not give sufficient emphasis to the organic aetiology of many psychiatric disorders (Noak 2001).

There is no clear established model for secure services for adolescents, particularly those with neuro-cognitive disabilities. There are, however, some principles derived from research evidence that are likely to be important when working with this inpatient population. It is important to recognise that there are limitations to importing standard models of forensic care for adults (predominantly suffering from functional psychoses) and applying them to adolescents, particularly those with complex combinations of developmental disorders.

There are some challenges to models of care that are common across forensic populations. The adversarial nature of the criminal justice process can promote an authoritarian style of therapeutic interaction in secure settings. In patients who spend long periods in secure settings it can be easy to recreate an authoritarian style of relationship via the process of transference (Felthous 1984). A high degree of interpersonal skill is required to manage aggressive behaviour (Crowhurst and Bowers 2002). Unfortunately a confrontational style of interaction in some forensic settings is common (Kaye and Franey 1998; Rask and Levander 2001).

Patients in secure settings have typically had very negative relationships with parental and authority figures (McCann et al. 2000) and this is probably even more true of adolescents with developmental disabilities. Offending and antisocial behaviour can place additional stress on these already strained family relationships (Tsang, Pearson and Yuen 2002). Levels of self-efficacy and self-esteem among these patients can be very poor (Rask and Hallberg 2000).

The nature of the risks means that these patients can spend comparatively long periods of time within secure settings. They tend to be complex individuals with a variety of needs and treatment can be lengthy (Badger et al. 1999). Improvements can be slow and erratic with intermittent relapses.

Any model needs to try to prevent and manage the phenomenon of malignant alienation where there is a progressive deterioration in the relationship between the patient and others where the individual is seen as provocative, unreasonable or over-dependent (Watts and Morgan 1994). Staff may fall into a degree of therapeutic nihilism when faced with the prospect of a long period coping with very disturbed and needy young people whose prognosis is perceived as poor. The problems of staff 'burnout' are well recognised in secure settings (Beer, Paton and Pereira 1997).

There are ethical issues for staff who look after these patients, particularly around the balance between care and control (Kaye and Franey 1998). In adolescent populations this can mean a split between staff predominantly delivering therapy or who have a 'developmental' perspective and those whose main role is in maintaining security and who see themselves as 'forensic' (Clarke 1996; McCann et al. 2000). These divisions can significantly accentuate the tensions between different professional groups. These interdisciplinary tensions rank as the highest source of stress for staff working in secure settings (Whyte and Brooker 2001).

Improved communication between staff and the opportunity to develop new working methods are associated with positive working relationships (Molyneux 2001). Models that explicitly guide staff in both planned and spontaneous interaction with patients improve the perceptions of an inpatient setting for both patients and staff (Furst *et al.* 1993).

An appropriate model for this population has to get the right balance between maintaining security and safety and being developmentally appropriate. However, it is important to remember that without security and safety there can be no therapy and progress is much more uncertain. Maintaining safety is a key goal in young people who have not only engaged in high risk behaviours, but who themselves have been exposed to significant violence and neglect.

Impaired social ability may play a more significant role in offending than factors like intellectual ability (Kearns and O'Connor 1988). Treatments targeting relational abilities have been shown to be effective (Goodness and Renfro 2002). For young people with complex developmental disorders like autistic spectrum disorder (ASD), models that combine pharmacotherapy with other interventions are more effective than treatment with medication alone and may allow lower doses of pharmacological agents to be used (Aman *et al.* 2009).

Nutrition is rarely discussed as an issue in models of secure care for young people. This is surprising as nutritional deficits have been implicated in the development of behavioural disturbance, antisocial personality disorder, hyperactivity and impaired cognitive function (Dani, Burrill and Demmig-Adams 2005; Liu *et al.* 2004; Raine *et al.* 2003; Walker *et al.* 2007). For further exploration of this issue please see Chapter 11.

PRACTICE ISSUES

Psychological interventions

Population

Young people with developmental disabilities (DD) and forensic presentations are not a homogeneous group. Difficulties experienced in this population are often a combination of one or more of the following: developmental and learning disability, early trauma and associated attachment difficulty, social and adaptive deficits, mental health and emotional issues and forensic presentations with associated risk behaviours (e.g. aggression, inappropriate sexual behaviour and fire setting). Furthermore, adolescence is a key developmental milestone and a time of great change and transition with young people often acting out their difficulties and distress leading to problems with behaviour. It is also common to find co-morbid difficulties in childhood and adolescence and it is a time when enduring mental health problems such as psychosis and mood disorders begin to emerge. To fully address the needs of this population a flexible, individualised and multimodal approach is essential (Schwartz *et al.* 2006). This will ensure that individual needs, the systems they are within and the environment are encompassed within the interventions.

There is a limited evidence base for interventions that are effective with adolescents with DD and in particular those that also have forensic or co-morbid mental health needs (Adamson 2010; Schwartz *et al.* 2006), even though those with DD are more likely to develop mental health difficulties than the general population (Dosen and Day 2001; Schwartz *et al.* 2006). Currently, research for the DD population focuses on interventions aimed at addressing the DD rather than the co-morbid mental health or forensic needs. The general practice involves adapting interventions for mental health or forensic needs by using the evidence base from the adult and non-DD literature and adapting after considering the cognitive and communication deficits (Schwartz *et al.* 2006). On the other hand trying to adhere rigidly to established models of therapy may exclude those with a DD from receiving an appropriate intervention (Royal College of Psychiatrists 2004). Hence individual needs must be considered when adapting interventions (Waitman and Reynolds 1992; Whitehouse *et al.* 2006).

Assessment

Professionals are often working with a number of complexities; it is important to keep in mind when completing assessments that all areas are covered, as there is often an emphasis placed on risk behaviours. Please refer to Chapter 10 for more details relating to risk assessments. Assessments usually include information gathered from clinical interviews, case history review, psychometric assessment, observations and collateral sources.

Clinical interviews

Clinical interviews can be either structured or unstructured, with both including information such as family history and early history (including developmental factors), onset and course of problems, previous interventions and factors involved in the maintenance of the problem.

Psychometrics

There is a range of psychometrics that can be used to assess cognitive, social and adaptive functioning, mental health issues and forensic presentations. It is important to emphasise when considering using a psychometric tool that it needs to be appropriate for the specific age and population. There can be a lack of psychometric tools that are designed for and validated on young people who have DD and co-morbid mental health difficulties (Benson and Ivins 1992; Taylor 2002). Therefore, it is more likely that psychometric tools designed for use with non-DD adolescents are sourced and adapted as appropriate. However, this may impact on the validity of the scoring. There will also be limitations to consider when using self-report psychometrics with this population including the young person's communication and literacy skills, levels of understanding and insight into his or her difficulties (Taylor 2002).

Other assessment methods

What is becoming clear is that interventions need to be guided by valid assessments. Due to some limitations of the methods outlined above, the majority of assessment may be completed indirectly by gathering information from family members and professionals. This will primarily be collecting information on developmental history and observable behaviours using the ABC (antecedents, behaviour, consequences) model within frameworks such as functional analysis, and behavioural monitoring to provide information on triggers (antecedents) for behaviour and the impact of interventions (consequences). With this in mind the usefulness for functional analysis for a range of difficulties is being recognised outside the realm of challenging behaviour (Harvey *et al.* 2009).

Formulation

Formulations draw together all available information from which hypotheses are developed that aid in the understanding of how difficulties have developed and are currently being maintained. On the basis of this understanding intervention targets can be identified which can break maintenance cycles and highlight potential barriers and limitations that may occur in treatment. Formulations are often a complex process using biopsycho-social theories to inform evidence-based practice (Johnstone and Dallos 2006).

The cognitive and social abilities listed below are key areas that require close attention when formulating difficulties in this population as they are likely to increase the risk of mental health difficulties (Schwartz *et al.* 2006) and engagement in risk behaviours (Farrington 1989).

BOX 17.1: KEY COGNITIVE AND SOCIAL ABILITIES TO CONSIDER WHEN FORMULATING, AND THEIR IMPACT ON THE YOUNG PERSON

- Impaired memory – ability to retain information

- Problem solving deficits – difficulty in generating and implementing a range of strategies

- Impulsivity, poor planning and judgement – not considering consequences

- Reduced ability to understand abstract concepts and language

- Impaired communication skills – for example, expressive language difficulties

- Suggestibility and compliance – easily led by others

- Poor attention and concentration

- Social skill deficits – difficulties reading others' behaviour and body language

- Empathy or theory of mind deficits

Intervention

Traditionally interventions applied to this population have been informed by behavioural theory and medication (Hurley, Tomasulo and Pfadt 1998; Schwartz *et al.* 2006). There is mounting evidence that other treatment approaches may not be particularly effective, such as social skills training, and instead there should be a focus on skills acquisition (Schwartz *et al.* 2006), as well as consideration of ecological and systemic factors. Furthermore, there is an increasing evidence base that cognitive behavioural therapy (CBT) can be effective with this population (Stenfert Kroese, Dagnan and Loumidis 1998; Willner 2006), but it is intellectually challenging and must be adapted to the correct cognitive and communication level for the individual (Schwartz *et al.* 2006; Willner 2006). It will often be more directive to use persuasion, suggestion and reassurance (Hurley *et al.* 1998; Stavrakaki and Klein 1986) rather than traditional guided discovery (Whitehouse *et al.* 2006). For example, CBT has been found to be more effective for those with a DD who are more able in terms of their cognitive and communication abilities. However, the effectiveness of this approach with those who are less able can be increased if additional time is spent educating the young person about the differing components for the treatment approach, such as being able to distinguish between thoughts, emotions and behaviour and the impact they have on each other (Dagnan, Chadwick and Proudlove 2000).

Psychological formulation often highlights a number of target treatment areas. It is important to give serious consideration to the order in which difficulties should be addressed, even though there is often a pressure to focus on areas linked to the risk behaviours. For example, it would not be advisable to offer anger management before a young person has learnt to label and identify different emotions in him- or herself or work on past trauma before a person has learnt coping skills and a degree of emotional regulation. Most young people will require some emotional or self-monitoring work as their initial interventions (McCabe, McGillivray and Newton 2006).

Due to the fact that young people may often enter into patient settings with a high degree of distress and aggressive behaviour, they may also need to go through a period of behavioural stabilisation. They must be able to regulate their behaviour to a degree before they can start working on the difficulties for which they were admitted. This will also provide an opportunity to begin to develop a therapeutic rapport with the young person.

Therapeutic relationship

The therapeutic relationship is key when working with adolescents with DD (Whitehouse et al. 2006) and can often be a useful tool in modelling and teaching appropriate relationships and social behaviour (Stavrakaki and Klein 1986). However, this relationship can often be slower to develop (Whitehouse et al. 2006) as the young people will often have low self-esteem, based on previous experiences (Willner 2006). Therefore, it is important when developing the relationship to set simple realistic goals, and that the expectations from the team are achievable (Schwartz et al. 2006; Stavrakaki and Klein 1986).

There can often be a lot of preparatory work that requires completion before the young person can progress to the stage where they are ready to engage in structured work that focuses on specific problem areas related to mental health (anger management, self-esteem work, mood swings) or risk behaviours. When it is deemed appropriate to deliver structured therapeutic interventions there are a number of factors that need to be taken into consideration including the young person's motivation to change and level of engagement. Young people may not be willing to engage as they do not feel they have the skills to be able to achieve change or they may have the skills but lack motivation to change as they do not consider that their behaviour is problematic (Rollnick 1998;

Willner 2006). If this difficulty to engage arises, the use of functional analysis and motivational interviewing techniques can be effective.

Due to the fact the these young people are in an institutional setting and often have attachment issues the professional must always keep in mind boundary issues and use supervision appropriately. It may also feel to professionals that they are not doing any useful interventions because they are spending a long time gaining trust and rapport building. This can often involve being very flexible and open minded and getting involved with the young person in activities which are not focused on addressing his or her difficulty, such as going for walks, playing games, or other sessional work (Dagnan 2007).

Staff

Psychological interventions and programmes are often delivered by a different staff group to the professionals who developed them. This is particularly the case with nursing staff administering behavioural modification programmes. Furthermore, when structured interventions are delivered by psychologists or occupational therapists, members of the nursing team can play a key role in supporting these interventions by reinforcing the transference of skills learnt in this context to the ward environment (Willner 2006). However, for this to be effective the staff may need training in the particular therapeutic model in order to believe in its effectiveness and be motivated to apply it (Taylor 2002; Willner 2006). Often staff may hold negative beliefs about the difficult behaviour the young person is displaying which can impact on their interactions with him or her, and possibly lead to displays of high expressed emotions by staff and the young person (Dagnan 2007). Training can also help to address this issue as can formulation meetings with the entire team which can be influential in developing a shared understanding of how the difficulties have developed and the interventions that are required.

Other factors

There are a number of adaptations that need to occur regarding structured interventions that are delivered to young people with a DD. It may not be possible to deliver therapeutic interventions in the traditional sense to this population.

Often the process of change or recovery can be a long process due to the complexity of cases (Adamson 2010). The factors related to delivery of interventions such as shorter duration of sessions and the need for extensive repetition can also add to the length of time need required. Particular areas that need to be considered in terms of adaptation to intervention are summarised in Box 17.2 below:

> ## BOX 17.2: FACTORS TO CONSIDER WHEN DELIVERING STRUCTURED INTERVENTIONS TO A YOUNG PERSON WITH A LEARNING DISABILITY
>
> * Presenting information in a variety of ways, e.g. role plays, visual aids
> * Generalisation of skills from one context to another
> * Extensive rehearsal and aide mémoires
> * Simplification of concepts
> * Modelling of appropriate behaviour
> * Frequency of sessions (once or more per week)
> * Duration (not too lengthy)
> * Providing concrete information
> * Checking understanding
> * Getting multidisciplinary team involvement
> * Providing a range of activities within one session
> * Pitching information at the right level of ability
> * If group work, considering membership of the group
> * When and where sessions occur (time of day, day of week and environment)

In addition to the adaptations above, when facilitating group sessions further considerations include: the abilities and individual difficulties of group members, pitching the information to meet the needs of young people with varying levels of cognitive ability, attention and concentration and confidentiality issues. However, despite the challenges of group interventions they have the potential to increase social connectedness (McCabe *et al.* 2006) and the group members can support and learn from each other.

Overall treatment models

A model for this complex patient population requires four main principles:

* structure, with clear goals and transparent risk related decisions
* flexibility to be tailored to meet individual need

- recognition that all therapies and interactions (including micro-interactions) are valuable

- comprehensiveness – crossing all developmental domains.

It is likely, particularly with adolescents, that there is significant interaction between interventions; they are not operating a single channel with a clear input/outcome relationship. Physiotherapy intervention on balance and coordination has been shown to positively affect reading ability (Reynolds, Nicolson and Hambly 2003). It is there likely that a system's theory approach is more likely to be useful in understanding complex inpatient adolescent populations (Setterberg 1991).

The model needs to be flexible to take into address a wide range of needs amongst the patient population. The programme has to cover a wide range of domains including remedial education, and physical activity including physiotherapy, speech and language and occupational activity. The environment has to be configured to allow a wide variety of programme activities within a safe and secure environment. Young people demonstrating the riskiest behaviour have some of the greatest needs and a programme must be flexible enough to deliver interventions safely to these young people. This may mean that educational input will need to be delivered flexibly in the residential living environment rather than in a designated school setting. For patients with significant autism the programme may need to be structured along appropriate principles like Treatment and Education of Autistic and Related Communication Handicapped Children (TEACCH) (Crocombe *et al.* 2001; Mesibov, Shea and Schopler 2005).

Disruption of attachment appears to be a key issue underlying many of the symptoms of young people with conduct disturbance (Holland *et al.* 1993; Moretti, Holland and Peterson 1994). Unsurprisingly interventions by multiple agencies with different personnel can actually worsen outcomes for youth with conduct disorder (Shamsie, Sykes and Hamilton 1994). Conventional rehabilitation systems for adults with mental illness that rely on moving through multiple settings with changes in personnel and progressively reduced security may be problematic for these young people with attachment difficulties who have often already been in multiple care settings prior to admission.

A significant proportion of the population is likely to be on the autistic spectrum, and find change difficult and anxiety provoking. For those young people the stress of the transitions can lead to an individual remaining in the most structured and familiar environment due to preference, or due to the recurrent relapse of a co-morbid mental illness. Young people with autistic spectrum disorders (particularly those with sensory sensitivities) may engage in behaviours that they know will result in them being moved to low stimulus environments like seclusion. Systems that rely on the minimum of disruption with a single well planned structured transition from a secure setting into the community under an appropriate legal framework are preferable. This approach may raise questions about the flexibility of some systems of secure care for adolescents and young adults.

The issue of managing the touch needs of the adolescent patient population is a good example of the need to have some divergence from adult forensic models. Forensic services are likely to have policies that limit physical touch in view of patients who have histories of inappropriate sexual behaviour and which try to prevent staff themselves being accused of inappropriate physical contact. However, touch is a requirement for normal brain development in children. Primates who are deprived of touch develop a range of abnormal and aggressive behaviours (Harlow and Suomi 1971). Many developmentally disabled young people who come into forensic settings have histories of abuse and neglect (Doyle and Mitchell 2003). This may be complicated by histories of sexual offending and inappropriate patterns of sexual arousal. Some individual adolescent patients can engage in a variety of inappropriate behaviours in order to meet their physical touch needs, including deliberately precipitating physical restraint, which risks injury to both the young person and staff. A programme therefore needs to develop 'safe' ways for adolescents to meet touch and sensory needs specifically via a sensory programme as discussed in Chapter 3 on sensory integration and Chapter 11 on developmental traumatology.

Issues centring on managing personal care are common in young people with developmental disabilities, particularly those with autistic spectrum disorders (Gillberg 2002). These are not uncommonly related to sensory sensitivities. This can be related to the odour of particular shower gels, soaps or shampoos or the sound of electric razors or toothbrushes. It can relate to the sensation of water or other items on the skin, or be related specifically to discomfort upon using a toothbrush on the gums, or cutting nails or hair. Not uncommonly a parent or carer may have reacted inappropriately to what may have been considered wilful resistance, which can complicate the process with a memory of a traumatic experience. In severe cases the young person may have symptoms consistent with post-traumatic stress disorder (PTSD). It is very important that models of care are able to assess sensory sensitivities fully and design modified routines that allow a young person to master issues like personal hygiene. This understanding of the importance of micro-enviromental interaction is becoming increasingly recognised as vital in the care of complex patients (Tyrer et al. 2007).

One of the core issues that adolescent services must address is how a developmentally disabled young person will within his or her programme construct a core of self-identity that is positive and pro-social. Symbolic interactionism places particular importance on the interpretation of micro-interactions between individuals and has been the basis for criticism of inpatient psychiatric care, particularly regarding excessive control (Goffman 1961). For those with histories of offending behaviour a model must also allow transition into a supported community service, including legal frameworks.

The delivery of some treatments (e.g. for sex offending or arson) can be additionally hampered by a patient's inability to tolerate the negative cognitions and emotions associated with the examination of past offences. Any treatment programme therefore needs to have a balance between examining past related risk issues and activities that are more positive and future focused.

Solution focused model

Solution focused ideas are potentially helpful for a model for adolescent residential or inpatient care (Durrant 1993). The authors would argue that this is particularly true for our developmentally disabled population. Solution focused therapy stems from a tradition different from many psychotherapies practised in forensic settings. It is not as interested in 'insight' as it is in disrupting the 'problem pattern' that has proved ineffective and harmful.

Solution focused brief therapy was developed in the US in the 1980s from research into disordered communication patterns in patients and families with schizophrenia. It is an approach based on solution building by exploring the patient's own resources and developing realistic future goals. The key is creating a climate where there is an expectation of change. The solutions lie in changing interactions in the context of the unique constraints that surround the person (De Shazer *et al.* 1986). It is a flexible approach and appears to be an effective therapeutic intervention across a range of presentations including inpatient psychiatric settings, residential treatment for adolescents, young offenders institutions and adult prison populations (Durrant 1993; Gingerich 2000; Hagen and Mitchell 2001; Iveson 2002). Solution focused work does not require the understanding of abstract ideas or sophisticated concepts. It can be delivered to people of more limited cognitive ability including children and adolescents, and patients with mild and moderate learning disability. It is also suitable for patients who have had cognitive decline associated with severe mental illness and active psychotic symptoms (Hagen and Mitchell 2001).

Solution focused interventions are felt to increase the cohesiveness between staff, assist staff–patient interaction, help set goals and improve outcomes when introduced into psychiatric inpatient settings (Mason, Breen and Wipple 1994). It has also been used as a model for the supervision of staff working in mental health services (Triantafillou 1997). A solution focused model shares some features with DBT and the Tidal Model but may be less complex to deliver.

Here are some of the key concepts.

PREFERRED FUTURE

A 'preferred future' for patients in a secure forensic setting almost invariably involves moving into a less secure setting and having more access to the community. It is therefore a key goal shared between patient and staff. However, this goal may need to be broken down into smaller stages. The stages must be realistic, concrete, observable and significant to the patient. Achievement is recognised as a beginning rather than an ending.

PROBLEM-FREE TALK

Problem-free talk indicates an interest in the person rather than the problem and involves initial discourse with the patient on subjects other than the problem area. It can help break out of a cycle of a patient presenting with a 'problem' as the key to interacting with staff. Some patients can find their personal identity substantially defined by their problem. This can make them reluctant to seek solutions and can therefore complicate attempts at treatment.

EXCEPTIONS

A solution focused approach recognises that many patients are already doing at least a component of the solution to a problem. There may have been times when patients have been faced with a particular trigger or situation of increased risk where they have maintained safe behaviour. It is important that patients are reminded of these times, particularly when these triggers occur. Their capacity to maintain safe behaviour is acknowledged and when these strategies are successful it can give patients a sense of mastery.

NOTICING SUGGESTIONS

Solution focused therapy seeks to identify small positive changes. It is important that these 'noticing suggestions' are regularly observed and communicated to the patient. Nothing is potentially too small to be remarked upon, as small changes can herald the onset of larger ones.

It is unlikely that many of these complex patients are going to make substantial improvements in small periods of time. However, incremental improvements in a number of areas can cumulatively over time produce a meaningful transformation. Such improvements can make the difference between continued secure inpatient care and living in a supported community setting.

RESOURCES

Solution focused methods are always looking for 'resources' (i.e. skills and abilities that the patient already possesses). Even the most disturbed and damaged individuals have resources that can be usefully engaged. The goal is to use these resources as a foundation and seek to generalise solution focused behaviour into other areas.

Applying a solution focused model

The current framework for delivering psychiatric care in the UK (including forensic or secure services) is the care programme approach (CPA). Any model must therefore be compatible with CPA. A core component of the process of CPA is the assessment of 'need' and the planning undertaken to meet these needs. However, the needs of developmentally disabled young people in a secure setting are often extensive and can seem overwhelming.

Some of the needs, particularly around issues external to the person (e.g. disrupted family relationships), may be insoluble even with infinite resources. Recurrently discussing needs for which there are no realistic solutions can be counterproductive to treatment. A solution focused approach would always seek to make goals achievable and the needs relevant to the patient. So rather than trying to arrange repeated interventions to meet the needs of an intractable external problem a solution focused approach would seek to help the individual patient use and develop the mature coping strategies he or she already has for dealing with the distress that these problems cause.

Staff dealing with these patients (especially nurses) need a framework to deal with the multiplicity of situations that can arise when other staff are unavailable. There may be concern that 'ad hoc' interventions may interfere or not be compatible with work that is being undertaken by others. An advantage of the solution focused model is that it remains neutral with respect to therapeutic interventions, particularly those that focus on examining past events. An entire programme including other psychotherapeutic or group interventions can be incorporated into a solution focused model, all working toward an appropriate preferred future. Brief informal interactions are seen as important as formal psychotherapeutic interventions.

Solution focused interventions are flexible enough to be delivered in very short time scales. Meaningful work can sometimes be done in just a few minutes. The principles of the approach can be devolved to staff who have had little experience in delivering more formal therapeutic interventions. Staff often find that much of what they do that is helpful is already 'solution focused' in nature.

A solution focused approach is particularly helpful in redefining the nature of the relationship between staff and patients. It 'steps sideways' out of an authoritarian and potentially confrontational relationship with a patient and enters a more collaborative one. Instead of saying 'You should do this because I/we think you need to' staff say 'You need to do this because it will get you where you want to be.' The goal of a solution focused model would be to have as many staff interacting in this way with patients as often as possible. Even a small improvement like the reduction in struggling during safe patient restraint can be helpfully fed back to the patient in a solution focused way.

Measuring outcomes

Outcome measures for treatment programmes are desirable but their interpretation in a complex population requires some sophistication. Overall change is difficult to measure with a single outcome tool, and a range of measures depending on the needs and risk of an individual is more appropriate. There are a range of specific outcome measures outlined in previous chapters like formal examinations for educational attainment, changes in the Model of Human Occupation Screening Tool (MoHOST) (Parkinson *et al.* 2006) or the Vineland ABS (de Bildt *et al.* 2005) for occupational therapy, the Modified Overt Aggression Scale for reductions in violence (Alderman, Knight and Morgan 1997) and the St Andrew's Sexual Behavior Assessment (SASBA) (Knight *et al.* 2008) for monitoring sexually inappropriate behaviour.

We routinely use the Health of the Nation Outcome Scales for Adolescents (HoNOSCA) (Gowers *et al.* 1999) and HoNOS Secure (Dickens, Sugarman and Walker 2007). HoNOSCA was devised for an outpatient population. Its use has to be adapted for inpatient settings and can be relatively insensitive to change in some of our young people, particularly those with histories of sexual offending. The Children's Global Assessment Scale or CGAS (Shaffer *et al.* 1983) is another overall measure but its overall inter-rater reliability without a high level of training is modest at best (Lundh *et al.* 2010). There is currently no one appropriate global outcome measure for adolescents with developmental disabilities detained in secure psychiatric settings.

Case description

Stephen was a 15-year-old adolescent with mild learning disabilities (Full Scale IQ 63) and had been recently diagnosed with co-morbid ADHD probably as a result of foetal alcohol syndrome. His mother had significant problems with alcohol substance misuse and he was taken into care on the grounds of neglect at the age of two years. Stephen was very difficult to manage due to his hyperactivity and aggressive behaviour and had a number of failed foster placements. At the age of 14 he was moved into a residential children's home. While in the home Stephen had access to inappropriate sexual material by downloading adult films on his mobile phone. He was apprehended after coercing two eight-year-old boys into penetrative sexual activity in the wooded area of a local park. Stephen was already serving a community sentence for an earlier but less serious sexual offence with a younger boy who was a resident in the home.

Stephen presented initially as very distractible, sexually inappropriate and socially intrusive; there were a number of incidents in the first few weeks where he needed restraint. His personal hygiene skills were very poor and he had serious gum disease. He refused to wear any clothing that was not soft and was aggressive if staff tried to take his favourite tracksuit away when it became full of holes.

An assessment using the Autism Diagnostic Observation Schedule (ADOS) (Lord et al. 2000) confirmed that he was on the autism spectrum. A formal sensory analysis identified him as predominantly sensation seeking but having a variety of sensory perception problems including not tolerating a hard toothbrush or clothing that was 'too stiff'. Stephen had an occupational therapy sensory programme to meet his sensory needs. An appropriate soft electric toothbrush and more socially appropriate soft clothing was obtained. He also has a visually structured personal skills programme to improve his personal care, and a programme to teach other skills including clothes washing and cooking. He had physiotherapy input after he was identified with significant developmental dyspraxia. His ADHD and autism were treated with a combination of long acting methylphenidate and low dose risperidone.

Stephen slowly engaged in remedial education and made progress, particularly in English and Maths where he obtained Entry Level qualifications. He underwent social skills training and aggression replacement training. Although Steven did not engage with art psychotherapy he was an enthusiastic participant in the drumming and music group. His aggressive behaviour was monitored using the Modified Overt Aggression Scale (MOAS) (Alderman et al. 1997) and sexually inappropriate behaviour using the SASBA (Knight et al. 2008). There were progressive declines in both measures over time. He underwent group and individual work in the Adapted Sexual Offender Group. Initially he found it difficult to attend and staff helped remind him that his progress back into the community was dependent on improving his 'safety skills'.

Twelve months later, at the end of the programme, he had made significant improvement on the outcome measures. Stephen developed a particular interest in animal care and was placed on the programme looking after rabbits and guinea pigs. Steven expressed the view that he would like a job working with animals. Stephen also had some supervised telephone contact with his mother and worked toward a facilitated visit to the hostel where she was living. Stephen progressed his interest in animal care into a part-time course at a local agricultural college. He also engaged in the Duke of Edinburgh Programme, went on several expeditions, and obtained his Bronze Award. He was discharged under a community treatment order into a highly structured residential placement with a service for adults specialising in young people with autistic disorders and was engaged in part time work at a local stables.

CONCLUSIONS

A model working with adolescents has the challenge of integrating the staff team so that all activities are working toward a common purpose and all are seen as valuable within the overall treatment programme. A key mantra should be that *every interaction with a young person, no matter how brief, has the potential to be therapeutic.*

Permission was kindly given to reproduce material previously used in an article by one of authors in the British Journal of Forensic Practice (2006) 8, 1, 24–30.

REFERENCES

Adamson, L.G. (2010) *Investigating the Assessment and Treatment of Violence in Adolescents with Developmental Disabilities.* Unpublished Doctor of Forensic Psychology thesis. Birmingham: University of Birmingham.

Alderman, N., Knight, C. and Morgan, C. (1997) 'Use of a modified version of the overt aggression scale in the measurement and assessment of aggressive behaviours following brain injury.' *Brain Injury 11*, 503–523.

Aman, M.G., McDougle, C.J., Scahill, L., Handen, B. *et al.* (2009) 'Medication and parent training in children with pervasive developmental disorders and serious behavior problems: Results from a randomized clinical trial.' *Journal of the American Academy of Child and Adolescent Psychiatry 48*, 12, 1143–1154.

Badger, D., Vaughan, P., Woodward, M. and Williams, P. (1999) 'Planning to meet the needs of offenders with mental disorders in the United Kingdom.' *Psychiatric Services 50*, 12, 1624–1627.

Barker, P. (2001) 'The Tidal Model: Developing an empowering and person centred approach to recovery within psychiatric and mental health nursing.' *Journal of Psychiatric and Mental Health Nursing 8*, 233–240.

Beer, M.D., Paton, C. and Pereira, S. (1997) 'Hot beds of general psychiatry: A national survey of psychiatric intensive care units.' *Psychiatric Bulletin 21*, 142–144.

Benson, B.A. and Ivins, J. (1992) 'Anger, depression and self concept in adults with mental retardation.' *Journal of Intellectual Disability Research 36*, 169–175.

Boles, M. (2004) 'Clinical Governance in an Adolescent Forensic Inpatient Service.' In S. Bailey and M. Dolan (eds) *Adolescent Forensic Psychiatry*. London: Arnold.

Clarke, L. (1996) 'Covert participation observation in a secure forensic unit.' *Nursing Times 92*, 48, 37–40.

Crocombe, J., Carter, S., Jabarin, Z. and Gralton, E. (2001) 'Maple House – an autistic-friendly NHS facility.' *Psychiatric Bulletin 25*, 109–111.

Crowhurst, N. and Bowers, L. (2002) 'Philosophy, care and treatment on the psychiatric intensive care unit: Themes, trends and future practice.' *Journal of Psychiatric and Mental Health Nursing 9*, 6, 689–695.

Dagnan, D. (2007) 'Psychosocial interventions for people with intellectual disabilities and mental ill-health.' *Current Opinion in Psychiatry 20*, 456–460.

Dagnan, D., Chadwick, P. and Proudlove, J. (2000) 'Toward an assessment of suitability of people with intellectual disabilities for cognitive therapy.' *Cognitive Therapy and Research 24*, 627–636.

Dani, J., Burrill, C. and Demmig-Adams, B. (2005) 'The remarkable role of nutrition in learning and behaviour.' *Nutrition and Food Science 35*, 4, 258–263.

De Bildt, A., Kraijer, D., Sytema, S. and Minderaa, R. (2005) 'The psychometric properties of the Vineland Adaptive Behavior Scales in children and adolescents with mental retardation.' *Journal of Autism and Developmental Disorders 35*, 1, 53–62.

De Shazer, S., Kim Berg, I., Lipchik, E., Nunnally, E. *et al.* (1986) 'Brief therapy: Focused solution development.' *Family Process 25*, 207–222.

Dickens, G., Sugarman, P. and Walker, L. (2007) 'HoNOS-secure: A reliable outcome measure for users of secure and forensic mental health services.' *Journal of Forensic Psychiatry and Psychology 18*, 4, 507–514.

Dosen, A. and Day, K. (2001) 'Epidemiology, Aetiology and Presentation of Mental Illness and Behaviour Disorders in Persons with Intellectual Disabilities.' In A. Dosen and K. Day (eds) *Treating Mental Illness and Behaviour Disorders in Children and Adults with Intellectual Disabilities*. London: American Association Books.

Doyle, C. and Mitchell, D. (2003) 'Post traumatic stress disorder and people with learning disabilities: A literature based discussion.' *Journal of Learning Disability 7*, 1, 23–33.

Durrant, M. (1993) *Residential Treatment: A Co-operative Competency Based Approach to Therapy and Program Design*. London: Norton.

Farrington, D. (1989) 'Early predictors of adolescent aggression and adult violence.' *Violence and Victims 4*, 79–100.

Felthous, A.R. (1984) 'Preventing assaults on a psychiatric inpatient ward.' *Hospital and Community Psychiatry 35*, 12, 1223–1226.

Furst, D.W., Boever, W., Dowd, T., Daly, D.L., Criste, T. and Cohen, J. (1993) 'Implementation of the Boys Town psychoeducational treatment model in a children's psychiatric hospital.' *Hospital and Community Psychiatry 44*, 9, 863–868.

Gillberg, C. (2002) *A Guide to Asperger Syndrome*. Cambridge: Cambridge University Press.

Gingerich, W. J. (2000) 'Solution focused brief therapy: A review of the outcome research.' *Family Process 39*, 477–498.

Goffman, E. (1961) *Asylums: Essays on the Social Situation of Mental Patients and Other Inmates*. New York, NY: Doubleday.

Goodness, K.R. and Renfro, N.S. (2002) 'Changing a culture: A brief program analysis of a social learning program on a maximum-security forensic unit.' *Behavioural Sciences and the Law 20*, 5, 495–506.

Gowers, S.G., Harrington, R.C., Whitton, A., Lelliott, P. *et al.* (1999) 'Brief scale for measuring the outcomes of emotional and behavioural disorders in children: Health of the Nation Outcome Scales for Children and Adolescents (HoNOSCA).' *British Journal of Psychiatry 174*, 413–416.

Hagen, B.F. and Mitchell, D.L. (2001) 'Might within the madness: Solution-focused therapy and thought disordered clients.' *Archives of Psychiatric Nursing 15*, 2, 86–93.

Halpern, J. (2003) *Empathy and the Practice of Medicine: Beyond Pills and the Scalpel.* New Haven, CT: Yale University Press.

Harlow, H.F. and Suomi, S.J. (1971) 'Social recovery by isolation-reared monkeys.' *Proceedings of the National Academy of Science of the United States of America 68*, 7, 1534–1538.

Harris, J.C. (2000) 'Multimodal Interventions for Developmental Neuro-psychiatric Disorders.' In C. Gillberg and G. O'Brien (eds) *Developmental Disability and Behaviour.* London: Mac Keith Press.

Harvey, S.T., Boer, D., Meyer, L.H. and Evans, I.M. (2009) 'Updating a meta-analysis of intervention research with challenging behaviour: Treatment validity and standards of practice.' *Journal of Intellectual and Development Disability 34*, 67–80.

Holland, R., Moretti, M.M., Verlaan, V. and Peterson, S. (1993) 'Attachment and conduct disorder: The response program.' *Canadian Journal of Psychiatry 38*, 6, 420–431.

Hurley, A., Tomasulo, D.J. and Pfadt, A.G. (1998) 'Individual and group psychotherapy approaches for persons with intellectual disabilities and developmental disabilities.' *Journal of Developmental and Physical Disabilities 10*, 365–386.

Iveson, C. (2002) 'Solution-focused brief therapy.' *Advances in Psychiatric Treatment 8*, 149–157.

Johnstone, L. and Dallos, R. (2006) *Formulation in Psychology and Psychotherapy: Making Sense of People's Problems.* London: Routledge.

Kaye, C. and Franey, A. (1998) *Managing High Secure Psychiatric Care.* London: Jessica Kingsley Publishers.

Kearns, A. and O'Connor, A. (1988) 'The mentally handicapped criminal offender: A 10-year study of two hospitals.' *British Journal of Psychiatry 152*, 848–851.

Knight, C., Alderman, N., Johnson, C., Green, S., Birkett-Swan, L. and Yorston, G. (2008) 'The St Andrew's Sexual Behaviour Assessment (SASBA): Development of a standardised recording instrument for the measurement and assessment of challenging sexual behaviour in people with progressive and acquired neurological impairment.' *Neuropsychological Rehabilitation 18*, 2, 129–159.

Liu, J., Raine, A., Venables, P.H. and Mednick, S.A. (2004) 'Malnutrition at age 3 years and externalizing behavior problems at ages 8, 11, and 17 years.' *American Journal of Psychiatry 161*, 2005–2013.

Lord, C., Risi, S., Lambrecht, L., Cook, E.H. *et al.* (2000) 'The Autism Diagnostic Observation Schedule – Generic: A standard measure of social and communication deficits associated with the spectrum of autism.' *Journal of Autism and Developmental Disorders 30*, 3, 205–233.

Lundh, A., Kowalski, J., Sundberg, C.J., Gumpert, C. and Landén, M. (2010) 'Children's Global Assessment Scale (CGAS) in a naturalistic clinical setting: Inter-rater reliability and comparison with expert ratings.' *Psychiatry Resarch 177*, 1–2, 206–210.

Mason, H.W., Breen, R.Y. and Whipple, W.R. (1994) 'Solution focused therapy and inpatient psychiatric nursing.' *Journal of Psychosocial Nursing 32*, 10, 46–49.

Mason, T., Williams, R. and Vivian-Byrne, S. (2002) 'Multi-disciplinary working in a forensic mental health setting: Ethical codes of reference.' *Journal of Psychiatry and Mental Health Nursing 9*, 5, 563–572.

McCabe, M.P., McGillivray, J.A. and Newton, D.C. (2006) 'Effectiveness of treatment programmes for depression among adults with mild/moderate intellectual disability.' *Journal of Intellectual Disability Research 50*, 239–247.

McCann, R.A., Ball, E.M. and Ivanoff, A. (2000) 'DBT with an inpatient forensic population: The CMHIP forensic model.' *Cognitive and Behavioural Practice 7*, 447–456.

Mesibov, G.B., Shea, V. and Schopler, E. (2005) *The TEACCH Approach to Autism Spectrum Disorders*. New York, NY: Kluwer Academic/Plenum.

Molyneux, J. (2001) 'Interprofessional teamworking: What makes teams work well?' *Journal of Interprofessional Care 15*, 1, 29–35.

Moretti, M., Holland, R. and Peterson, S. (1994) 'Long term outcome of an attachment-based program for conduct disorder.' *Canadian Journal of Psychiatry 39*, 6, 360–370.

Noak, J. (2001) 'Do we need another model for mental health care?' *Nursing Standard 16*, 8, 33–35.

Parkinson, S., Chester, A., Cratchley, S. and Rowbottom, J. (2006) 'Application of the Model of Human Occupation Screening Tool in an acute psychiatric setting.' *Occupational Therapy in Health Care 22*, 2–3, 63–75.

Raine, A., Mellingen, K., Liu, J., Venables, P. and Mednick, S.A. (2003) 'Effects of environmental enrichment at ages 3–5 years on schizotypal personality and antisocial behavior at ages 17 and 23 years.' *American Journal of Psychiatry 160*, 1627–1635.

Rask, M. and Hallberg, I.R. (2000) 'Forensic psychiatric nursing care – nurses' apprehension of their responsibility and work content: A Swedish survey.' *Journal of Psychiatry and Mental Health Nursing 7*, 2, 163–177.

Rask, M. and Levander, S. (2001) 'Interventions in the nurse–patient relationship in forensic psychiatric nursing care: A Swedish survey.' *Journal of Psychiatry and Mental Health Nursing 8*, 4, 323–333.

Reynolds, D., Nicolson, R.I. and Hambly, H. (2003) 'Evaluation of an exercise-based treatment for children with reading difficulties.' *Dyslexia 9*, 48–71.

Rollnick, S. (1998) 'Readiness, importance and confidence: Critical conditions of change in treatment.' In W.R. Miller and N. Heather (eds) *Treating Addictive Behaviors*. Second edition. New York, NY: Plenum.

Rose, J. (2004) 'The residential care and treatment of adolescents.' In P. Campling, S. Davies and G. Farquharson (eds) *From Toxic Institutions to Therapeutic Environments*. London: Royal College of Psychiatrists.

Royal College of Psychiatrists (2004) *Psychotherapy and Learning Disability: Council Report: CR116*. London: Royal College of Psychiatrists.

Schwartz, C., Garland, O., Waddell, C. and Harrison, E. (2006) *Mental Health and Developmental Disabilities in Children: A Research Report Prepared for Child and Youth Mental Health British Columbia Ministry of Children and Family Development*. Vancouver: Simon Fraser University.

Setterberg, S.R. (1991) 'Inpatient child and adolescent therapy groups: Boundary maintenance and group function.' *Group 15*, 2, 89–94.

Shaffer, D., Gould, M., Brasic, J., Ambrosini, P. *et al.* (1983) 'A Children's Global Assessment Scale (CGAS).' *Archives of General Psychiatry 40*, 11, 1228–1231.

Shamsie, J., Sykes, C. and Hamilton, H. (1994) 'Continuity of care for conduct disordered youth.' *Canadian Journal of Psychiatry 39*, 7, 415–420.

Stavrakaki, C. and Klein, J. (1986) 'Psychotherapies with the mentally retarded.' *Psychiatric Perspectives on Intellectual Disabilities 9*, 733–743.

Stenfert Kroese, B., Dagnan, D. and Loumidis, K. (eds) (1998) *Cognitive Behaviour Therapy for People with Learning Disabilities.* London: Routledge.

Taylor, J.L. (2002) 'A review of the assessment and treatment of anger and aggression in offenders with intellectual disability.' *Journal of Intellectual Disability Research 46*, 57–73.

Triantafillou, N. (1997) 'A solution-focused approach to mental health supervision.' *Journal of Systemic Therapies 16*, 4, 305–329.

Tsang, H.W.H., Pearson, V. and Yuen, C.H. (2002) 'Family needs and burdens of mentally ill offenders.' *International Journal of Rehabilitation Research 25*, 25–32.

Tyrer, P., Kramo, K., Miloseska, K. and Seivewright, H. (2007) 'The place for nidotherapy in psychiatric practice.' *Psychiatric Bulletin 31*, 1–3.

Waitman, A. and Reynolds, F. (1992) 'Demystifying Traditional Approaches to Counselling and Psychotherapy.' In A. Waitman and S. Conboy-Hill (eds) *Psychotherapy and Mental Handicap.* London: Sage Publications.

Walker, S.P., Chang, S.M., Powell, C.A., Simonoff, E. and Grantham-McGregor, S.M. (2007) 'Early childhood stunting is associated with poor psychological functioning in late adolescence and effects are reduced by psychosocial stimulation.' *Journal of Nutrition 137*, 2464–2469.

Watts, D. and Morgan, G. (1994) 'Malignant alienation. Dangers for patients who are hard to like.' *British Journal of Psychiatry 164*, 11–15.

Whitehouse, R.M., Tudway, J.A., Look, R. and Stenfert Kroese, B. (2006) 'Adapting individual psychotherapy for adults with intellectual disabilities: A comparative review of the cognitive-behavioural and psychodynamic literature.' *Journal of Applied Research in Intellectual Disabilities 19*, 55–65.

Whyte, L. and Brooker, C. (2001) 'Working with multidisciplinary teams in secure psychiatric environments.' *Journal of Psychosocial Nursing 39*, 9, 26–34.

Willner, P. (2006) 'Readiness for cognitive therapy in people with intellectual disabilities.' *Journal of Applied Research in Intellectual Disabilities 19*, 5–16.

Wix, S. (2003) 'Dialectical behaviour therapy observed.' *British Journal of Forensic Practice 5*, 2, 3–7.

CONTRIBUTORS

Lucy Adamson is Chartered Forensic Psychologist at Malcolm Arnold House, St Andrew's Healthcare, Northampton. Lucy has worked at St Andrew's Healthcare since 2006. Prior to this, she had experience of working with families at a parenting assessment centre and worked for three years in a secure training centre with adolescents who had offended. She studied her Doctorate in Forensic Psychology Practice (ForenPsyD) at the University of Birmingham. Her thesis explored the assessment and treatment of violence in adolescents with developmental disabilities. Lucy has a specific interest in investigating the applicability of established risk assessment tools for young people with developmental disabilities.

Mary Barnes is Art Psychotherapist at Malcolm Arnold House, St Andrew's Healthcare, Northampton. Mary is a registered art psychotherapist who worked for many years in CAMHS and in special schools before coming to St Andrew's in 2007. Mary has a background in the fine arts, and after graduating from the Royal College of Art worked as an artist, teacher and parent before training as an art psychotherapist in 1996. She is particularly interested in attachment theory and how creativity within a therapeutic relationship can facilitate change and recovery from early traumatic experience.

Sarah H. Bernard is Consultant Psychiatrist in Learning Disabilities for the National and Specialist CAMHS Learning Disability Team, Michael Rutter Centre, Maudsley Hospital, London. Sarah has a special interest in offending behaviour, the assessment of risk, fitness to plead, capacity, and behavioural problems associated with epilepsy. She also has an interest in behavioural phenotypes, transition and service development. She is a member of the Examinations Sub-Committee of the Royal College of Psychiatrists, Champion for Child Learning Disability Services.

Melanie Dixon is Lead Teacher at Malcolm Arnold House, St Andrew's Healthcare, Northampton. Melanie has worked as a teacher at St Andrew's Healthcare for over 20 years and has been a lead teacher for the Adolescent Service since 1997. She has vast experience of working with young people with developmental disabilities and challenging behaviour, many of whom have a forensic history. Melanie has led on the significant expansion of education provision at St

Andrew's, with many young people achieving outstanding improvements according to Ofsted inspection.

Teresa Flower is Senior Lecturer in Child and Adolescent Forensic Psychiatry in the Department of Psychological Medicine, Monash University, Melbourne, Australia. Teresa is a consultant psychiatrist with a special interest in adolescents with developmental disabilities who offend, the incarceration of adolescents, and the legal context for young people with offending behaviour.

Ernest Gralton is Lead Consultant Forensic Psychiatrist in Developmental Disabilities at St Andrew's Healthcare, Northampton, and Senior Research Fellow at the Institute of Psychiatry, Kings College London. Ernest completed specialist training in both lifespan learning disability psychiatry and forensic psychiatry and has a special interest in adolescents with developmental disabilities with a variety of offending behaviours. He has worked at St Andrew's Healthcare as a consultant psychiatrist since 2000.

Yve Griffin is Chartered Clinical Psychologist at Malcolm Arnold House, St Andrew's Healthcare, Northampton. Yve has worked at St Andrew's Healthcare since 2009. She studied her Doctorate in Clinical Psychology (ClinPsyD) at the University of East Anglia. Prior to this she graduated from the University of Birmingham with an MSc in Forensic Psychology Practice. Her thesis explored the social information processing model and the assessment methods used to detect hostile attribution bias in adolescents. Yve has a specific interest in autistic spectrum disorders and their relationship with risk and offending behaviour. She is also a Research Fellow at the Institute of Psychiatry.

Hilary Haynes is Senior Physiotherapist at Malcolm Arnold House, St Andrew's Healthcare, Northampton. Hilary trained as a physiotherapist in Western Australia at WAIT (now Curtin University of Technology). She has a BSc from Leicester University, an MSc from the University of Northampton and a qualification in Basic Body Awareness Methodology from Bergen University College, Norway. She has worked in a variety of settings in Australia and the UK and has been a clinical specialist in neuro-rehabilitation, paediatrics and learning disability services. Her current interests are in dyspraxia, body awareness and the interconnectedness of physical and mental health.

Belafonte Hosier is Senior Occupational Therapist at Malcolm Arnold House, St Andrew's Healthcare, Northampton. Belafonte gained a BSc (Hons) degree in Occupational Therapy in 2003 at Northampton University. His career began working with the community adult learning disability team in Northwest

Leicestershire until 2005. He continued on to work in the adolescent service at St Andrew's Healthcare, initially with young people with complex mental health needs at Lowther Adolescent Service. His current post working with adolescents with developmental disabilities, challenging behaviours and mental health needs at Malcolm Arnold House was taken up in 2006.

Anupama Iyer is Consultant Child and Adolescent and Learning Disability Psychiatrist at Malcolm Arnold House, St Andrew's Healthcare, Northampton. Anu has trained in learning disabilities and child psychiatry and has been working as an inpatient consultant in a medium secure unit for adolescents with developmental disabilities in the UK. She is involved in developing inpatient care for young people with moderate learning disabilities, significant challenging behaviours and co-morbid developmental and mental health concerns. She also has a research interest in behavioural phenotypes in children with inherited metabolic disorders.

Anne McLean is Consultant Clinical and Forensic Psychologist at St Andrew's Healthcare, Northampton. Anne has training in both clinical and forensic psychology, and has a special interest in risk management and offending behaviour programmes for young people.

Margaret Mills is Senior Social Worker at St Andrew's Healthcare, Northampton. Margaret is a Principal Social Worker who qualified as a social worker in 1993 having gained the Diploma in Social Work. She has since returned to academic learning, achieving a BA (Hons), and is completing an MSc in Child and Adolescent Mental Health. Her professional experience is within the area of mental health with a particular interest in adolescent males that offend.

Jackie O'Connell is Senior Occupational Therapist at Malcolm Arnold House, St Andrew's Healthcare, Northampton. Since qualifying in 1997, Jackie has worked in both community- and hospital-based positions; for the past ten years she has worked with adolescents who have a variety of diagnoses, including mental health conditions, autistic spectrum disorders and forensic histories. Jackie's specific area of interest is working with sensory integration needs and she has completed the sensory integration training, using this knowledge to develop a sensory integration clinic with a colleague. This has proved beneficial in engaging patients, assessing sensory needs and using techniques to meet these needs in an effort to reduce challenging behaviours, and has increased individuals' abilities to produce adaptive responses to everyday stimuli.

Carol Reffin is Specialist Speech and Language Therapist at Malcolm Arnold House, St Andrew's Healthcare, Northampton. Carol has worked as a speech and language therapist since 1989. She worked in the NHS for 15 years as a specialist for young people with specific language impairment within mainstream education. She has worked in the Adolescent Service at St Andrew's Healthcare for the last two years. Her area of specialism is working with adolescents with speech, language and communication needs with associated mental health issues. She completed an MA in Applied Health Studies in 2006. Her dissertation was a qualitative study to explore the perceptions of speech and language impaired adolescents towards leaving school and entering adulthood. Carol is particularly interested in developing awareness of the role of speech and language therapy within the multidisciplinary team and in helping others to understand the nature and overall developmental significance of language acquisition and communication in childhood and adolescence.

Marilyn Sher is Senior Charted Forensic Psychologist at St Andrew's Healthcare, Northampton. Marilyn worked in the Adolescent Service at St Andrew's from 2005 to 2010. Due to the complex nature of the client group, she placed considerable emphasis on adapting and developing offence-related assessment and treatment procedures to meet their unique needs. She has also played an integral role in developing standards of effective implementation of risk assessment procedures and in delivery of training to staff hospital-wide. She is the lead researcher in a pilot of the START-AV (Adolescent Version) that is currently being undertaken.

Cheryl Smith is Specialist Autism Teacher at Malcolm Arnold House, St Andrew's Healthcare, Northampton. Cheryl has specialised in autism for the past 13 years. At St Andrew's Healthcare she has been responsible for setting up a structured education programme for young people with autism in a bespoke classroom which uses the TEACCH (Treatment and Education of Autistic and related Communication-Handicapped Children) approach.

Charlotte Staniforth is Chartered Clinical Psychologist at Malcolm Arnold House, St Andrew's Healthcare, Northampton, and Research Fellow at the Institute of Psychiatry. She completed a BA in Psychology and an MA in Clinical Psychology from the Eötvös Loránd University of Budapest in 2002. Since then she has achieved a Post Graduate Certificate in Mental Health and completed the Doctorate in Clinical Psychology from Coventry University and the University of Warwick in 2005. She has been working in the adolescent developmental disability service at St Andrew's healthcare since qualifying in 2008. Her special interests include the impact of trauma on personality development and offending behaviour in young people with developmental disabilities.

Ekkehart Staufenberg is Consultant Forensic Neuropsychiatrist and Senior Lecturer at the University of East Anglia. Ekkehart has a particular interest in epilepsy, autism offending and acquired brain injury.

Lesley Tebbutt is Senior Occupational Therapist at Malcolm Arnold House, St Andrew's Healthcare, Northampton. Lesley gained a Diploma in Occupational Therapy in 1979. Since 1993 she has worked at St Andrew's Healthcare with adolescents with developmental disabilities, mental health problems and challenging behaviours, and runs its Duke of Edinburgh scheme. She has special interests in the areas of spirituality, animal-assisted therapy, and developing vocational skills.

Claire Underwood is Lead Occupational Therapist, Adolescent Division, at St Andrew's Healthcare, Northampton. Claire has worked in the adolescent services for the past 12 years. Prior to this she worked in the NHS for five years in adult mental health, learning disabilities and elderly mental health. Within her current role she is responsible for leading a team of 25 occupational therapists and technical instructors. She also remains clinically involved in delivering specialist interventions such as sensory integration, sensory attachment intervention and Theraplay®-based interventions across the adolescent services. Claire has presented at many conferences to promote occupational therapy, with a highlight being hosting the OT CAMHS Conference at St Andrew's Healthcare in 2006.

Phil Webb is Principal Social Worker at Malcolm Arnold House, St Andrew's Healthcare, Northampton. Phil is a qualified Registered Nurse in Mental Health (RMN) and a GSCC registered social work practitioner. Phil has worked in health and social service settings both in nursing and social work and has worked for St Andrew's Healthcare as Principal Social Worker attached to the adolescent service for 17 years. His specialism is working with children and adolescents with developmental disabilities and mental health disorders who have been detained in medium secure settings. Prior to coming to St Andrew's, he worked in a number of fields including drug and alcohol outreach, adoption, and community and hospital social work.

SUBJECT INDEX

AUTHOR INDEX